THE FASHION ENCYCLOPEDIA

First edition for North America published in 2015
by Barron's Educational Series, Inc.

Styles and Components of Dress and
Textiles and Embellishments Text © Emily Angus, 2015
Design, Tailoring, and Stitching Text © Macushla Baudis, 2015
Fashion Terminology Text © Philippa Woodcock, 2015
Design © Carlton Books Ltd 2015

All inquiries should be addressed to:
Barron's Educational Series, Inc.
250 Wireless Boulevard,
Hauppauge, New York 11788
www.barronseduc.com

ISBN: 978-0-7641-6767-6

Library of Congress Control Number: 2014941315

Printed in China

9 8 7 6 5 4 3 2 1

Senior Executive Editor: Lisa Dyer
Managing Art Director: Lucy Coley
Picture Researcher: Emma Copestake
Production Manager: Maria Petalidou
Copy Editor: Allie Collins
Designer: Emma Wicks
Illustrator: Fatima Jamadar

THE FASHION ENCYCLOPEDIA

A VISUAL RESOURCE FOR TERMS, TECHNIQUES, AND STYLES

EMILY ANGUS   MACUSHLA BAUDIS   PHILIPPA WOODCOCK

BARRON'S

INTRODUCTION

Answering countless questions relating to fashion history, the design and construction of clothing, textiles, and decoration, this comprehensive catalogue not only demystifies key fashion terms and explains the techniques employed today, but also looks at the building blocks upon which the industry stands.

The last one hundred years have seen seismic shifts in the way we create and wear our clothes. Once dictated by court dress and haute couture, fashion is now fast and mass-produced with little time or few funds available for fine craftsmanship. It is also energetic, vibrant, and opportunistic. But even the newest or most anarchic of trends is underpinned by tradition, and fashion develops almost equally in opposition as in imitation of what went on before.

Each chapter addresses a specific area of interest to those who want to increase their knowledge: the artistic, social, and political movements that gave rise to fashion trends; historical and modern articles of clothing; the construction and stitching of clothing from bespoke tailoring to home dressmaking; and the fibers and textiles as well as the surface embellishment that can be used to transform them. By exploring the links between the historical and the contemporary, by pinpointing technical developments that have impacted fashion, and by including background on key figures that influenced the course of fashion – from Issac Singer and his sewing machine to Vivienne Westwood and the punk movement – this reference provides a breadth of information, both practical and conceptual.

▶ Laser-cutting, 3D printing, and tailoring create a new hybrid of suit in Iris van Herpen's Voltage haute couture collection, spring/summer 2013.

▼ On February 12th, 1947, Christian Dior presented two lines in his collection, En Huit and the Corolle, the latter was to be named the New Look, after Carmel Snow, editor of *Vogue* magazine, declared " It's quite a revolution, dear Christian! Your dresses have such a new look." Subsequently, Dior ushered in a flurry of new silhouettes for the 1950s, including the A-line in 1955, all inspired by the shape of the letter.

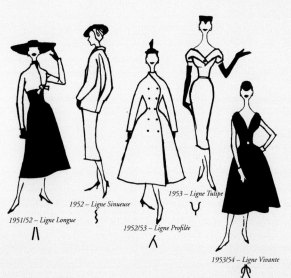

1951/52 – Ligne Longue

1952 – Ligne Sinueuse

1952/53 – Ligne Profilée

1953 – Ligne Tulipe

1953/54 – Ligne Vivante

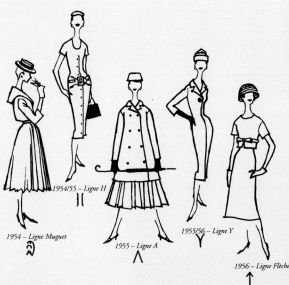

1954 – Ligne Muguet

1954/55 – Ligne H

1955 – Ligne A

1955/56 – Ligne Y

1956 – Ligne Flèche

CONTENTS

DESIGN, TAILORING, AND STITCHING 156

MACUSHLA BAUDIS

TEXTILES AND EMBELLISHMENTS 234

EMILY ANGUS

FASHION TERMINOLOGY

Modern fashion – whether it be haute couture, prêt-à-porter, chain store, or upcycled – reflects the influences bearing on the designer, fused with their erudition, interests, and artistic aims. As a result, the consumer is faced with the choice of a seemingly infinite variety of designs. When each runway collection is received by the fashion press, a slew of words seeks to identify its sources, as well as to explain the designer's "creative genius". The following chapter aims to briefly explain the terms most frequently used to describe the styles of clothing we have worn, and the influences and events that continue to have a bearing on the clothes we currently wear. Covering the vocabulary with which we group stylistic inspiration and adherents into movements, and the most striking silhouettes that dominate our clothing, it will explore the sometimes fantastic hyperbole and seemingly coded language that so often characterize fashion journalism.

We can see that there is an unbreakable link between fashion and social history: movements of cultural protest like the beatniks or hippies demonstrate that clothing has been used as an identifier, and can become a uniform to define a generation. Styles such as the flapper fashions of the 1920s illustrate how fashion links to the social changes that liberated young women after World War I. Clothing has also been a mirror to political change, with trends in Russian-inspired fashion reflecting this country's experiences of different government regimes.

Equally, fashion is an art, and we see a symbiosis with the decorative and fine arts in fashion movements and common terms. Trends and cuts have been directly created by artists and their entourages, while art has inspired fashion designers to work to artistic ideologies, or even to directly incorporate works of art in print or conceptual form. Indeed, such is the close link that certain terms, such as the "belle époque" loosely refer to a historical period, an era of distinct artistic change, as well as a range of iconic clothing and silhouettes. Furthermore, clothes that draw on an imaginary past – perhaps an era of bucolic peace – allow us to tell stories about our own past and identity.

An overall view of the terminology shows that at a linguistic level, there is a close link between clothing, evocative fantasy, and the past. We use resonant onomatopoeic language to describe the shocking and new – "punk" – but also draw on history to suggest that fashion has roots and antecedents, with modern-day designers still referencing the ancient regime or the Baroque.

Finally, the stunning engineering terms we apply to differentiate silhouettes show how fashion has interacted with the human body, just as we humans have changed our environment and architecture. Terms such as H-line or S-bend reflect the technical expertise involved in creating silhouettes, which not only change the way the human body is dressed, but the range of physical movement and liberty it is practically capable of.

In conclusion, the following terminology is a shorthand to describe the rainbow variety of fashion, and how it interprets other human cultures and achievements.

▶ Whistler's model typifies the elongated form of artistic dress (*see* page 23), where the simple fabric, high waistband, and stiffened puff sleeves recall elements of medieval costume, such as the bliaud. Her loosely styled hair echoes depictions of virgin saints.

▶▶ Martin Margiela's fall/winter 2014–15 collection juxtaposes clashing shapes and sizes of textile with segments of tailored garments and oversized feature seams to expose the methods of clothing construction (*see* Deconstruction, page 13), simultaneously challenging preconceptions of what a finished, saleable item of clothing should be.

FASHION MOVEMENTS

INTRODUCTION

Fashion movements not only refer to the styles of clothing worn by their members, but also reflect influences such as the movement's relationship with the prevailing contemporary culture, the musicians or artists who promote and wear the movement's "look", and the politico-economic circumstances. Fashion movement terms are frequently used to identify a decade, particularly after 1900.

These terms also reveal fashion's importance to human society – movements have been born out of disaffection and political protest as much as being driven by the aesthetic programs of artists or propagandists or the runway designs of haute-couture designers. Indeed, movements might be born from the disenfranchised or poorer members of society, as much as an elite avant-garde, while youth groups have been disproportionately influential in creating fashion movements, which are later adapted to bourgeois customers.

While some movements are associated with novelty and invention, others subvert existing styles or propose new ways of thinking about and creating fashion. Indeed, there are anti-fashion movements that haute couture has struggled to subsume into its economic model, rarely with success. Finally, some movements included here describe a more eternal attitude to style and dress, by which connoisseurs of fashion attempt to live their lives in style.

▲ Varvara Stepanova's 1923 for a national sports costume incorporates the Constructivists' devotion to modernism, geometry, and practicality (*see* Cubism, page 13): every costume would effectively convey a shared identity, as well as efficiently use material resource and be appropriate to the activity performed.

▶ Pierre Cardin's 1968 silver vinyl space-age outfits reflected contemporary public interest in space exploration (*see* Space Age, page 18), as well as the minimalist modernity of the youth movement. His designs for tunics and trousers could also be adapted to unisex wear, and their utilitarian character is embodied in the use of innovative fabrics created from new technical processes.

Art Nouveau

ART NOUVEAU

A style of decorative and applied arts that was popular *c.*1890–1910: it was formed in reaction to the deliberately medieval styles, such as the pre-Raphaelites, and its graphic organic forms, heavily influenced by Japanese art, are a precursor to early modernism. Dominant motifs were inspired by elongated botanic forms, based on elegant stems rather than petals, as well as the "decadent East". Fashions had a sinuous, curving silhouette, which relied on the S-line, or swan-bill corset; this was superseded by a more columnar outline *c.*1910. Long narrow skirts, with prominent bustles, and high-necked, lace-trimmed blouses further exaggerated the S-bend. Art Nouveau is particularly associated with designers such as Jeanne Paquin, Jacques Doucet, and Paul Poiret whose ateliers were customized by famous actresses as well as infamous royal mistresses.

BEATNIK

An anti-materialist, minimalist youth fashion of the late 1940s to early 1960s that rejected the clean and wholesome American preppy look. Instead, it worshipped the unconventional and, in particular, French Left-Bank intellectuals and members of the American Beat Generation: William S. Burroughs, Jack Kerouac, and Allen Ginsberg. Female icons included Jean Seberg, Brigitte Bardot, and Audrey Hepburn. The beatnik look was based on an unadorned monochrome, black wardrobe, with gamine hairstyles, berets, rolled-up jeans, black turtleneck sweaters, heavily made-up eyes, dark glasses, and leather jackets. It is an early forerunner of the hipster movement.

BELLE ÉPOQUE

Often synonymous with Art Nouveau, this covers the period of European peace (*c.*1871–1914), when women became more emancipated, and the rounded Victorian silhouette was rejected for a more columnar or S-shaped figure. The model of the modern couture house began when the British designer Charles Frederick Worth established his salon in Paris, and the first runway show took place in Lady Lucy ("Lucille") Duff Gordon's salon. Parisian-sewn couture gowns were bought by European royalty and the American super-rich, while greater social emancipation was emphasized in female sporting outfits, including the bifurcated skirt.

CUBISM

Early twentieth-century Cubist artists such as Picasso and Braque represented nature using geometric forms: contemporaneously, the sinuous S silhouette was rejected in favor of the linear flapper figure, the geometric bob haircut, and the cloche hat. In particular, Cubism had a great influence on fashion illustration *c.*1910–1930, and on the clothing designs of the Russian Constructivists. Their manifesto emphasized the role of technology in clothes production, thus the reduction of patterns to rational, geometric forms was perfectly Cubist in philosophy, as illustrated by Varvara Stepanova's 1923 design for a sports costume composed of three rectangles and a circle segment (*see* page 10).

DANDYISM

Men who take exquisite interest in their appearance for the sake of aesthetics, and promote an elegant, refined comportment may receive the moniker of "dandy". It was

Dandyism

inspired by the impeccably stylish Beau Brummell, who set a model of male dress and courteous behavior in Regency London, inspiring fashionable society to mimic him. Unlike the macaroni (an eighteenth-century dandy who mimicked Continental fashions), the term is neither derogatory nor questioning of sexuality. Dandyism is associated with the upholding of traditional values and immaculate, if updated, gentlemanly dress, and has thus centered on the British tailoring of Jermyn Street and traditions of appropriate dress for town and countryside.

DECONSTRUCTION

Influenced by the French philosopher and philologist Jacques Derrida, deconstructivist fashion aims to show the process of construction within the garment itself, playfully emphasizing the unfinished, as well as mocking the self-regarding nature of fashion. Seams and stitches might be a visible feature. Derrida's idea of the engineer as a *bricoleur* (odd-job man) is applied to fashion by the use of recycled materials and the haphazard use of tools and implements: the "unfinished" pieces might be in the process of unraveling or be made from imperfect fabrics, with twisted, compromised seams. Key designers include Martin Margiela (*see also* page 8), Comme des Garçons, Yohji Yamamoto, and Issey Miyake.

Flapper

DISCO

After the anti-materialistic counter-culture of the 1960s, disco was a movement of excess, in reaction to the economic crisis of the 1970s. Its fusion of Latino, funk, and soul music with new electronic music was associated with sequin-covered glamour and the hedonistic lifestyle typified by New York's Studio 54, but adopted equally by working-class Americans, as depicted in the movie *Saturday Night Fever*. Second-skin leotards and leggings reflected the growth of the "body beautiful" fitness craze, while models like Jerry Hall and Marie Helvin, in clinging Halston halter-neck dresses, exemplified the more sophisticated end of the look.

FAUVISM

The Fauvists' iconoclastic disregard for artistic rules led to their being dubbed "wild beasts" (*Fauves*): indeed, artists such as Henri Matisse and Henri Rousseau employed a bright, tropical palette, combining Impressionist, Modernist, and Cubist styles. In fashion, Fauvists Sonia and Robert Delaunay designed costumes for the movie industry: their constructivist designs use vividly printed and woven fabrics, and clients included Hollywood's Gloria Swanson. In the 1920s Sonia established her own label, and her geometric prints could be seen as the forerunner of psychedelic prints. Fauvism has translated into contemporary trends for fashion's fluorescent brights, vivid color blocking, and bold silhouettes.

Goth

FESTIVAL CHIC

Drawing on the original music festival fashions of Woodstock and the Isle of Wight in the late 1960s, understated festival chic is an irreverent mix-and-match style, which has nonetheless become an outdoor uniform for the British summer time. Dogged by unpredictable weather, the field-based festival season requires Wellington boots – preferably brightly colored Hunters, worn with knee socks for comfort. Jean shorts or maxi dresses are perfect daywear, worn with layers of strappy T-shirts, plaid shirts, and plentiful beads. The look is associated with model and serial festival-goer Kate Moss.

FLAPPER

The modern interpretation of flapper style is inspired by the most daring elements of late 1920s fashion: a straight silhouette, with dresses cut for boyish flat chests and slim hips; a knee-length (or higher) fringed or handkerchief hemline; jeweled reticules; Louise Brooks bobbed hair; cloche hats; and belted short jackets. The original flapper herself, named for the boots worn with the short dresses, which would allegedly flap open, was a symbol of post-war social change. This liberated young woman smoked, attended clubs unchaperoned, danced to the Charleston, wore heavy makeup, and rejected the corsetry of her mother's generation.

GLAM ROCK

The British antidote to the 1970s economic crisis, glam rock was an explosion of flamboyant theatricality, adopted by musicians Elton John, T-Rex, and Slade. It had an androgynous element, as men wore capes, high-heeled stacked platform shoes from Terry de Havilland's boutique Cobblers to the World, clinging satin, heavy makeup, long permed hair, and all-in-ones: the "Ziggy Stardust" leotard by Kansai Yamamoto served to emphasize David Bowie's unspecific sexuality. The art-school group Roxy Music incorporated conceptual art, glamorizing historic fashions and sexual fetish. Glam rock mixed the rich velvets, plums, and electric blues of the historical dandy with cartoonish primary colors.

GOTH

Modern goth style is inspired by tailored, dramatic Victorian fashion. Nineteenth-century mourning etiquette meant that many people wore dark, somber clothing for extended periods and dwelled on the death of their loved ones by wearing jewelry made from the deceased's hair. The goth look celebrates this macabre chic, with many adherents wearing deathly pale foundation, contrasted with strikingly dark eyes, lips, and nails. Typical clothes include long-tailed coats, flowing skirts, and corsetry, cut in decadent velvets and trimmed in scarlet and purple. They are particularly showcased in "haute goth" couture by John Galliano and Christian Lacroix as well as the cinematic costumes of Tim Burton.

GRUNGE

Allied with deconstructivism, this anti-fashion movement was inspired by the 1990s Seattle alternative music scene, led by Nirvana and Pearl Jam. Grunge clothing expressed disenchantment with corporate Western society, and runway interpretations were rarely successful. Traditional ideals of beauty were eschewed for unwashed long hair; facial hair; mass-produced checked shirts; donkey jackets; and loose, disheveled jeans with kicked around Doc Marten boots. The sub-culture was more successfully translated by the fashion industry into "undone" or "heroin" chic, as exemplified by the young Kate Moss's 1993 *Vogue* "Under Exposure" spread and Calvin Klein campaign of the same year.

New Romantic

HIPPIE

The ultimate anti-materialist youth movement, the hippies of the 1960s demonstrated their alternative lifestyle – and their idea of a peaceful, united world – by sourcing clothes from global travels and tribal societies, preferring natural fabrics and ethnic accessories, a flowing silhouette, and, above all, bold pattern. Kaftans, smocked shirts, loose tiered skirts, long hair, and beads exemplified the half-vagabond gypsy, half-tribal elder look. Despite the anti-consumerism of the counterculture, it was transferred to the boutique by "hippie deluxe" designers such as Ossie Clark, Zandra Rhodes, and Celia Birtwell. Emilio Pucci's psychedelic-print kaftans are now iconic of the period, but are far removed from the original hippie aesthetic.

JAPANESE STREETWEAR

Led by young women, Japanese streetwear is based on a pastiche of school uniforms, exaggerated cartoon character fashion, and a rejection of the traditional idea of Japanese female beauty – that is, pale skins and dark hair. Instead, the 1990s saw the ganguro look develop, which mimicked the tans and blonde hair of the All-American girl, with intimidatingly bright clothing and arresting white makeup. Street fashion is divided into subgroups and style tribes in Japan, which link to their geographical roots and shopping preferences; for example, the core Lolita style is linked to Tokyo's Harajuku district, but subgroups have specialist shops elsewhere in the capital.

Punk

NEO-CLASSICAL

Inspired by Ancient Greece, this look integrated details of classical design such as the Greek key motif. Although worn by Marie-Antoinette at her model farm, it is nevertheless particularly associated with post-revolutionary France, and expressed the regime's break with a royal past. However, the fashions for muslin, empire-line dresses trimmed with ribbon and Eastern cashmere shawls spread across early nineteenth-century Europe. Women's hair was dressed in tight Grecian curls and piled high, while low-heeled, ballet-style slippers were worn indoors. Male dress adopted plainer fabrics and military details, inspired by the armies who battled in Europe until Napoleon's fall in 1815.

NEW LOOK

Dior's Corolle line, or "New Look", revolutionized post-war fashion in 1947. In contrast to the utility clothes of ration-era Europe, Dior described the designs as being for "flowerlike women, with rounded shoulders, feminine busts, and hand span waists". He used abundant lengths of decadent material to create full skirts over light crinoline petticoats, trimmed with luxury materials, furs, and jewels: in contrast, a wasp waist finished a tightly fitted torso. Neat hats topped immaculately dressed hair, and mid-heel shoes and matching handbags were deemed most ladylike. Although initially provoking moral outrage at such extravagance, the silhouette was widely copied and became synonymous with glamour.

NEW ROMANTIC

Vivienne Westwood led punk's aesthetic of decay, but her 1981 Pirates collection also epitomized the New Romantics' "post-punk theatricality". Fashion and music now took a far more playful and joyous attitude, creating costumes inspired by pre-industrial historical renegades, carefree gypsies, marvelous macaronis, and lace-clad maidens to create a "born of the dressing-up box" (Marnie Fogg, *Fashion The Whole Story*, 2013) cult. London-centric and led by fashion students and musicians like Spandau Ballet, Duran Duran, and Boy George, the New Romantics congregated at clubs and art colleges.

PUNK

Spearheaded by Vivienne Westwood and Malcolm McLaren's Sex boutique, and McLaren's prodigies the Sex Pistols, this was an anti-fashion movement that challenged bourgeois values. Its confrontational palette of red, black, and plaid, clashing with fluorescents, reflected the deteriorating British economy in the late 1970s. Sex sold a mix of unusually tailored tartan and bondage gear, but punk also insisted on recycled clothing as well as politically aware items like Westwood's Anarchy shirt (1976). Punk culture and Mohican haircuts became emblematic of 1980s London. Westwood's work transferred to the runway in 1981, but the spirit of punk protest continues in her support for nuclear disarmament.

Space Age

SPACE AGE

Russian and American space exploration, and advances in synthetic materials, in particular from DuPont, were the source of 1960s futuristic fashion. Pared down silhouettes in André Courrèges' Space Age collection (1964), color blocking, and metallic trims mimicked the imagined space suits of cosmonauts and astronauts, while patent white boots and oversized white "goggle" sunglasses echoed the heat-reflective materials and equipment of space travel. Unisex design characterized collections like Pierre Cardin's Cosmo Corps, while Paco Rabanne experimented with "space age" materials to produce clothing formed of components, rather than cut from patterns. Additional futuristic glamour was added by these designers' work in the movie industry, such as Rabanne's designs for *Barbarella* (1968).

STEAMPUNK

Fusing technology and historical romance, this is a modern fantasy interpretation of Victorian *de luxe*, crossed with nineteenth-century invention and a post-apocalyptic future. For example, a Victorian bustle might support a cutaway skirt, exposing stockings and garters, or aviator goggles might accessorize a Folies Bergère bodice. Steampunk began as an underground movement, popularized by fans of authors and illustrators in the genre, such as H.G. Wells and Jules Verne. It has crossed over to couture in the work of Chanel, while the Prada fall/winter 2012 campaign presented Gary Oldman and Willem Dafoe as characters from the *League of Extraordinary Gentlemen*.

STREETWEAR (HIP-HOP)

Socially aware hip-hop culture has attracted street and youth followers, as well as the commercially aware fashion houses, becoming big business in the 1980s. Its styles have expressed political and artistic agendas. For example, the black empowerment movement adopted the traditional kente cloth, while the sportswear labels worn by hip-hop groups, such as Kangol, Adidas, and Nike, have become cult objects for those wishing to identify with their favorite musicians. Graffiti style has been adopted by high-end fashion at Louis Vuitton and Vivienne Westwood, while hip-hop artists have established their own labels at Wu Wear or Jay-Z's Rocawear.

SURREALISM

Surrealist art and fashion aims to unsettle, placing ordinary objects in odd situations. In 1937 Salvador Dalí's hand-painted trompe l'oeil lobster and parsley sprig – carefully innocuous in their own right – were made extraordinary in an Elsa Schiaparelli ball gown. Surrealism was particularly allied with knitwear: Schiaparelli's knitted swimsuits brought the topically absurd to bathing, with tops decorated with bobbing angelfish. Elsewhere in Paris, accessories – hats and bags by Anne Marie of France – were made in the shape of everyday objects like the Bakelite telephone. Jewelry might mimic live insects, suggesting that the wearer was encrusted with crawling beasts.

YOUTHQUAKE

The extraordinary social and cultural changes that took place in 1960s London are predominantly associated with a younger generation of artists, designers, and musicians, allied with the Labour government of Harold Wilson. In this period, homosexuality and abortion were legalized, counterculture became mainstream, and Britain led the world musically and visually. According to Diana Vreeland, the editor of British *Vogue* at the time, this new landscape had been determined by a youthquake that celebrated individuality and talent as no generation had before. Key figures in youthquake fashion included The Beatles, Mick Jagger, Twiggy, Jean Shrimpton and Mary Quant, Vidal Sassoon, and the photographer David Bailey.

Youthquake

Steampunk

COMMON TERMS

INTRODUCTION

The following terms seek to outline a selection of some of the historic styles of dress, national and transnational folk influences, persistent additions, new inventions, particular types of utilitarian dress, as well as non-costume sources drawn from art and popular culture, that are said to have inspired couture design and street fashions. Collectively, they show that the "other" – tribal, ethnic, folkloric – is particularly tantalizing to Western fashion. Influences have arrived through travelers who wear foreign discoveries for their own pleasure, Art Nouveau designers who changed an era's silhouette to titillate with erotic nuances of the harem, as well as modern runway collections based on folklore and ethnic fashions that are quite different from the West's design history.

Equally, commentators like to collect designers together in schools, even if each of their collections is idiosyncratic and bears only the slightest relationship to their contemporaries' work. However, designers who come from the same continent or who have a similar interest in the use of particular textiles are frequently grouped together. Finally, the style of clothes people have traditionally worn and their modern interpretation in "looks" are also gathered together under one name, allowing fashion historians to trace the development of a particular idea.

▲ Rebecca Rimmer's trompe l'oeil designs (*see* Trompe L'oeil, page 32) demonstrate how both tailoring and printed fabrics can convince the eye that it is viewing an alternative silhouette to the reality. Here we see how the impression of an hourglass, frilled-hemmed dress is projected onto a more voluminous geometric form, and an orange cape is projected onto a simpler top.

▶ Duro Olowu's fall/winter 2011–12 presentation at Milk Studios showcases contemporary afrocentric style (*see* page 22). It perfectly combines tailoring with a European heritage, as this nineteenth-century-style coat and Halston-inspired dress, with arresting print and palettes inspired by traditional African textiles. Here the contrasting fabrics allow the precisely tailored forms to be clearly appreciated.

ACADEMIC DRESS

Developing from medieval houppelandes and mantles, traditional academic dress is now only generally worn on ceremonial occasions. The wearer's gowns indicate intellectual status upon having obtained a college degree. Hoods and gowns can be trimmed with multiple-hued silks, velvets, or furs, each combination indicating institutional affiliation and the subject of expertise. Equally, headgear indicates academic achievement: a mortarboard for the first degree and a squashy, sixteenth-century cap for the Ph.D., worn with colored robes. The tailoring of academic dress is associated with traditional, London-based firms such as Ede and Ravenscroft, which also supplies legal robes.

AESTHETIC DRESS

Developed from artistic dress, aesthetic dress, like the Arts and Crafts movement of the 1880s, rejected mass-produced textiles. It favored a natural palette, or "greenery yallery", of hand-embellished or block-printed designs, featuring natural forms such as the peacock feather in the Liberty print by Arthur Silver. The cut was inspired by European historical costume, as well as Japanese traditional dress. Clothes for both men and women were loose, displaying the gorgeous Liberty prints and heavy velvets, and idealistically ending body-deforming fashion. It was promoted by figures such as Oscar Wilde, the author Mary Eliza Haweis, and the artist Whistler.

AFROCENTRIC

In post-colonial Africa the fusion of traditional cloths like kente and kanga with Western fashions created a distinctive, dynamic scene, led by Nigerian, Malian,

Avant-garde

and South African designers. Shade Thomas Fahm's 1960s *iro complete* mixed Yoruba dress with a European-style blouse. This tradition of vivid African print and modern tailoring is continued by contemporary designers Duro Olowu and Lisa Folawiyo, whose Jewel label clashes geometric textiles with modern club

Anime

style. While North African influence was evident in Algerian-born Yves Saint Laurent's 1968 safari suit, Max Azaria and Azzedine Alaïa have taken Africa onto the global haute-couture stage.

ANDROGYNOUS
Indicating gender neutrality in clothing and silhouette, androgynous fashion is particularly associated with twentieth-century modernism, whose geometrical aesthetic influenced the design of straight-cut "flapper" dresses of the 1920s, through to the functional androgyny of pre-war Russian constructivism and the workwear of totalitarian regimes, and on to the material modernism of the 1960s. Equally, clothing has become interchangeable between the sexes: for example, Yves Saint Laurent's Le Smoking tuxedo for women of 1967, and the gorgeous young men of glam rock. The sexual androgyny of Marlene Dietrich and David Bowie, and the lean boy-like figure of Jean Shrimpton, typified androgyny.

ANIME
Japanese anime animates Manga graphic novels and features characters with notably wide, child-like, highly emotive eyes and unrealistically colored hair. Their facial expressions are drawn from a set "dictionary" recalling Ancient Greek theater. Female characters dress in a precociously sexualized Lolita/cheerleader style, complete with hair bows and frilled ankle socks. For some characters, pastel clothes predominate, with midriff-revealing capri pants and ra-ra skirts, while others make reference to the steampunk movement and contemporary chain store fashions. Such styles appear in Japanese street

and fan fashion, and a subculture of anime "dressing up" has become popular as a blogging and social activity.

ARTISTIC DRESS
Inspired by the medieval, draped costumes of the Pre-Raphaelites, this style was associated with the artists, their mistresses, and models. Active in mid-nineteenth-century Britain, the Pre-Raphaelites idealized a very languid femininity. Jane Morris (the wife of William, the leader of the Arts and Crafts Movement) and Lizzie Siddal adapted the medieval bliaut, a type of tunic robe that was fitted to the upper body. Unlike mainstream Victorian fashion, corsetry was eschewed, and an elongated figure was emphasized with a high waistband; a loose skirt; and wide, floor-length sleeves. A rich primary palette was preferred, and hair was worn loose and long.

AVANT-GARDE
A pioneering fashion design that stands apart from the mainstream, the avant-garde is progressive, is individual, and changes ideas. Some elements of the design are adopted more widely, and the idea itself becomes mainstream. Equally, avant-garde may refer to a particularly unusual or extreme creation where form is given precedence over function: for example, the surrealist Skeleton dress by Elsa Schiaparelli (1938) combined a perfect cut with an integrated, tailored skeletal frame, while many of Alexander McQueen's runway collections (*see* fall/winter 2009, opposite) could not be practically worn but were extremely beautiful. The aim is to present new concepts by challenging the conventional notions of how a garment is meant to function or look.

Baroque Style

BAROQUE STYLE

Baroque fashion takes its inspiration from the formalized excess of the absolutist courts of the seventeenth and eighteenth centuries, especially at Versailles. It is characterized by historically inspired tailoring in decadent silks or heavy brocades, with lavish embellishment. For fall/winter 2012–13, Dolce & Gabbana offered the Baroque Romanticism collection (*see* right), which reflected Spanish Golden Age styles: black, heavily textured capes festooned with gold rococo embroidery and contrasted with enameled jewels. Vivienne Westwood's *Les femmes ne connaissent pas toute leur coquetterie* 1996 collection was directly inspired by Watteau gowns and robes à la française, with classic silks contrasted with more iconoclastic tartans and bare shoulders.

BODY CON

Body con (concept) includes form-fitting "second skin" clothing and dresses in heavily elasticated and Lycra-rich knitted and woven fabrics, sometimes with concealed, form-shaping undergarments. Noted designers include Azzedine Alaïa and Roland Mouret (the Galaxy dress), while Hervé Léger's bandage dress has remained a key part of his collections since 1989 and is a ubiquitous part of the female celebrity wardrobe. The fashion was popularized in the 1980s as designers were influenced by sportswear and the "body beautiful" keep-fit movement. At the same time, advances in science led by DuPont allowed materials to retain their shape, improving longevity.

BOHEMIAN

Bohemians live unconventional lives and are named after a marginalized artistic class whose rootless existence recalled the bohemian gypsy. The term covers any alternative movement and its fashions, including the Arts and Crafts Movement and even the beatniks. Bohemian fashion as an indicator of anti-establishment feeling was perfected by the hippie movement and reflected an interest in the historically free lifestyle of travelers; Ossie Clark and Thea Porter captured this ethos in the 1960s and 1970s while Anna Sui reworks the style season after season. On the street, boho fashions mimic a romantic ideal of gypsy and hippie fashion, mixing often deluxe maxi dresses with intricate, ethnic jewelry and luxury goods from brands felt to reflect an artistic tradition, such as Mulberry.

CAD

Computer-aided design software has contributed greatly to pattern making and design in fashion: prototypes were developed in the 1960s, but the first mass-market CAD packages appeared in the 1980s, alongside the spread of desktop computing. Such software helps reduce inefficiency in pattern production and cutting and allows for clearer visualization of designs. CAD software can model designs in different fabrics and simulate draping, as well as indicate the effect upon proposed garments of different fittings. Training in CAD is essential for many designers and pattern cutters: it can be studied at college or during on-the-job training.

COURT DRESS

Court dress is the precise standard of costume required by rulers at formal occasions. Historically, social status, wealth, and proximity to the ruler were expressed in the materials permitted to the wearer by sumptuary laws: for example, cloth of gold could only be worn above the rank of viscount at the Tudor court, but anyone who was decently dressed could enter the palace. The king or queen could set the style to be worn – for example, the *grand habit*. Certain couturiers gained renown by appointment to the monarch; for example, Rose Bertin for Marie-Antoinette or Norman Hartnell for the young Elizabeth II.

DIRECTOIRE

The Directoire period followed the bloodiest period of the French Revolution, when a council of five directors governed France from 1795 until 1799. Artistically "neoclassical", it rejected royal visual excess, and fashion symbolically referred to Greek democracy. For women, empire-line muslin gowns were worn with Indian cashmere shawls. Hair was worn piled in ringlets in the Grecian style or under a turban. Male clothing was now cut in sober, plain colors with military details, referring to Revolutionary France's campaigns in Europe. The aesthetic was subverted by the Incroyables and Merveilleuses, who exaggerated Directoire costume to indicate their displeasure with the government.

ETHNIC

European fashion has experimented with the traditional dress of non-Western and "primitive" societies ever since their first contact. Then, as now, the art of *luxe povera* – producing derivative and costly Western versions of traditional dress – indicates the wearer's global knowledge. Designers who have a non-Western design tradition, or who seek to mix textiles and tailoring from different cultures, have been among fashion's avant-garde. In the early twentieth century, Paul Poiret adapted Japanese dress to Western costume, and his harem pants titillated and liberated women's evening dress. Kenzo and Sonia Rykiel continue to interpret ethnic design, juxtaposing global materials and traditions.

Directoire

FOLKLORIC
Drawing on the legends of Northern European society, folkloric fashion is a high-end version of bohemian style. Equally, the hedonistic abandon of the 1960s – the spirit of Mick Jagger and Marianne Faithfull – with astrakhan coats, knee-high boots, and *luxe povera* patchwork feed this look in which male and female clothing are equally sumptuous. In 2012 Valentino and Etro produced mosaic prints, inspired by the Orthodox Church, woven into Boyar coats and shawls and styled with heavy, bear-like furs. Animal skins are patched into skirts and waistcoats. Delicate chiffons are juxtaposed with tapestry and butter-soft leathers, and hairstyles reference the hirsute 1960s.

GRANNY STYLE
Inspired by the craze for vintage, granny is a very self-aware style, which includes updated versions of the archetypal British ladies' wardrobe. It celebrates midi-length tweed skirts worn over opaque or heavy-denier flesh-colored hosiery, knitted cardigans – with a deliberate hint of the homemade – sensible button-to-the-neck coats, and round-neck or pussybow blouses. Brogue shoes, crocheted brooches, and pearls accessorize the look. Granny style, like 1940s chic, represents a trend of making new clothes look deliberately retro, and was popularized by designers Marc Jacobs and Louis Vuitton in 2011, followed by Nina Ricci's demure twinsets of 2013.

GYPSY DRESS
Traditional gypsy dress is a highly decorated fusion of exotic print, daring color, and practical layering. Voluminous, long, tiered skirts are teamed with cotton blouses, many-textured shawls, and, for married women, headscarves, or *diklo*. Skirts and shawls might be trimmed with coins, or *galbi*.

The Western image of the gypsy woman was both exotic and erotic, and has concentrated on the scantily clad dancing girl in long embellished skirt and cropped, tightly fitting blouse. The modern "streetwear" gypsy mixes historically inspired and vintage pieces,

Gypsy Dress

such as the justaucorps waistcoat, voluminous blouses, tiered skirts, and extravagant gold and folk jewelry. A contemporary icon of the gypsy look is singer/songwriter Stevie Nicks of Fleetwood Mac.

HAUTE COUTURE

Born in nineteenth-century Paris with the pioneering business model of British couturier Charles Frederick Worth, haute couture re-emerged after World War II under Christian Dior and Hubert de Givenchy. Their elegant "houses" could show biannual collections and had ateliers where garments were hand-sewn. In London, Hardy Amies and Norman Hartnell provided couture designs for the British "season". Couture garments are developed from sketches or draping cloth, but their designs must be original. They will be ordered by individual clients and are never mass-produced by the House (*see also* pages 158–63).

MAGYAR DRESS

Traditional Hungarian costume, worn up until the late nineteenth century, continues to influence modern "folk" fashions. It is composed of embroidered white cotton blouses with puffed virago sleeves, contrasting embroidered loosely laced bodices, and full skirts. The skirt itself is plain to mid-thigh and heavily decorated below, either with embroidery, tiered rows of color, or contrasting traditionally woven material. A close-fitting, heavily decorated cap is worn over the hair. Thanks to Hungary's historic position within the Austro-Hungarian Empire, this style of dress was occasionally adopted by the Hapsburg empresses, and the decoration was made in silver and gold thread.

Minimalism

MILITARY

Military styles have influenced the cut and detail of many designers, particularly in menswear collections. Indeed, during World War II, civilian fashion took on the leaner lines and smart headwear of service uniforms, reflecting political circumstances as well as rationed cloth. Perestroika was reflected in a vogue for Princess or Russian military great coats and furred chapkas. On the runway, military appears in strong structured coats in felted wools, the use of khaki and serge, with details such as embossed gold buttons, epaulettes, or dog tags. American GI dress has been interpreted in combat pants and leather bomber jackets.

MINIMALISM

Minimalist designs rely on simply cut clothes with an absence of detail, print, or embellishment. In contrast to the sumptuous New Look, late 1950s designs by Givenchy and Balenciaga for shift dresses and pilgrim pumps exemplified a very feminine minimalism, and were worn by Audrey Hepburn and Jackie Kennedy. The 1960s space-age minimalism of Pierre Cardin and André Courrèges employed new fabrics, while in the 1990s Jil Sander, Ann Demeulemeester, Calvin Klein, and Helmut Lang offered unembellished yet beautifully cut items in "noble fabrics" (*see* page 268), suggesting their essential nature. The Prada tote bag has become an icon of minimalism, in plain but recognizable Pocone fabric.

Op Art

MOD

The Mods were a British youth movement of the late 1950s and 1960s that defined itself in opposition to the Rockers. They expressed their identity through a preference for short hair and Italian slim-cut tailoring (as well as Italian scooters) as sold in the U.K. by Cecil Gee. The style became more flamboyant, with hip-hugging pants worn over Chelsea, or heeled, boots; vivid close-cut shirts; and the hooded parka that was an essential for scooter travel. Women wore simply cut minidresses and long boots. The mod look was popularized by London groups like The Kinks and The Who.

OP ART

Op (Optical) Art includes modernist paintings from the 1930s to the 1960s by artists such as Victor Vasarely and Bridget Riley, where blocks of color or simple repetitions of forms are used in the composition, rather than more traditional ideas of depth and narrative. As such, an optical illusion is created for the viewer. This visual style perfectly suited the minimalist, simply cut minidresses and A-line dresses of the 1960s by designers such as Yves Saint Laurent and Betsey Johnson. Op Art also appears in the psychedelia of the later 1960s, Paco Rabanne's space-age "Twelve Unwearable Dresses in Contemporary Materials", and Pierre Cardin's houndstooth tunics.

ORIENTALISM

For Europe, the East was a point of eternal fascination, and European fashion has tried to interpret its perceived exoticism, whether through the gentleman's banyan coat, the Egyptian motifs of neoclassical fashion, or the erotic gypsy dancing girl costume. In the early twentieth century, Mario Fortuny, Erté, and Paul Poiret used Eastern opulence in a new, looser silhouette for eveningwear, with kaftans, tunic robes, and harem pants made from silks and stiffened organza, topped with turbans and exotic egret feathers. Equally, the Japanese unisex kimono has influenced Western tailoring, as seen at Galliano for Dior for spring/summer 1998, Vivienne Westwood for spring/summer 2012, and Etro for spring/summer 2013.

PANNIER

A pannier is a basket form worn under skirts to give them greater or exaggerated fullness. They appeared in early modern fashion, in particular in the eighteenth-century *robe à la française* that was popular until the French Revolution of 1789. Here, a two-dimensional silhouette was created by panniers of three to five whalebone or willow strips: these panniers were tied around the waist, and further petticoats were laid on top to create the form. Some pannier skirts could be several feet wide, but very narrow when seen in profile. Arm panniers were also used to achieve the exaggerated sleeves of the Romantic era (1830s).

PEASANT STYLE

Peasant style is a vintage look, based on reinterpreting an idea of traditional European rural dress such as the dirndl, as well as the alternative culture of the 1960s and 1970s. It presents a romanticized, bucolic image of the past and is related to gypsy dress, festival chic, boho, and folkloric style. Simple, off-the-shoulder, tiered maxidresses and minidresses, colorful floral prints, cheesecloth blouses, and Magyar-style shirts might be teamed with

Peplum

animal-skin waistcoats and boots. Fringing, crochet, and embroidery decorate clothing. It has influenced recent runway collections by Oscar de la Renta and Dolce & Gabbana.

PEPLUM

The peplum is an extra frill of material added to the waistline of a skirt or to a jacket to exaggerate a small waist and the curve of the hip. It is derived from the Latin *peplos* (a shawl) and appeared in the frilled jackets of Victorian walking dresses and, later, bustles, as well as in 1930s Hollywood styles, 1940s suits, and Christian Dior's New Look. The peplum was typical of 1980s power dressing: for example, Claude Montana juxtaposed the peplum with extreme shoulder pads in fall/winter 1981–82, while the classic 1980s cocktail dress was nothing without a peplum. It has resurfaced in collections by Burberry and Bottega Veneta from 2012 to 2014.

Pop Art

POP ART

Originating in the 1950s, pop artists such as Andy Warhol, Jasper Johns, and Roy Lichtenstein celebrated the mundane, elevating everyday objects to the status of High Art and relying on primary colors, print, and bold lines. Pop Art links to Warhol and Studio 54 habitués like graffiti artist Basquiat: in 1984 Stephen Sprouse applied graffiti to his balloon-cut coats and in 2001 he created the Speedy Bag at Louis Vuitton. Elsewhere, Moschino's 1987 skirt suit was embellished with an appliquéd comic book "Whaam" and hats made of everyday objects. Versace's Warhol Print dress (1991) used the artist's technicolor Marilyn Monroe print.

POWER DRESSING

In the 1980s designers took inspiration from women in the workforce and society: power dressing was its answer to female parity and a response to the male suit. Rather than the softer lines of New Romantics, the new silhouette offered a sharp triangular upper-body line, which simultaneously accentuated the hourglass. Shoulders were enhanced with massive padding, and waists minimalized in contrast with peplum jackets. Skirts and pants were slim fitting and ideally worn with spiked stiletto heels, aspirational accessories by Hermès or Chanel, and immaculate bold makeup. Such "glamazons" could be seen in the television show *Dynasty*.

PREPPY

The modern preppy look is associated with designer Ralph Lauren. It offers an all-American, youthful, healthy lifestyle for clean-cut WASPs (White Anglo-Saxon Protestants). Originating on American Ivy League college campuses and in private preparatory ("preppy") schools, it offered a sense of social standing and identity. For women, bobby sox, full skirts, and round-neck sweaters were de rigueur, while young men wore natural-cut blazers in tweed, buttoned-down Oxford cloth shirts, and flat-fronted pants in gray flannel or ribbed corduroy. Letterman sweaters also indicated your collegiate status. Modern preppy includes khaki pants/chinos, polo shirts, linen suits, and double-breasted blazers and cashmere sweaters.

PROM STYLE

As teenagers developed their own cultural identity in the 1950s, American high schools marked the transition to adult life with the "prom", where couples of senior students danced under the surveillance of their teachers. The archetypal prom dress was strapless, with a sweetheart neckline. The bodice was fitted to the waist, where the skirts flared out in layers of tulle petticoat. As the prom has become ubiquitous in the West, prom gowns offer girls a range of classic ball gowns and cocktail dresses. However, the vintage look of the 1950s remains popular, and original gowns command high prices among collectors.

READY-TO-WEAR (PRÊT-À-PORTER)

Ready-to-wear indicates the more affordable yet still design-led end of fashion. It originated in the 1940s in the U.S. and developed in France in the 1960s and 1970s, when Yves Saint Laurent split from Dior to launch his Rive Gauche boutiques. A rebellion against haute couture, it reflected a world in which customers no longer had the time for individual fittings but wanted distinctive, quality, ready-made clothing "off the rack" ("off the peg"). This model was followed by the top fashion houses, where haute couture remained as a flagship activity, but prêt-à-porter, and increasingly accessories, became the more lucrative output.

RESORTWEAR

Originally marketed to a post-war international jet set who could enjoy a year-round summer lifestyle, resortwear is inspired by the Mediterranean and its visual traditions. It originated on the French Riviera in the 1950s and the daywear collections of Emilio Pucci and Chanel, as worn by celebrities such as Jackie Onassis and Brigitte Bardot. Clothes must be suitable for leisure and more relaxed soirées, and suggest a casual elegance, using lightweight fabrics. It also includes deluxe swimsuits, fitnesswear, and accessories. Brightly colored and nautical prints are prevalent. Many brands now offer a resortwear runway collection.

ROBE DE STYLE

In contrast to the androgynous silhouette of the 1920s flapper dress, Jeanne Lanvin's mid-decade robe de style offered a more feminine alternative, with references to historical court dress and with couture finishing. Combining the typical 1920s flat front and an often somber palette with a partially dropped waist, it adapted the eighteenth-century pannier to support midi-length cloche skirts that revealed calves and ankles. Lanvin was particularly known for lavish ancien regime embellishment, using art deco motifs such as the peacock feather or Egyptian forms, embroidered in metallic threads, beading, and tiny jewels. The robe de style was available to couture customers.

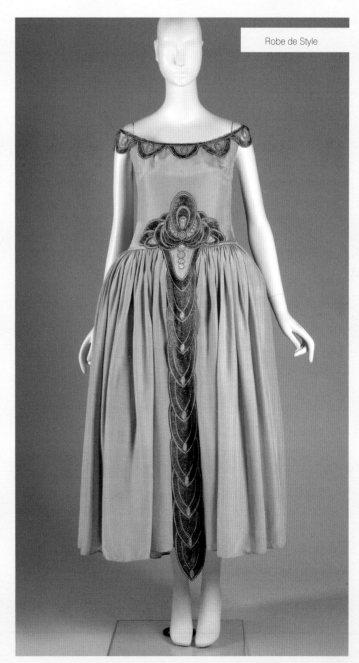

Robe de Style

Tribal

RUSSIAN STYLE

Inspired by peasant and elite traditions and colorful prints, as well as the heavy embellishment and rich mosaic fabrics and furs of the Russian Empire, Russian style is tempered with the structured coats and shiny trimmings of the military. The term can also refer to the influential Russian constructivism of the 1920s and 1930s. The most seminal reference to this style was Yves Saint Laurent's 1976 collection which juxtaposed folkloric with luxury fabrics, but many fall/winter collections are influenced by Russian myth and tailoring: Dolce & Gabbana's 2012–13 Tapestry and 2013–14 Byzantine Icon collections reflected the costumes of Russian empresses; Alexander McQueen 2008–09 collection was inspired by the Romanov court, while his 2014–15 collection (*see* image below) showed brocaded, fur-collared coats from the Steppes.

SPORTSWEAR/ATHLETIC WEAR

The development of specific clothing for active wear in the past century has depended on advances in materials technology, particularly in knitwear. It originated in underwear by designers such as Jaeger and John Smedley, who sought to design healthy clothing for a body liberated from corsetry. When Spandex and elastanes were added to cottons, fine wools, and synthetic fibers, the shape-retaining swimwear and close-fitting gym wear that we now take for granted were born.

TRIBAL

Tribal cultures have contributed vastly to modern Eurocentric fashion, with runway collections influenced by unusual woven textiles, ostrich feathers, and bold block prints once again on show at Alexander McQueen spring/summer 2014. Counterculture movements like the hippies have also contributed to this process, diffusing traditional fabrics in accessories such as backpacks, while tribal-style jewelry using natural materials has remained popular since appearing in the 1960s. "Tribal" is often used as a catch-all term for Afrocentric and ethnic fashion. Equally, it can refer to the fashion "tribes" who drive and characterize consumer taste in the fashion industry.

TROMPE L'OEIL

Literally "to trick the eye", trompe l'oeil art aims to convince viewers that they are viewing something in three dimensions, when it is actually a flat, two-dimensional surface. It was used particularly to decorate flat ceilings, creating the effect of domed surfaces or vaults open to the heavens. It has been employed in fashion in Op Art styles, or when designers use flat printed fabrics to create the effect of a textured surface or feature. For example, Mary Katrantzou's Perfume Bottle dresses (2009) use digital prints to suggest a distorted silhouette whose veracity is "confirmed" by real, 3-D jewelry.

Russian Style

TYROLEAN

Traditional Tyrolean style (*tracht*) has influenced a "folk luxe" style in fashion, especially for outdoors or hunting styles. Female dress

Unisex

– the dirndl – includes a long woolen or heavy fabric, ribbon-trimmed skirt. This is worn with a contrasting tightly fitted bodice top (*Leibl*) decorated with metallic buttons or braiding, over a white blouse. For men, traditional leather lederhosen are combined with felted jackets and a wool-felt hat (*Tirolerhut*). Primary colors – hunting green, red, and Prussian blue – are often used. Originally peasant dress, it was adopted by the late nineteenth-century aristocracy of the Austro-Hungarian empire as fashionable vacation wear.

UNISEX

Historically, unisex, non-gender-specific robes have existed such as the Chinese *hufu* or Japanese kimono, but unisex clothing has also been used to symbolize social change and sexual equality – for example, Rudi Gernreich's monokini (1964). Space-age exploration inspired Pierre Cardin to produce white all-in-ones for both sexes from close-cut knitted fabrics. Hollywood stars such as Marlene Dietrich and Anjelica Huston experimented with masculine dress: nowadays male celebrities are seen in sarongs and Céline blouses. Indeed, a great deal of everyday clothing could be said to be unisex, from sneakers to jeans, boyfriend cardigans, and long blazers.

UPCYCLING

Upcycled clothing is created from other pieces – vintage or modern – that might otherwise be thrown away. Some designs include more obviously recycled products, such as newspapers or plastics, and ask the fashion consumer to rethink their clothes' impact on the environment, as well as challenging their creativity. Upcycling is associated with the ethical fashion movement, and it has attracted collaboration with producers of ethical accessories and jewelry. Indeed, the ubiquity of the thrift/secondhand store and the growing popularity of sewing bees has shown how consumers enjoy creating their own look from previously owned clothing.

UTILITY

Utility clothing appeared in 1940s Britain and North America as materials were rationed. Alongside the "make-do-and-mend" campaign, utility clothing used minimal fabric and working time to produce functional clothes that retained a nod to fashion. For example, pockets were limited and pants did not have cuffs. Hardy Amies and Norman Hartnell, designers to the royal family, provided designs that were intended to be practical, as well as still appeal to the contemporary aesthetic, thus boosting morale. Utility clothing approached being a civilian uniform, as production runs were enormous, and all British products were stamped with CC41. Isabel Marant's dressed-down chic typifies the contemporary utility style, where military detail is matched with hardwearing fabrics in baggy cargo pants, chiffon khaki blouses, and jumpsuits.

SILHOUETTES

INTRODUCTION

Named after the "empty" fiscal policies of former French Finance Minister Etienne de Silhouette (1709–1767), the silhouette refers to the outlines of instantly recognizable styles in fashion, the forms of tailored clothing, as well as the human body itself. Today, one can buy clothes from a range of silhouettes – see the bridal catalogs, which propose dresses in any style – but, historically, fashion was dominated by successive silhouettes. This allows the fashion historian to compare the transition of styles and the development of tailoring. Key silhouettes also allow us to identify immediately the historical period to which certain clothing belongs.

A silhouette can be created by tailoring, the choice and drape of materials, or padding and corsetry, which enhances or distorts the natural human figure with bustles, peplums, and panniers. The end of the ancien regime is associated with the rejection of corsets and panniers, but they soon returned in Victorian bustles and the S-bend corset, while haute couture regularly includes form-changing engineering. In contrast, the new silhouettes of the 1950s and 1960s placed a geometrical form on the body, rather than emphasizing the body's own shape. The body now wore the clothes like a coat hanger. In the modern era, the silhouette refers more to the cut of an item, rather than its original period of wear, as "pure" silhouettes are adapted and accessorized away from their original form.

▲ The lavish use of luxury fabrics after wartime austerity and the return to a feminine silhouette contributed to the enduring popularity of Christian Dior's Corolle, or New Look, line. Here a silk taffeta dress with a tailored torso contrasts with a full skirt, exemplifying the role played by Paris as the leader of couture fashion.

▶ Dior's A-line updated the couturier's tailoring, and inspired 1960s silhouettes. Here, a narrow-shouldered jacket tapers gently down in a pyramidal form over a dropped-waist pleated skirt. The triangular form is emphasized by seams running from the bust to the hipline, and broad pleats. Dior's feminine ideal is maintained by matching accessories – hat, gloves, shoes, and umbrella.

A-LINE

Launched by Christian Dior in the spring of 1955, the A-line was identified with gently tapered, pleated-skirt suits, but was modernized by Yves Saint Laurent's Trapeze dress, while space-age fabrics allowed designers to make a structural A, typified by André Courrèges space-age A-line dress of 1967. The modern A-line dress has slim shoulders, a closely tailored torso and an elongated waist without a waistband, and the skirt gradually widens from waist to hem to stand away from the body, but without excessive fabric. Like the Princess Line, the silhouette is dependent on parallel seams that pass from the bust to the hip, rather than a horizontal waist seam.

COLUMNAR

The slim, columnar, waist- and hip-skimming silhouette first appeared in the empire line, Poiret's Oriental harem dress, and the 1920s flapper silhouette. Its futuristic simplicity appealed to the 1960s and suited new Spandex/elastane-rich materials as well as stiffer materials such as silks, velvets, or glazed cottons. Gowns might use single drops of draped fabric from bust to ankle, or combine a bodice and fitted skirt with a waist seam. The columnar silhouette is now ubiquitous as the strapless, body-skimming, red-carpet gown, perfected by Valentino. Its simple elegance is created by hidden corsetry, suggesting that the hips and bust of the wearer are perfectly matched.

COROLLE LINE

Christian Dior's 1947 Corolle collection was named after the open petals of a flower, and was in contrast to the military fashions of wartime Europe. The press dubbed it the New Look, and it was cut to emphasize a full bust, a narrow waist, and the curve of the hip, which is hidden under full skirts. It revisited

Dior Silhouettes

1951/52 – Ligne Longue

1952 – Ligne Sinueuse

1952/53 – Ligne Profilée

1953 – Ligne Tulipe

1953/54 – Ligne Vivante

1954 – Ligne Muguet

1954/55 – Ligne H

1955 – Ligne A

1955/56 – Ligne Y

1956 – Ligne Flèche

the crinoline silhouette by using interlining and wire to restrict the waist, and may employ slight padding over the hips to emphasize curves and make stand-away jacket hems – most iconically in the "Bar" suit of 1947, and robes à la française ball gowns.

EMPIRE LINE

The European vogue for the fashions of antiquity *c.*1800, popularized by the French Empress Josephine, favored muslin chemise dresses with a tight-fitting, crossover V-neck or scoop bodice, ending directly under the bust and thus negating form-shaping corsetry. The skirt fell directly down from the horizontal bodice seam, either as a column or a softly pleated, voluminous skirt. Representative of social change, the style was revived by Poiret's columnar silhouette, and the style was again popular in 1950s and 1960s teen fashion, as it emphasized youthful, boyish figures and modernity, and only required light underwear rather than the controlling girdles of the mature woman.

H-LINE

In contrast to his curving Corolle line, Dior's 1954 H-line or "French-bean" silhouette was deliberately modern and slim-fitting, with a columnar torso. Dior adapted the "H" form to a narrow-cut skirt suit, in which the jacket or tunic top fell to mid-thigh. The top had a square neck, or a V covered with a modesty panel, worn over a pencil skirt. Sleeveless versions were appropriate for evening dress, while the silhouette developed into a dropped waist, flapper-esque dress. Reactions to it were mixed, with one newspaper declaring, "Dior has abolished bosoms", but it nonetheless became a common silhouette (*Vogue*).

PRINCESS LINE

Created by Charles Frederick Worth in the 1870s, the gown experimented with tailoring by using a continuous linear seam from shoulder to hem, cut from lengths of fabric, rather than sewing a separate bodice to the skirt at the waist as in former fashions. As voluminous crinolines became less fashionable *c.*1865, a gored skirt allowed for a slimmer figure at the hips, with fullness at the hem: the bodice was now molded to the torso, and a fitted, leaner upper body was tailored from shaped panels. Modern interpretations retain a fitted, long-line torso and slightly flared, gored skirts of various lengths.

Dior's A-, S- and H-Lines

Robe à la Française

Dame in Reifrock.

ROBE À LA FRANÇAISE

A standard of formal aristocratic dress *c.*1720–1790, adapted from the restrictive *grand habit*. It had a flat-fronted, two-dimensional silhouette, with width created by pannier petticoats. A richly embroidered, trimmed-mantle, open-fronted gown was pinned to a contrasting, elaborate stomacher, itself pinned to a whalebone corset, which gave the silhouette an extremely small waist in comparison to the panniered hips. An equally lavishly trimmed underskirt was displayed under the mantle. The wearer displayed their wealth in the use of expensive silks, gold trimming, and reams of tiered lace *engageante* sleeves. The robe also integrated a low sack-back or Watteau cape.

THE SACK

While Dior's A-, H- and Y-lines were modernizing the silhouette, Cristóbal Balenciaga and Hubert de Givenchy concurrently developed the Sack dress, which was made famous in Federico Fellini's *La Dolce Vita*. Focusing on the shoulders and pelvis, rather than the curves, Balenciaga's 1957 Sack was a broad-shouldered, slim-hipped, drop-waisted loose shift, which tapered to the knees and was cut architecturally to form a geometrical diamond shape. It also influenced overcoat fashions, with width needed to wear this slouchy beltless style. Like the Trapeze dress, it heavily influenced the 1960s mini dress silhouette, as adapted by Mary Quant.

S-BEND

Distorting the elongated Princess line, *c.*1900 the mode for bustled skirts, exaggeratedly slim waists, and thrust-forward breasts was created by the elongated S-bend corset. Straight-fronted, this garment began just below the breasts and tilted the upper body forward. It compressed the breasts into a "pouter pigeon" mono-bosom wobbling on top of the corset, displayed in sleeveless evening dress or exaggerated by lacy blouses. The hips were pushed backward and thus the bottom was pushed out, steatopygously. The S-bend corset, also known as the swan-bill or health corset, was felt to ameliorate the problems of tight lacing with earlier corsets.

Y-Line

TRAPEZE

Yves Saint Laurent's first collection at Christian Dior (1958) introduced the Trapeze-line dress: a softer, more voluminous and definitely iconoclastic adaption of Dior's A-line. It flared outward from the shoulders – skimming over the bust – with a loose waistline, ignoring the hips. The skirts could accommodate pockets without compromising the silhouette. Finishing at knee length, hemlines rose in the 1960s, leading to the baby-doll dress and trapeze-cut coat. While early trapeze dresses were demurely trimmed with round collars or bows, or adapted in rich velvet for eveningwear, the 1960s saw the trapeze become synonymous with large bouffant hairstyles, accentuating the pyramidal effect.

V-LINE

The V-line refers to the geometrically exaggerated tailoring of 1940s formalwear, and is particularly associated with the work of the Hollywood costume designer and couturier Adrian, who experimented "with clean tailoring, seeing how far he could take a clean line without making it complicated" (Drake Stutesman in *Fashion in Film*, 2011). He launched his own ready-to-wear line in 1941 and offered a slim, modern silhouette, with broad-shouldered, slim-waisted suits. Collarless jackets ended in a dramatic V, which projected over the fitted skirt as a stiff-front peplum. Adrian eschewed embellishment other than geometrical detail, such as asymmetrical pockets.

WATTEAU

The Watteau, robe volante, or sack-backed dress was a relatively informal style of the early eighteenth century, in which a front-fastening loose robe displayed an elaborate chemise and petticoats worn underneath. At the back, a box-pleated demi-cape fell to the ground, adding to the voluminous skirts, themselves supported by a light pannier. The design allowed for the display of the modish large floral printed silks inspired by the Orient. The Watteau cape was revived in aesthetic dress, and was famously seen in Vivienne Westwood's 1996 Watteau Les Femmes collection, adapted for daywear and eveningwear.

Y-LINE

Christian Dior introduced his Y-line collection in 1955, answering Chanel's charges that his historically inspired New Look designs were too backward-looking. Rather than curves, this modern silhouette was characterized by a straight, narrow cut to knee length and reflected the move away from heavy girdles. The impression of a Y-form was enhanced by relatively broad shoulders, a high waistline, and a V-neck. The Y-line contributed to greater informality in day dress, but could be adapted for glamorous eveningwear. Off-the-shoulder necklines were achieved by hand-shaping luxury fabrics, rather than structural boning, while belts replaced hidden corsetry.

S-Bend

STYLES AND COMPONENTS OF DRESS

The history of apparel is one that began with functionality: garments were worn initially as protection from the elements and to provide modesty. As civilization became more established and complex – with survival no longer the main preoccupation – the notion of choice and style through the cut and shaping of clothes emerged, facilitated by various inventions such as the eyed needle and the weaving loom. By the time of the Ancient Egyptians, before 1500 BCE, clothes were more than just mere protection; they were signifiers of status, power, and taste, designed to be "read" by the society around the wearer. The idea that clothes project meaning has prevailed until the present day, when the styles of clothes one chooses to wear carry a plethora of sociological and cultural implications.

There are essentially 12 components that may go toward completing an outfit: the pants (trousers), the skirt, the shirt, the dress, the top, and the coat or jacket, accessorized by hats, bags, and shoes, with underwear underpinning it all. Each component may be fashioned in a variety of ways depending on the type of cloth used, the way in which the fabric is cut and tailored, how it is trimmed or embellished and how the components are assembled. All of these things are choices that may be made by anyone in any era, but they operate within a strict parameter of the prevailing accepted taste and style (and sometimes even within the law, when one considers the various sumptuary laws that have been issued throughout history in an attempt to manipulate the fashions and fabrics worn by certain classes).

Fashionable clothing was the preserve of the social elite until the Industrial Revolution, and the introduction of new technology in clothing production, such as the retailing of "readymades" in the late nineteenth century. ("Readymade" was a retail term used before the implementation of "ready-to-wear". It was widely adopted by the clothing industry and used to describe items that were purchased as a finished garment.) New styles were disseminated through the burgeoning number of periodicals throughout the following century, as well as through travel, movies, and runway shows. Dressmakers and tailors to the aristocracy, such as Louis Hyppolite Leroy, who introduced the empire line to the Empress Josephine in the eighteenth century, were forerunners of the designer as auteur, and the ones responsible for dictating trends.

The arrangement of various seams and woven or knitted pieces of fabric is subject to the design process, potentially leading to unlimited diversification. Certain designers are associated with various styles, fabrics, and cut of garment; for example, Madeleine Vionnet and the bias cut, Coco Chanel and bouclé tweed, Cristóbal Balenciaga and the dolman sleeve, Christian Dior and the hourglass silhouette, and Mary Quant and the miniskirt.

The language of clothes has a limited yet versatile vocabulary of styles and components. The juxtaposition of these elements, and the plundering of traditional tailoring techniques, together with contemporary innovations in both fabrics and embellishment, promulgates new ways of clothing the body that go beyond the purely protective.

▶ A satirical image from the 1860s, France. This photograph is part of a series that was taken to demonstrate the extreme impracticality of the steel crinoline at its widest, with the wearer having to be helped into it by an assistant.

JACKETS

INTRODUCTION

A jacket is a short, lightweight overgarment generally made up of sleeves and some form of collar with a center-front fastening, closed by a variety of means. The length, fabric, cut, and purpose of the jacket has evolved throughout the centuries, from its origin as the doublet of the Middle Ages to the vest and knee-length coat ensemble championed by King Charles II and, eventually, the tailored garment of contemporary fashion. While the elite continued to prefer the long coat as a formal garment, the laboring classes wore a shorter jacket for reasons of practicality. By around 1840 the shorter jacket was considered acceptable informal wear for the gentleman, particularly with the introduction of sporting jackets such as the Norfolk jacket.

Before the nineteenth century, women tended to only wear shawls, mantles, or cloaks outdoors. However, the Victorian-era Rational Dress Movement, which espoused the wearing of practical clothing in place of the restrictive corsets and crinolines, popularized the tailor-made jacket that was based on masculine tailoring. From this point onward, the jacket remained a key element in every woman's wardrobe.

▲ This single-breasted women's jacket from the quintessentially 1960s designer Ossie Clark – with print sections designed by his wife Celia Birtwell – has the wide lapels and form-fitting silhouette typical of womenswear at the time.

▶ Robert Dudley, first Lord of Leicester, was a leading member of the Elizabethan court. Dating from *c*.1575, this portrait shows Dudley's silk doublet with fashionable slashing on the body and sleeves (*see* Doublet, page 45).

Blazer

BLAZER

An informal jacket appropriated from male sporting dress, the term "blazer" is thought to have originated in England with the red sports jacket of the Lady Margaret Boat Club (1825), the rowing club of St. John's College, Cambridge. Loosely cut to allow greater movement in play, the colors may indicate affiliation with a college or university, a British independent school, or a sporting club. The three-colored striped blazer was worn by mods, a British youth subculture, in the 1960s, and is the favored garb of the preppy. Single- or double-breasted, with flat brass buttons, the blazer, in contemporary fashion, is an essential item of both men and women's wardrobes.

BLOUSON JACKET

So-called because the loose, informal shape resembles a blouse, the blouson is a twentieth-century jacket that is voluminous in shape but is pulled in around the waist with an elasticated or drawstring hem at the base. The arms are also typically voluminous with a similar elastication at the cuffs. They are usually fastened with a zipper and have a small, upright collar.

BOLERO

A short jacket, the bolero is usually worn open and features a curved center front. It originated in Spain, and became popular in the mid-eighteenth and early nineteenth centuries when it was worn over a princess-line gown, exposing the parallel vertical seams and emphasizing the waist. During this period it was frequently decorated with elaborate military-style passementerie (trimmings and edgings such as tassels or fringing) or beading.

Bolero

The bolero also became part of a dress-and-jacket combination in matching fabric, popular during the 1950s.

BOMBER JACKET

Leather flight jackets with high wraparound collars and zipper closures with wind flaps, frequently lined with fur, were first distributed by the U.S. Army with the establishment of the Aviation Clothing Board in September 1917. The D-1 leather flight or "bomber" jacket was first worn by the U.S. Air Force in World War II, designed for the uninsulated cabin of airplanes. The jacket was appropriated by hip-hop stars in the 1980s, and is similar in style to the preppy varsity jacket.

DONKEY JACKET

An item of British workwear, the utilitarian credentials of the donkey jacket reside in the coarse woolen cloth and the reinforced panel across the back of the shoulders. Reputedly created by John Key of Rugeley, for the Manchester Ship Canal Company in 1889, the name may derive from "donkey work", meaning grueling, menial labor. The donkey jacket was worn in the 1950s as a declaration of solidarity with the workers and the "angry young men" of the era.

DOUBLET

The doublet was the staple component of the male wardrobe from the beginning of the fifteenth century to the second half of the seventeenth century (*see* page 43). Cut from velvet or satin, the waist-length jacket was worn with a codpiece, created to cover the genital area. In 1570 padding was introduced to the doublet – mimicking the lines of contemporary plate armor – and was stuffed with bombast, rags, horsehair, and flock to form an overhanging "peasecod" belly. Modern takes on the doublet include Franck Sorbier's fairy-tale jacket, pictured below, for his fall/winter 2013–14 couture collection.

Doublet

DRAPE JACKET (TEDDY BOY)

Edwardian aristocratic dress revived by the tailors of Savile Row in the 1950s was appropriated by the British working-class youth subculture, the teddy boys. Similar in style to the zoot suit (*see also* pages 56–57), this long-line jacket had a drape front and was cut in bright-colored fabrics, with narrow velvet lapels. A steel tail-comb featured in the breast pocket, used both as a weapon and to groom the signature D.A. ("Duck's Arse") quiff. The jacket was worn with string ties, narrow "drainpipe" jeans, and crepe-soled shoes, known as "brothel creepers".

HACKING JACKET

Worn by both men and women, the single-breasted tweed hacking jacket was initially designed for horse-riding, or "hacking". The name is derived from the word "hack" or "hackney", a saddle horse chosen for informal pleasure as opposed to a horse used for jumping or hunting. Tailored with long single or double vents at the back to accommodate the rider sitting astride, the jacket features slanted flapped pockets. American designer Ralph Lauren produces contemporary versions in his appropriation of British aristocratic dress.

MANDARIN JACKET

This style originated from a Western interpretation of dresses worn by mandarins in Imperial China, especially during the Qing Dynasty, as part of the traditional garment of Manchu. Following the Chinese revolution of 1911, a black mandarin jacket and a blue long gown were officially designated as a ceremonial outfit. The short, unfolded stand-up collar of the jacket – typically rising

vertically from between 1 and 2 inches (2 and 5 centimeters) – is a style frequently adopted by contemporary designers.

MOTORBIKE JACKET

A perennial symbol of youthful rebellion, the black leather motorbike jacket was adopted by the motorbike gangs of the 1950s, epitomized by Marlon Brando in László Benedek's 1953 movie *The Wild One* (*see* opposite). The motorbike jacket was first introduced in 1928, and Brando reputedly wears the Perfecto Model 618, a lancer-fronted jacket designed by Irving Schott and named after his favorite cigar, the Perfecto. The leather motorcycle jacket had military connotations and was adopted by the Army Air Corps prior to World War II.

Drape Jacket

Motorbike Jacket

Mandarin Jacket

NEHRU JACKET

The Nehru jacket was created in northern
India, possibly in Jodhpur, Rajasthan, in the
1940s as the *band gale ka* (Hindu-Urdu for
"closed neck coat"). The high-standing collar
of the Nehru jacket, based on the collar of
the *achkan* – historically the royal court dress
of Indian nobles – is cut close to the neck.
Named after, and popularized, by Sir Pandit
Jawaharial Nehru (1889–1964), the first prime
minister of independent India in 1947, the
Nehru jacket first gained popularity in the
West in 1966, following the adoption of the
style by musicians such as the Beatles.

NORFOLK JACKET

An item of British sporting dress, the tweed
single-breasted Norfolk jacket is constructed
with vertical box pleats at the back to facilitate
raising the arm to fire a gun. Endorsed by the
sartorially influential Edward, Prince of Wales
(later King Edward VII), the oldest son of
Queen Victoria and Prince Albert, the Norfolk
jacket was named after the county of Norfolk,
the site of his country residence.

Safari Jacket

Zouave Jacket

SAFARI JACKET

First seen in the late nineteenth century, the safari jacket is based on the British khaki drill uniforms worn in warm climates. The belted jacket features the distinctive "bellows" pocket, with an expansion pleat, applied to the outside of the garment. It was subsequently adopted by big game hunters such as Denys Finch Hatton before Parisian designer Yves Saint Laurent rendered it fashionable when he introduced the safari jacket in neutral linens in 1968. It was particularly popular with the release of such films as Sydney Pollack's 1985 movie *Out of Africa*.

SMOKING JACKET

In 1860 Edward, Prince of Wales, requested that Henry Poole, Savile Row's most prominent tailor, cut off the tails of his evening suit to create a more comfortable smoking jacket, thus creating the first modern dinner jacket. In 1886 James Potter wore a version of the jacket to his club in Tuxedo Park, New York, resulting in the style being called the "tuxedo" in the United States. Parisian designer Yves Saint Laurent introduced the female version of "Le Smoking" in 1966.

SPENCER (ETON) JACKET

This waist-length style of jacket first appeared in the 1790s, when George, Second Earl Spencer, removed the tails from his tailcoat. It was adopted as part of mess dress – military formal eveningwear – and in 1820, the prestigious British independent boarding school Eton College appropriated the jacket for first-year students' uniforms. The style was adopted by bellhops and waiters, and the jacket continues to be used as part of military mess dress and in the service industries.

WINDBREAKER (WINDCHEATER)

Designed to resist wind chill, the lightweight windbreaker, more commonly known as the "windcheater" in the U.K., features elasticated cuffs and waist – occasionally formed from ribbed knitted fabric – and a center-front zipper fastening. The term "windbreaker" was the brand name of gabardine jackets produced by the John Rissman company of Chicago. They are now made in high-performance fabrics for comfort and durability.

ZOUAVE JACKET

Throughout the nineteenth century, civilian clothing for men and women imitated military uniforms in cuts and decoration, including the zouave jacket, based on the French Zouave uniform. The short embroidered jacket or bodice, cut with or without sleeves, gained the most popularity during the 1850s, when French Zouaves were fighting in the Crimean War, and during the American Civil War in the 1860s.

SUITS

INTRODUCTION

Representing authority and an emblem
of official power, one that suggests a life
free from physical toil, the suit creates a
professional identity that is essentially male.
The three-piece suit, allowing for differentials
of cut and fabric, has been the basis of the
male wardrobe since the last quarter of the
seventeenth century, when King Charles II,
on the restoration of the British throne in
1660, appeared in a knee-length coat, vest
(the seventeenth-century term for a waistcoat
that is still used in the U.S.), and breeches.
Throughout the eighteenth century, the
comfortable and practical coat, waistcoat, and
breeches, mostly made of wool, underwent
little alteration. By the 1780s this style of dress
was correct for all but the most formal of
occasions and obligatory court appearances.
By 1806 the first tailor was established in
Savile Row in London, with the emphasis on
fit and sculptural seaming and construction.
Ready-to-wear versions of the suit were worn
by city workers, and by the 1920s, it was worn
for all business events, and so the suit became
the all-purpose male costume of the twentieth
and twenty-first centuries. With the advent
of 1980s power-dressing, women began to
adopt elements of male dress, wearing an
approximation of the male suit in the pantsuit
(trouser suit).

▲ Exemplifying fashionable androgyny, Yves Saint Laurent introduced the three-piece
tailored suit for women, further emphasized by the masculine styling.

▶ Coco Chanel models a suit of her own design on the rue du Faubourg St. Honoré in
Paris in 1929. The relaxed fit and soft silhouette of the iconic cardigan suit (*see* page 52),
worn with her trademark rope of pearls, is typical of Chanel's aesthetic.

Double-breasted Suit

DOUBLE-BREASTED SUIT

A suit defined by its jacket, which has an overlapping front panel that usually crosses from left to right. The overlap is held in place by two vertical rows of buttons. Double-breasted jackets should not be worn unbuttoned, as this will spoil the line of the suit. The length of the lapels can vary, sometimes reaching even to the bottom button of the jacket.

SINGLE-BREASTED SUIT

A single-breasted suit has a straight front opening that only just overlaps, enough to allow a single row of buttons to hold the sides of the jacket together. The lapel length and the number of buttons can vary according to fashion, but it is not common to have more than two or three. The single-breasted suit was at its most elegant in the 1960s, when Brooks Brothers created slimline suits that were worn by successful men such as President Kennedy and the advertising men of Madison Avenue. The look was revived in the 2010s when the television series *Mad Men*, set during the 1950s and 1960s, became popular.

CARDIGAN SUIT

The cardigan suit was first designed by Coco Chanel, and it encapsulates all that was revolutionary about her designs. Loose-fitting, this three-piece in knitted jersey fabric included a long-line, edge-to-edge jacket, a "pullover" beneath, and a calf-length skirt that matched the jacket, rather than the sweater. Accessorized by the pearls for which she became famous, the cardigan suit represented a liberating garment that was easy to put on and wear but that retained a sense of respectable elegance and modernity.

JUMPSUIT
(BOILERSUIT/SIREN SUIT)

Also more simply known as an overall, this one-piece garment with a front fastening (usually a zipper) on the torso is commonly worn by manual laborers, either alone or over their own garments, to protect them from dirt. The boilersuit is sometimes adopted by people who are not involved in manual work as a political statement, with many feminist women wearing the garment during the 1980s. During World War II, the "siren" or "shelter" suit was popularized as a practical garment to be worn during an air raid. Its invention is generally attributed to Winston Churchill, who commissioned a garment from his tailor, Turnbull and Asser, that could quickly be thrown on over pajamas. The siren suit was given a couture spin with designers such as Elsa Schiaparelli and Digby Morton producing their own glamorous versions.

Jumpsuit

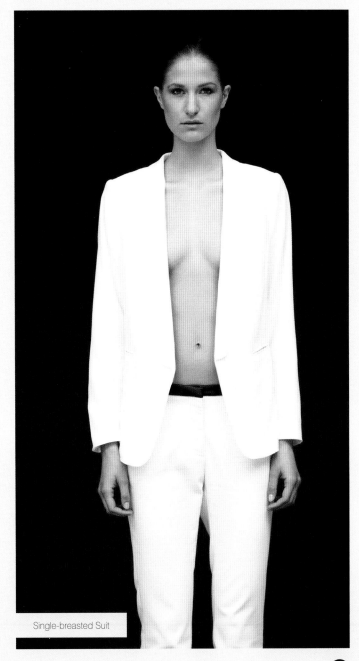

Single-breasted Suit

Tailormade

Mao Suit

LOUNGE SUIT

The lounge suit gained favor around 1850 to 1860, as a development of the paletot, a loosely cut jacket without a waist seam worn with a matching vest (waistcoat) and pants. A single-breasted suit with a straight front opening that only just overlaps, it was initially worn after lunch and only in private, and never on formal occasions or in the city. However, by 1920 ready-to-wear versions were worn by finance workers, and the lounge suit was subsequently worn for all business scenarios.

MAO SUIT

The Mao, or *zhongshan*, suit had first been worn in China in the early part of the twentieth century as a compromise between

historical costume and Western attire, mostly by a government keen to appear modern and forward-thinking. After the Cultural Revolution in 1966, it seemed politically expedient for both sexes to wear the suit preferred by Chairman Mao. It came in only three colors – gray, green, or blue – with a high, turned-down collar and military-style buttoned pockets.

PANTSUIT (TROUSER SUIT)

A specifically female ensemble, the pantsuit is derived from men's suiting. Groundbreaking figures such as Marlene Dietrich and Katharine Hepburn first dressed in menswear in the 1930s as a symbol of their emancipation and individuality. However, pantsuits specifically tailored to the female form were not made commercially available until 1966, when Yves Saint Laurent designed "Le Smoking" – a sleek three-piece pantsuit that was inspired by Dietrich. However, it was not considered a modern classic until Helmut Newton photographed a version of the YSL suit in 1976.

TAILORMADE

The tailormade suit specifically refers to a type of day suit bought from a tailor rather than a dressmaker, popularly worn by women at the end of the nineteenth century. Women's clothing was becoming more simplified in this period, taking on elements of masculine tailoring. The tailormade was a simple suit jacket, cut to fit the female form, worn with a long flared skirt in a matching fabric (usually in plain linen or serge weave). A shirtwaister blouse of white cotton was worn underneath.

TROTTEUR (WALKING SUIT)

A woolen suit for women first seen in the 1890s, but that continued to be popular well into the twentieth century. Coinciding with the greater freedoms women were experiencing, it was specifically designed to enable them to move about freely when taking part in outdoor activities such as hill-walking. The trotteur suit was first produced by a company called Redfern, based in France. The skirt was shorter than usual, which allowed for freedom of movement, and was worn with a loose jacket cut in a masculine style.

Pantsuit

TUXEDO

Known as a dinner suit, or colloquially a "DJ" (for dinner jacket) in the U.K., the tuxedo is a semi-formal suit to be worn in the evening. The suit consists of a black jacket, a black bow tie worn over a starched white dress shirt and a black trouser with satin or grosgrain stripes on the outside seam, often with a cummerbund around the waist. Although it is a design classic, components of the tux can adjust with the prevailing fashion – from the width of the lapels (which should always be in satin or silk) and shoulders to the general cut (double- or single-breasted) or type of shirt worn underneath.

VEST (WAISTCOAT)

One of the oldest tailored garments, the term vest was first used in the very early sixteenth century to describe a close-fitting, buttoned-up garment worn under a doublet (*see* page 45). By the end of the eighteenth century, the waistcoat was short at the back and had long decorative panels to the front, almost reaching the knee. In the twentieth century it had become a plainer garment, matching the fabric of the outer jacket, and could be worn alone with pants or as part of a three-piece suit.

ZOOT SUIT (ZAZOU)

A suit in which all the elements are exaggerated. The shoulders are wide, the jacket long – even sometimes reaching the knee – the waist is cut small, and the trousers are "peg" (loose at the top, narrowing to a tapered ankle). A key garment for African-Americans, Italians, and Hispanics during the Swing age, the zoot suit was at its height of popularity toward the end of the 1930s. Not only was

the tailoring eye-catching, but so was the cloth from which they were made, which was colorful and sometimes patterned.

Tuxedo

PANTS

INTRODUCTION

Modern pants, or trousers, replaced breeches in the early 1800s. It was at this point that they began to be made from fabric that matched the jacket or coat, creating the early precursor to the suit. At around 1840, pants began to be fitted with a fly-front fastening – a much neater construction than the traditional front-flap opening of earlier pantaloons. One of the most influential fashion leaders in this transitional period was the Prince of Wales, the future King Edward VII, who made many changes to the established male wardrobe, introducing a new informality. These innovations included moving the pant creases from the front to the sides – as in the German style – and the adoption of a turned-up cuff to protect the hem from dirt. For women, pants were not an option until the late nineteenth century, and even then they were only embraced by a small minority of daring women. It was not until the socio-political changes after World War II, when women entered the workforce in large numbers, that pants as womenswear became socially acceptable, and even then only on informal occasions.

▲ One of the first brands to embrace the idea of designer jeans in the 1980s, Calvin Klein used provocative imagery and the famous tagline "Nothing gets between me and my Calvins" to sell jeans – via teen beauty Brooke Shields – to the fashion-conscious masses (see Jeans, page 63).

▶ Appropriating the cut of traditional equestrian dress, Ralph Lauren for fall/winter 2012 tailors the jodhpur for everyday outerwear (*see* Jodhpurs, page 63).

Capri

BIB OVERALLS (DUNGAREES)

Bib overalls, otherwise known as dungarees, have their origins in workwear and were designed to be worn over normal clothing when doing dirty jobs to protect the garments underneath. The overalls are made up of a pair of pants with an attached bib at the front, leaving the arms and shoulders uncovered. Bib overalls made of denim are the most ubiquitous, but the name "dungarees" comes from the calico fabric they were often made of, from the Dongari Killa region of India.

CAPRI

The capri – a mid-length, narrow women's trouser, usually side-fastening – is named after the Italian island that became popular as a jet-set holiday destination in post-war Europe. Emilio Pucci embraced the resortwear market by producing capri pants in bright colors, to be worn with his print shirts. Recently, the capri, when made of luxury fabrics such as silk brocade, has been worn as part of a pantsuit. An even shorter version of the capri is the pedal pusher – also known as clam diggers.

CIGARETTE PANTS

A slim-fitting narrow trouser similar to the capri (and also popular during the 1950s), but ankle length rather than cropped, it resembles the columnar silhouette of a slim cigarette. The waistline is high and the trouser follows the line of the hip closely before tapering slightly to the ankle. To keep the look sleek, cigarette pants have a side fastening and are often worn with a crease ironed down the front to elongate the silhouette.

CULOTTES

A type of loose, casual trouser that was deemed socially acceptable womenswear in the early twentieth century. The bifurcated garment had been a solely male garment for millennia; however, the increase in political and social freedom experienced by women in the 1930s meant that they could wear pants in certain situations without controversy. Culottes were the perfect compromise, as they appear as a skirt when static, only revealing their bifurcation when movement occurs.

DRAINPIPES

Drainpipe trousers are a very closely fitting garment worn by both men and women, close in appearance to skinny jeans but with a straighter line beneath the knee. They are most

Bib Overalls

frequently made of denim and are worn as jeans – although designers such as Hedi Slimane took the drainpipe silhouette and used it in formal suiting. Their origins can be seen in the *churidar* leggings worn as part of the traditional *shalwar kameez* of India and Pakistan, a look that was passed on to formal male dress in the early nineteenth century. Since the silhouette was revived in the 1950s, a form of drainpipes has been in fashion almost constantly, with many subcultures adopting it including teddy boys, mods, punks, and 1980s rock bands.

FLARES

Flares, or bell-bottoms, are inextricably linked to the hippie movement of the 1970s, although bell-bottomed trousers were also popular in the 1930s – particularly as naval uniform – and they also had a revival in the "Summer of Love" in 1989. Flared pants are narrow and tight-fitting at the waist and either flare out from the thigh or from the knee. While the suiting of the 1970s featured somewhat modest flares with small circumferences, youth culture embraced the aesthetic with increasingly wider circumferences – with those at the greatest extent known as "loon pants".

Cigarette Pants

Gaucho Pants

GAUCHO PANTS

For the nineteenth-century Latin American cowboys who originally wore them (calling them *bombachas*), gaucho pants were a key part of their traditional dress. They were a loose-fitting, wide-hipped trouser belted with a loincloth, which was better for riding horses. Today, a gaucho pant is essentially a cropped, fitted trouser that is tight around the waist but loose around the legs, ending abruptly at the knees.

HAREM PANTS

These wide-legged pants, which have a narrow cuff at the ankle and a gusset that hangs down as far as the knees (or even as far as the ankles), appear in fashion whenever there is a revival of the hippie bohemian aesthetic, such as in Paul Poiret's jeweled Jupes Culottes from 1911. Originally from Turkey and the Arabian Peninsula, these skirt/pant hybrids were worn by women in the harem court. The early harem pants were designed to completely cover and disguise the body shape of the wearer, being vast and voluminous.

HIPSTERS (BUMSTER)

Hipster trousers, which were ubiquitous during the 1990s and early 2000s and so called because they sat on or below the hips, have a clear and definitive genesis. Alexander McQueen, wanting to show off as much of the lower back as possible, in 1996 produced a trouser known as the "bumster", which sat below the natural top of the bottom, revealing an area of "bottom cleavage". This extreme version was watered down and adapted by the mainstream and worn as the hipster.

Jeans

Hipsters

JEANS

Jeans, along with the T-shirt, have been an
informal multi-generational uniform for
decades, and have gone from being functional
workwear worn by the laboring classes to
expensive, high-end designer garments. The
first jeans, made from blue denim fabric, were
worn in the American West in the nineteenth
century, as they were hardwearing trousers
suitable for heavy labor. The youth cultures
of the 1950s adopted the jean in a spirit of
rebellion, and from this point the jean has
gone on to be embraced by all generations
and all strata of society. In recent decades,
jeans have been a key garment in a designer's
diffusion line, and many designer denim
brands are established luxury goods brands.

JODHPURS

Specifically designed for horseback riding,
jodhpurs can take two forms. One, more
commonly worn for casual riding, is the
jodhpur that clings to the leg throughout its
length, from thigh to ankle, with suede patches
at the inside of each knee to protect from wear
from the saddle. The other, a more formal and
traditional jodhpur, has a baggy section from
thigh to knee. Either style can be worn with
short ankle or knee-high boots.

KNICKERBOCKERS (PLUS-FOURS)

The knickerbocker (Dutch for "knee-pants") is a loose men's trouser, invariably made from tweed, that is curtailed just below the knee, where the fabric is gathered into a close-fitting cuff. Initially a military garment from the 1860s, the garment was adopted for country pursuits such as shooting and golf, as they allowed plenty of freedom of movement. Plus-fours are a variation on a knickerbocker, with an extra 4 inches of fabric in the overhang around the cuffs to add further volume.

Knickerbockers

Leggings

Oxford Bags

Palazzo Pants

LEGGINGS

Historically, leggings were known as *braies*, or hose, and were simple bifurcated garments that were cut close to the leg and worn by men. These garments were never particularly tight, as there was no Lycra or elastic to make them cling. The modern version of the legging has its origins in the sportswear fashions of the 1970s – when Lycra leotards and other exercise wear were worn in clubs such as Studio 54 before the trend then spread to daywear.

OXFORD BAGS

A men's flannel trouser popular in the 1920s, the Oxford bag was a controversial garment at the time. They are straight-legged but excessively wide (up to 40 inches/1 meter) from waist to foot and were generally worn with blazers or a pullover and shirt. They were part of a movement toward informality of dress, instigated by a generation that rejected the formality of the pre-war years. As such, the bags represented a type of youthful rebellion against their elders and were named after the Oxford students who first wore them.

PALAZZO PANTS

Like many fashions, the wide-legged, high-waisted palazzo pant was first seen on Hollywood movie stars in the 1930s before being embraced by the masses. Initially designed by Coco Chanel, the pajama trouser, or beach pajama, was designed as resortwear, and had its origins from a visit she paid to Venice in 1920 when she wore a wide-legged sailor's trouser that was a far more practical garment for getting in and out of gondolas (*see* right). She called the trouser the "palazzo pant" for the palaces that she saw in Venice.

PEG TOPS

A pant that has a high waist and voluminous shape around the hips and tapers into a carrot shape as it reaches the ankle, the volume being created by adding pleats and panels of fabric. Originally a style of men's pant, having its origins in the early nineteenth century, the peg top was adopted by women in the early twentieth century, as they were particularly practical for women who found themselves working in factories during World War I (*see* below). The name "peg" came from the method of pegging the narrow hems of the pant legs.

SALOPETTES

The salopette, a variation on bib overalls, is most commonly associated with skiwear today and is usually made from waterproof, synthetic, high-performance fabrics and padded for insulation. The word is derived from the French term for workmen's trousers. The pants have a high bib at the front and reach high up the back, in order to stop snow from gathering underneath, and are held in place by elasticated suspenders (braces). The pants are flared at the ankles, usually with a short zipper, in order to fit over ski boots.

Peg Tops

SHORTS

A bifurcated garment usually tailored in the same way as pants, but shorter in length – typically falling to the knee or higher – with those that only just cover the buttocks being known as hot pants. The modern shorts, as opposed to the short breeches of the past, were first worn by men in the 1930s, and were designed to be worn when taking part in summer activities. However, their appealing practicality means they are now worn by all ages and genders in hot weather.

STIRRUP (SKI) PANTS

With its origins in sportswear (both equestrian and snow sports), the ski pant was a key garment during the 1980s, when fashion adopted many sports garments for everyday wear. They are a close-fitting style of trouser with a tapered ankle with straps that run underneath the foot to hold it in place. The narrowness of the leg is balanced by the flexibility of the fabric, which allows for freedom of movement, and most ski pants have elastane or Lycra in their fabric mix.

TOREADORS

A toreador is a Spanish bullfighter, hence toreador pants are a garment that resembles the close-fitting, cropped-to-mid-calf trouser worn by such men when performing in the bull ring. What distinguishes them from plain cropped pants or clam diggers is the decoration – they usually appear with a slight kick at the bottom, which is emphasized by buttoned cuffs or embroidery. Toreador pants are also often bicolor, with the external panels of the legs being heavily embroidered.

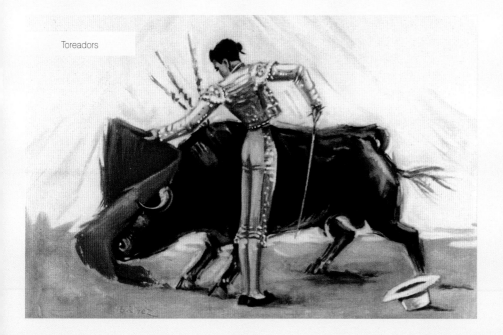

Toreadors

DRESSES

INTRODUCTION

The term "dress" to describe a woman's outfit only began to be used in the nineteenth century – when the fashion changed from a garment made up of a separate bodice and skirt to one constructed in one piece. Generally, between the twelfth and sixteenth centuries women wore a gown, or a **houppelande** – essentially a loosely cut, long garment with long, decorative sleeves, with the material gathered at the waist or under the breasts with a belt. By the sixteenth century, a woman's outfit had fragmented into several elements: the "pair of bodies", or stays; a bodice; a stomacher; and the skirt. The bodice went around the back and sides of the torso. It was either laced up at the front with a stomacher panel concealing the lacing or, more commonly, it was laced onto a separate triangular-shaped boned stomacher panel that helped to flatten the body's shape. The fabric of the skirt was then attached along the bottom edge of the bodice. The sleeves were also a separate entity.

Although the shapes, lengths, and variety of fabrics changed, these elements remained essentially the same until around 1800, when Empress Josephine promulgated the fashion for a one-piece empire-line gown (*see also* page 73). A rejection of the ancien regime and its increasingly extravagant ensembles, the empire line was a delineating marker between the past and the Early Modern Period when a simple dress could be worn.

▲ Two day dresses in the empire-line style, from the turn of the nineteenth century. The simplicity of the empire-line dress bypasses the natural waist with ingénue crossover bodices and columnar skirts (*see* Empire-line Dress, page 73).

▶ Petrus Christus's 1449 painting of a young aristocratic couple buying a wedding ring in fifteenth-century Bruges, *A Goldsmith in His Shop*, depicts a bride wearing an extremely ornate example of a houppelande gown, with its high waist and gold brocade fabric.

꙰ *... per ꭓpi me · fecit · aᵒ ⅰ₵₵₀ꙺ* ꙰

Bubble Dress

BIAS-CUT DRESS

A dress made from fabric that has been cut at an angle to the grain of the weave. This technique creates a draped garment that clings to the shape of the wearer, with the tension in the fabric allowing for flexibility. The bias cut reached its apotheosis in the 1930s, when it was pioneered by Madame Vionnet and popularized by Hollywood costume designer Adrian. John Galliano revived the fashion in the mid-1990s with his collections for Christian Dior.

BUBBLE (BALLOON) DRESS

This can refer to either a skirt or a dress with an inflated circular silhouette that resembles a balloon or bubble. The dress flares out, shaped by stiffened linings, from below the shoulders to reach a narrow hem, generally at the knee. The balloon skirt is narrow at the waist before flaring out at the hip with a narrow hem at knee length. The bubble/balloon silhouette was first seen in the collections of Pierre Cardin in the late 1950s, although there are less dramatic precursors in the collections of Paul Poiret, 50 years earlier.

CHEMISE (SACK DRESS)

Originally a loose linen unisex under-garment, the chemise evolved into a dress by the late eighteenth century, when it became a lightweight, unstructured dress secured at the waist by a wide sash. A variation was the Perdita chemise, which had button fastenings running along the entire front of the dress. By the 1920s the chemise had again mutated into a relatively casual dress that could be simply pulled over the head. It was worn unfitted and without fastenings.

Chiton

CHEONGSAM

A high-necked, slim-fitting dress with
a mandarin collar and an asymmetrical
fastening that runs under the arm, the
cheongsam was traditionally worn in China
but was adopted by Western women in the
1930s, when the mania for chinoiserie –
influenced by movies such as *Shanghai Express*
– was at its peak. The extreme narrowness
of the skirt necessitates one or two side slits.
The fabric is usually silk and decorated with
various Chinese motifs.

CHITON

The chiton is the term for the many varieties
of sleeveless tunics worn by both men and
women in Ancient Greece. It included
rectangular pieces of fabric that had no
tailoring or stitching, but were held in place
with brooches and pins or by being draped
over the shoulder. Typically women wore
ankle-length chitons and men wore them to
the hip, with both being belted at the waist,
although women often had an extra belt
under the breasts.

Cocktail Dress

COAT-DRESS

A dress designed to resemble a coat, sharing the same features such as front fastenings from top to bottom and long sleeves, along with other elements such as a collar and a belt, but in a lighter weight. The first coat-dresses were worn in the early twentieth century, but it was not until the 1980s that they became particularly fashionable, when Princess Diana was seen in a series of coat-dresses – for whom they were a particularly appealing combination of formal and feminine.

COCKTAIL DRESS

A dress designed for the cocktail hour when pre-dinner aperitifs were drunk – a habit first started in the decadent years after World War I and Prohibition in Europe and America. A cocktail dress must fall below the knee and be made from suitably luxurious fabrics, such as satin or silk, and is usually sleeveless, although gloves tended to be worn until the 1940s. The first designer to specifically label a dress as "cocktail" was Christian Dior in the early 1940s.

DJELLABA

A long, loose-fitting, hooded tunic traditionally worn by both men and women in North Africa, the djellaba was originally worn by the Berber tribes. The hood, named the *qod*, serves a dual purpose – to keep the head warm in the cooler mountains and at night and to keep the sun off the head during the day. The season dictates the textile used, with cotton djebellas worn in summer and wool worn in winter.

EMPIRE-LINE DRESS

Named after the Napoleonic era between 1800 and 1820, when this style was at its peak of popularity, the empire-line dress has a high waist that sits just under the breasts with an elongated, narrow silhouette. The look, led by the influential Empress Josephine, was inspired by the costumes of the classical democracies, which were political inspiration for the new French regime. It served as a desirable contrast to the tightly corseted dresses of the previous century and the ancien regime. *See also* page 68.

KAFTAN

A loose garment originally worn by men in the Middle East and North Africa before being adopted as a fashion garment and, ultimately, as a beach coverall. The kaftan is T-shaped, with wide sleeves. It can be hip-length or longer, and is sometimes belted at the waist. The neckline is round but with a V-shaped slot that is often decorated. The kaftan was periodically popular during the early part of the twentieth century, but was adopted enthusiastically in the late 1960s by people on the hippie trail to the East.

KIMONO

The traditional costume of Japan, the kimono is a T-shaped garment with wide, square arms that are cut in as part of the garment cloth. It is loose-fitting but usually worn with an obi belt or sash. The traditional gown is ankle-length, but modern fashion kimonos can be shorter. The highly decorated fabric is traditionally silk, but synthetics and cotton are now used, with the design either printed or woven. The kimono was first adopted in the West in the late nineteenth century, when companies such as Liberty began to import Japanese goods.

Kimono

Pinafore

PINAFORE (JUMPER)

The pinafore (so-called because it was "pinned afore") was originally a child's garment made up of a bib and straps that was worn over their clothes in order to protect them from dirt. By the twentieth century, a type of pinafore dress made of gray, navy, or other subdued colors was a school uniform staple, although by then it had gained a back and a pleated skirt. In the 1960s the pinafore dress was popularized by designers such as Mary Quant, worn by young women who were part of the Youthquake, where a youthful insouciance was ideal.

SACK

Another dress that has its origins in the surge of creativity that followed World War II, the sack first emerged in 1957 with several designers producing their own version, including Cristóbal Balenciaga, Hubert de Givenchy, and Jacques Griffe. The sack served as a contrast to the prevailing hourglass silhouette that had dominated couture since Dior's New Look collection of 1947 and consisted of a strong shoulder line that billowed out, bypassing the body before being gathered up again around the hem. It was loosely based on the *sacque,* or Watteau dress, from the eighteenth century.

Sari

SARI

A type of garment worn by Hindu women, composed of a long rectangular piece of cloth that is wrapped around the body and over the head, secured in such a way that does not require any additional fastening devices. In India, where the population is largely Hindu, the caste system has a dress code, and the number and style of folds to the sari denote the caste to which the wearer belongs. Saris can be plain or highly decorated with gold thread. The color palette is vivid, with pink being a popular choice. They are worn with a *choli* body beneath and *churidar* leggings.

SHEATH

A close-fitting dress that follows the contours of the body, but not to the extent that movement is restricted as with body-con dresses. The sheath, first seen in the early 1950s, is typically sleeveless, with a fastening at the back or side that leaves the front simply unadorned – revealing the darting seams that create the form-fitting shape – and usually falls at the knee or below. The simplicity of the cut makes it a flexible backdrop for more elaborate surface designs, or it can be left unadorned to create a clean, elegant garment. It can be worn during the day or at night, depending on the type of fabric used.

SHIRTWAIST DRESS (SHIRTWAISTER)

A dress that shares the same core features as a tailored shirt – with collar, cuffs, and center-front fastening to the hem – and typically knee-length. Also called a shirt dress, this was a popular garment in the early twentieth century when it was made in the "shirtwaist factories" in lower New York City. It is associated with the 1950s idealized housewife, who was usually depicted in the media wearing a version that was cut narrow around the shoulders, closely fitted at the waist before billowing out into a full skirt. In the more practical 1970s, the shirtwaister had evolved into a streamlined garment made of more clinging fabrics, with a narrower skirt.

Shirtwaist Dress

Tent Dress

SMOCK

Originally a T-shaped country laborer's garment made of cotton or linen, with long, voluminous sleeves caught up at the wrist and a gathered neckline, or a type of undergarment worn next to the skin like a chemise. By the late nineteenth century the smock had come to be inextricably linked with the pre-Raphaelite movement, which valued the aesthetics of the honest laborer and which adopted garments that reflected a pre-industrial age. Both men and women wore a more luxurious version of the smock, using naturally dyed fabrics.

TEA GOWN

The social ritual of tea drinking within the home emerged in the 1870s, and required a more informal type of garment. Boned corsets were abandoned and free-flowing garments known as *déshabillé* were worn. The comfort of the tea gown was soon adopted for other, more formal occasions, but continued to be worn mostly during the daytime. Invariably diaphanous, and frequently executed in a vibrant floral printed silk, the tea dress remains a popular style of garment in the twenty-first century.

TENT (TRAPEZE) DRESS

The trapeze line, first seen in the early collections by Yves Saint Laurent for Christian Dior, stood as a counterpoint to the 1940s waisted New Look. It was tailored to be fitted closely to the shoulders before flaring out to a wide trapezoid shape – bypassing the body entirely. Later, in the 1950s, the trapeze was diminished to a tent shape, with the use of fit-and-flare darting at the chest to create the classic A-line shift associated with the

Wrap Dress

miniskirt and the wardrobe of First Lady Jacqueline Kennedy in the 1960s. It again made a resurgence in the 1980s.

WATTEAU

Named after the eighteenth-century artist Jean-Antoine Watteau, who painted many subjects wearing this style of dress, it is recognizable thanks to the loose pleat that ran from the shoulders to the hem at the back of the dress, which gave the appearance of a cloak. Also known as the *robe volante* or *sacque*, it first appeared at the beginning of the eighteenth century, when it was a relaxed version of a more formal court gown. It was revived in the mid-nineteenth century and again in the 1950s.

WRAP DRESS

Although Diana von Furstenberg's name is synonymous with the wrap dress, this particular design was originally introduced by Claire McCardell, who was renowned for her practical and simple garments, including the wrap "popover" dress first seen in 1942. The wrap is characterized by its lack of fastenings; instead, the two front pieces of the dress are overlapped and held in place by an integrated belt, making dressing and undressing fast and efficient. The 1973 wrap dress appeared just as women were entering the workforce in greater numbers than ever before and required an easy working wardrobe: the cotton/rayon patterned wrap was the perfect solution.

Watteau

SKIRTS

INTRODUCTION

The costumes of earlier civilizations were all dependent on the simple method of using cloth to drape and wrap around the body, keeping it in place with a pin made from animal bone. Bifurcation is the act of dividing the lower half of the body in two, and in the Middle Ages men and women in rural communities dressed similarly. This changed with the advent of the French-inspired emphasis on contour and cut and the implementation of tailoring techniques in the fourteenth century, when men and women's costumes diverged. Since then, the skirt as the part of a dress below the waist – and the skirt itself – have been an essential element of female attire.

Historically, dresses were commonly made in two parts, from the sixteenth-century skirt, or *kirtle*, to the crinolines designed by couturier Charles Frederick Worth in 1860. Stand-alone skirts emerged with the popularity of the "tailormade" tweed walking suit and the shirtwaist and skirt worn by the early twentieth-century "Gibson girl". It was American designers such as Bonnie Cashin and Claire McCardell who popularized the skirt as an element of women's "mix-and-match" wardrobes in the early mid-century as a versatile alternative to the dress.

▲ Isabel Marant's leather wrap skirt from her fall/winter 2014 collection takes the informal structure of the wrap form but is cropped to mid-thigh (*see* Wraparound Skirt, page 84).

▶ Popular during the 1950s, the print circle skirt, with its narrow waist and wide mid-calf hem, features myriad decorative motifs.

Ballerina Skirt

BALLERINA SKIRT

This refers, in fashion terms, to skirts inspired by the soft, knee-length tulle net skirt worn by ballerinas, known as the romantic, or classical, tutu, rather than the stiff, horizontally protruding version, known as the platform tutu. Popular during the 1930s and 1950s, the ballerina skirt was made up of three or four layers of light fabric such as silk tulle for volume, which ended at mid-calf or just higher.

BARREL SKIRT

Similar to a balloon skirt, but with a less dramatic silhouette, the barrel skirt has a narrow waist and hem but a slightly voluminous middle. In some cases the barrel is closer to a bell shape, with the hem cutting off the curve of the middle before it narrows off. A barrel skirt also means a skirt decorated with two horizontal strips of pattern at the point where a barrel's metal hoops would lie.

BUBBLE (POUF) SKIRT

A bubble skirt is one that is gathered in and under at the hem, usually ending just below the knee, with the "bubble", or pouf, the result of an engineered inner construction. Christian Dior introduced a dress with a bubble skirt in 1956. It re-emerged in the collection designed by French-born Christian Lacroix, who, while at the couture house of Jean Patou, introduced *le pouf* – the bubble or puffball skirt – in 1986.

DIRNDL

Originally part of a traditional Austrian and Bavarian costume, the dirndl skirt is gathered onto a fitted yoke and cut to fall to below the knee or at mid-calf. The dirndl skirt was popularized in the mid-twentieth century when American designer Claire McCardell introduced it to a range of "separates", a capsule wardrobe of simple and practical pieces that could be put together in a variety of ways. The skirt frequently features vertical pockets set into the side seams.

FISHTAIL SKIRT

The undulating form of the fishtail skirt first appeared in the 1930s with the introduction of the bias cut, although fishtail trains existed from 1870 to 1879. The skirt closely follows the contours of the body, only splaying out at the hem. More usually seen on a full-length evening gown, daytime fishtail skirts tend to be more gently fluted. Further fullness at the hem may be attained with the insertion of godets or the manipulation of draped material.

Fishtail Skirt

Dirndl

HANDKERCHIEF SKIRT

The handkerchief-point skirt was a useful device to introduce longer hemlines at times of transition, such as when the tubular silhouette and short skirt of the 1920s evolved into the mid-calf length of the 1930s. The simplest method of creating a skirt with a handkerchief hem is to cut an opening in the center of a square of fabric for the waistband, with the four corners hanging down as points. Extra panels can be used to create a greater number of corners, or points, along the hem.

HOBBLE SKIRT

Generally considered to be responsible for releasing women from constricting corsets, Parisian couturier Paul Poiret instead introduced the hobble skirt into his tubular Directoire line in 1906, which limited a woman's stride to only few inches at a time. This necessitated the incorporation of a fetter made of braid, which was worn around the skirt under the knees to prevent the skirt from tearing when walking. There were also "hobble garters" worn beneath the skirt, which included two connected loops, one to be worn on each leg just below the knee.

KILT

Constructed from a distinctive checked tartan (plaid) worsted wool cloth, the kilt is synonymous with Scottish heritage. The weighty fabric is pleated into box or knife pleats, which are then stitched down to hip level. This is wrapped around the wearer's body, fastened at the flat apron front with straps and buckles and secured with a kilt pin. During the 1960s mini-kilts in bright pastel colors were popular, and they enjoyed a brief

Handkerchief Skirt

Kilt

revival in the 1990s, but more usually, kilts remain in the remit of childrenswear.

MAXI SKIRT

An ankle-length skirt worn during the day-time, as opposed to a full-length evening skirt, the maxi skirt has connotations of the 1960s free-spirited hippie when it was constructed from lightweight fabrics such as cheesecloth. Now frequently featuring vivid prints, the maxi skirt remains a popular option for sum-mer, reaching an apotheosis of ubiquity during the early parts of the twenty-first century with the trend for bohemian or "boho" fashions.

MIDI SKIRT

The mid-calf or "midi" is a skirt length popular when hemlines are in the process of either rising or falling, as in post–World War I and the change from Edwardian ankle-length skirts and dresses to the cropped chemise of the 1920s "flapper". Designers attempted to market the midi in the 1970s as a more wearable alternative to the miniskirt, but many women preferred the option of the then-popular pantsuit rather than giving up their freedom of movement.

MINISKIRT

With 1966 designated "the year of the leg", the A-line miniskirt reached new heights, with a hemline positioned at mid-thigh. Attributed to several designers, including Mary Quant and John Bates in the U.K. and the French designer André Courrèges, the miniskirt was only made wearable with the introduction of tights or pantyhose. The miniskirt was reimagined in the 1980s, but worn with stilettos rather than flat boots.

PENCIL SKIRT

With associations of the 1950s "sexy secretary", the pencil skirt closely adheres to the natural line of the waist and hips and ends on a narrow hem just on or below the knee. A small slit in the fabric is often introduced to the tailored pencil skirt at the center-back hem, unless the skirt is constructed from an elasticated fabric or jersey knit.

SARONG

A garment traditional to Malaysia, Indonesia, and the surrounding islands, a sarong, also known as a *sarung*, is a single length of fabric wrapped around the hips and tucked or tied at the waist at the side or center front to fall straight to the hem, usually to the ankles. Decorated by indigenous techniques such as batik or ikat dyeing, the contemporary sarong is a popular addition to the beach wardrobe, and is worn by both men and women.

SKATER SKIRT

Inspired by the costume traditionally worn by female ice dancers, a skater skirt is a flared skirt cut from a circular piece of cloth, with a central hole being cut to form the waist.

Usually constructed in a fairly stiff fabric to create an undulating hem, the skater skirt is designed to "flip" with movement and is essentially an ingénue style owing to its short mid-thigh length.

WRAPAROUND SKIRT

Constructed in a variety of weights and textures of materials, the wraparound skirt is a shaped length of cloth with side seams and fitting darts that wraps around the body before being fastened with a belt, sash, or button-and-loop. The front apron is left to fall free to provide ease of movement or to deliberately show a length of thigh.

Miniskirt

COATS

INTRODUCTION

An outer garment designed to be worn over layers, the coat provides both warmth for the wearer and protection for the clothes beneath. Following the universal adoption of the cloak or mantle, or the military-inspired greatcoat, bespoke tailoring for men emerged during the nineteenth century and was responsible for the wide variety of differing coat styles then prevalent. From the frock coat to the paletot, many styles evolved over the century to form the basis of male contemporary dress, all of which conformed to the strict prevailing dress codes. Constructed from wool and worsted cloth, which molded to the body, the coat exemplified formal dressing. During the 1860s women applied the principles of masculine tailoring to their outerwear, which they frequently had made at their husband's tailors. Initially made from hardwearing tweed, the coat was subsequently constructed from lightweight serge for winter and linens for summer. The design of the contemporary fashionable coat is no longer required to provide protection from the elements; it has become an important stand-alone item of a designer's collection.

▲ A favorite cut of British designer John Galliano, this coat resembles a redingote (riding coat) in the double-breasted front fastening and the way it is cropped at the waist, leaving two cutaway sides to hang on either side.

▶ The Burberry brand is synonymous with the trench coat, as shown on the right in the classic beige colorway, worn with the trademark Burberry check scarf. Other British classics produced by the brand include the duffle coat, shown on the left.

Car Coat

ANORAK

Also known as a cagoule, an anorak is a modern waterproof hooded coat made from synthetic fibers. Originally a garment worn by Inuits in Greenland and Canada, when it was called an *anoraq*, it was made from sealskin treated with various natural products such as fish oil to make it waterproof. The modern version, first produced when synthetic fibers began to be mass-produced in the 1920s, is lightweight, has elasticated cuffs, and usually has a drawstring around the waist.

BALMACAAN

Originally a men's garment from the nineteenth century, named after a Scottish estate, this knee-length overcoat is usually loose fitting in order to be worn comfortably over other layers of clothes. The single-breasted coat is defined by its raglan sleeves and small collar, and it is usually made from a heavy tweed. By the end of the nineteenth century the balmacaan was also considered a women's garment, cut to suit the female form.

CAR COAT

The increase in car ownership in the 1940s corresponded with the development of a new garment specifically designed to be worn while driving – the car coat. This was a loose-fitting, thigh- or hip-length coat that could easily be worn over other garments. Older motoring coats from the early days of car use were much sturdier and warmer, as early cars tended to be open-topped and more exposed to the elements. The garment evolved from a bulky garment designed for warmth to the briefly cut coat of the 1950s.

CHESTERFIELD

A long-length formal overcoat from the early nineteenth century, named after the sixth Earl of Chesterfield (1805–66), who first popularized the style. The Chesterfield is easily recognizable with its velvet collar, a lean silhouette with a slightly fitted waist, and one short back vent. They are typically furnished with two flapped side pockets and one left-breast pocket, with the later addition of a ticket pocket on the right-hand side. It is fastened with four or five buttons and is sometimes fly-fronted.

CLOAK OR MANTLE

A cloak of some form or other has been worn from as early as the Greco-Roman period and has remained more or less unchanged – with the exception of the addition of a hood or slits in the front for the arms to pass through. One of the oldest forms of overgarment, the cloak is a simple sleeveless garment that hangs from the shoulders and is held in place with a clasp at the shoulder or buttoned down the front. The cloak is more of a fashion statement in contemporary fashion, as it is a less practical garment in a modern urban environment.

Chesterfield

Cloak

COCOON COAT

At the turn of the nineteenth century, influenced by political and societal upheaval, many new styles and silhouettes were being produced by innovative designers such as Paul Poiret. Poiret was inspired by the art nouveau movement, with its dramatic sweeping lines and shapes influenced by natural forms, and his cocoon coat encapsulated all of these attributes, with its voluminous curved silhouette (echoing the shape of a butterfly cocoon), batwing sleeves that flowed into the body of the garment, and the folds of fabric that made up its volume.

CROMBIE

A Crombie is the name of a three-quarter-length wool coat produced by luxury British clothing manufacturers J&J Crombie Ltd. It is often used to refer to any coat that resembles the classic Crombie produced by the company, but the term should only technically refer to a coat made by the company itself. It was embraced by the youth cultures of the 1960s and '70s – but is largely worn by Establishment figures such as politicians, bankers, and royalty. It is a classic coat of thick wool with narrow lines and is usually single breasted. The upper lapel often has a velvet trim.

DUFFLE

Named after the coarse wool fabric from which is it made, the duffle coat was first worn in Britain in the late nineteenth century and was initially a garment worn by the British navy. However, after World War II, the surplus duffle coats were sold to civilians and they became a popular coat with the young. The coat is characterized by its wooden or horn

Duffle

toggle fastenings, large patch pockets, and hood, and was most famously worn by the fictional children's character Paddington Bear.

DUSTER

Originally worn by horsemen or carriagemen to protect their clothes from the dust of travel, this is a lightweight and loosely fitting long coat, usually made from linen or cotton in summer and wool or tweed (with a fur lining) in winter. With the invention of car travel in the early nineteenth century, the duster coat remained an important garment for protecting clothes. No longer used solely for protection against the elements, during the 1950s the loose-fitting duster was frequently worn over a dress in matching fabric.

FROCK COAT

A symbol of respectability, the frock coat has undergone several permutations since it first appeared in the early nineteenth century. Ostensibly a knee-length buttoned-down coat tailored to fit the waist closely, it could be either single- or double-breasted, although the latter was generally worn at more formal occasions. Initially an informal coat worn for sporting activities, the frock coat gained purchase as a formal suit by the mid-nineteenth century – when it had a Prussian collar and no lapels. By the end of the nineteenth century it had gained lapels and a waist seam.

Duster

Housecoat

HAORI

The haori is a type of Japanese coat to be worn over a kimono dating from around the seventeenth century (the Azuchi-Momoyama period), originally worn by men as part of their battle dress. The haori was adapted for everyday wear and was soon adopted by women. Worn long or hip length, the coat features deep square kimono sleeves varying in style according to the gender of the wearer. Unlike the traditional kimono worn for ceremonial use, the haori is not worn with an obi belt or a sash, but worn loose and open, or sometimes fastened with a himo tie. The material is usually highly decorative.

HOUSECOAT

The term "housecoat" has a variety of meanings. It can either be a type of formal dressing gown, worn by men or women upon waking or changed into before bed, in which case it is ankle or knee length and is secured by a belt, or an overall garment worn by women during the day to protect their clothes when undertaking domestic tasks. With both definitions, the understanding is that the garment is not designed to be worn outdoors.

MACKINTOSH

Initially, this term applied to any coat made from the eponymous fabric invented by Charles Mackintosh in 1822. The fabric was rendered waterproof by bonding layers of wool with dissolved India-rubber solution, with proof straps placed over the seams. By the mid-twentieth century the term applied to any waterproof coat, with the phrase "mac" being most commonly used.

PALETOT

A French term to describe various male and female coats in the nineteenth century, the paletot was produced in a variety of styles. In the first decades of the century it was used to refer to a man's short greatcoat with a wide, flat back. Several decades later the term described a loosely cut coat without a waist seam, the forerunner of the lounge suit. For womenswear, the paletot referred to a short pleated cloak until the 1860s, when it came to mean a long, figure-hugging coat with a lace trim designed to be worn outdoors.

PARDESSUS

From the mid-nineteenth century onward this term referred to any women's coat that fell to half or three-quarter length, was tailored to fit the waist, and had long sleeves. The word *pardessus* is French for "passed over" – in the sense that the coat hung over the voluminous clothes worn beneath. It had a similar silhouette to the paletot, but with fur or velvet banded decorations.

Paletot

Pardessus

Pelerine

Redingote

PEA COAT

The pea coat originated as a cold weather uniform in many European navies, most notably the British and the Dutch during the eighteenth century. It became part of the United States Navy's official dress during the early twentieth century. The term "pea coat" comes from the Dutch word *pij*, which is a type of cloth commonly used in the production of the coat. The typical pea coat is a short double-breasted jacket featuring broad lapels and vertical pockets and made from coarse wool. It remains a popular form of informal outerwear for both men and women.

PELERINE

From the mid-eighteenth century to the end of the nineteenth, the pelerine was a garment worn by women, composed of a short decorative cape that was cut in such a way that the long ends could be crossed over and wrapped around the body before being tied at the back. Usually made from a light muslin or lace in summer, or wool or fur in winter, it added a decorative layer and provided warmth. By the early twentieth century it had mutated to become a cape that hung over the shoulders without the wrapped element.

PELISSE (PELLICE)

A garment worn by both men and women from the eighteenth to the nineteenth century, the pelisse when worn by men was a fur-lined, waist-length cloak, and was a component of the Hussar uniform. For women, it originally referred to a longer cloak – usually three-quarter length – with a hood and an opening for the arms, decorated with silk linings and fur trims. As the nineteenth century progressed, the women's pelisse evolved into a long winter cloak made from rich fabrics such as velvet or brocaded silk, with loose sleeves.

PONCHO

The poncho was a garment synonymous with South and Central America before spreading into general wear in the twentieth century. It includes a large, usually square piece of knitted fabric with a hole in the center for the head and fringing around the hem. The fabric then hangs down over the shoulders and falls to the waist or the knee. South American ponchos are usually decorated with geometric patterns. Sharing the shape of a traditional poncho, modern versions can also be made in synthetic fibers and often act as a loose waterproof layer.

REDINGOTE (RIDING COAT)

Initially a term used to describe a man's double-breasted riding coat, by the nineteenth century a redingote also referred to a women's long coat (or gown that resembled a coat) that was tightly fitted on the torso and fastened with a row of functional or decorative buttons. The coat was cut high up on the waist – as was the fashion in the Regency or Empire period – but flared out into a full skirt and was often cut away to reveal the gown beneath.

Poncho

SWING COAT (SWAGGER/TOPPER)

The swing, or swagger, coat is a knee-length women's overcoat that fits the body at the shoulders but then flares out into a trapeze-line shape at the hem. First seen in the 1930s as a reaction to the straight-up-and-down silhouette of the previous decade, the swing coat has been variously popular throughout the twentieth century – particularly in the collections of Balenciaga in the 1950s and again in the 1980s. As a useful garment for wearing over other bulky clothes, it is also known as a topper.

TIPPET

In modern fashion terms, a tippet commonly refers to a short cape or scarf worn around the shoulders with the two ends left dangling from each side. The tippet may be made from various luxury materials such as velvet, silk, and lace but is most commonly found in fur – with a fox-fur tippet being an essential part of a woman's evening outfit in the 1930s. A tippet may also refer to the long strip of fabric worn over the shoulders by clergymen.

TRENCH COAT

In 1914, British company Burberry was commissioned by the British War Office to adapt its officers' coat to suit the conditions of contemporary warfare, resulting in the design of the "trench" coat. Made from gabardine – in which the yarn is waterproofed before weaving, a technique patented in 1888 by Thomas Burberry – the coat is double-breasted to provide another layer of waterproof fabric on the main part of the body. Epaulettes were designed to hold a folded hat or the strap of a satchel, or a pair of binoculars in place, and adjustable buckled straps on the sleeves prevented water from running down the arm. The revers of the high-standing collar can be fastened up to the neck, with further protection provided by a "storm flap" buttoned across the center front.

ULSTER

A heavy, long overcoat commonly found after 1870, with a detachable cape over the shoulders. The Ulster was popular outerwear for both men and women in the late nineteenth century and was first made in Northern Ireland in 1867. The coat is usually double-breasted and belted and made from a heavy cloth, known as Ulster cloth, or other similar tweed fabrics. The Ulster resides in popular public consciousness as the coat worn by Sherlock Holmes.

Ulster

SHIRTS AND TOPS

INTRODUCTION

Precursors of modern varieties of the shirt have evolved over the centuries in most cultures, gaining a wide catalogue of names. In a lasting transition from rudimentary undergarment to key wardrobe item – able to signify status, occupation, or leisure aspirations – the shirt has been called many things. In Asia, the *kameez* for men is a traditional loose garment for the upper body, constructed thriftily from rectangles of woven material to make the body and sleeves with an underarm gusset. In the traditions of Ancient Rome it was the equally simple *camicia* or *camisa*, mutating to the francophone *chemise* that is now chiefly used in the terminology of womenswear. The Anglo-Saxons preferred the words shift, smock, and, of course, shirt.

Until the nineteenth century, the shirt as underwear had the prime purpose of creating a washable barrier layer between the seldom-washed body and valuable outer garments, which could not be laundered. Often the long shirt served as the solitary undergarment, with the shirttails tucked down the legs to act as drawers. During the seventeenth century libertine tastes permitted the utilitarian shirt to flounce into view at the neck, and in due course this became the general fashion. From the Georgian era onward, gentlemanly style required an array of face-framing devices such as the neckcloth and cravat as a flourish around the collar and neck.

▲ A 1980s version of the tuxedo shirt (*see* page 105), with fine pin pleating on either side of the center front and a high wing collar.

▶ Hubert Givenchy's muse and one of the foremost models of her day, Simone Micheline Bodin (known as Bettina) is shown wearing the blouse that Givenchy named after her – with its Spanish-influenced sleeve flounces and shirt bodice (*see* page 100).

Balkan Blouse

BALKAN BLOUSE

In the 1910s Paul Poiret reinvented the fashionable female figure by adopting a columnar Orientalist silhouette. The Balkan blouse, named after the Balkan Wars of 1912–13, arose as a loose interpretation of regional peasant costume as presented in Sergei Diaghilev's Ballets Russes. With bishops' sleeves, the lace-collared, button-through blouse extended to the thigh, where it was pleated into a band, having been drawn in at hip level with a separate contrast sash.

BETTINA BLOUSE

Hubert de Givenchy launched his fêted Bettina blouse as part of his debut couture Separates collection in 1952, which was produced largely in inexpensive men's shirting. The name arose from the pseudonym of the renowned model and muse, Bettina Graziani (Simone Micheline Bodin). The fitted button-through blouse has an elevated open-neck collar, while the straight, set-in sleeve explodes with a garland of broderie anglaise around the elbow and forearm – a reference to Latin-American dancewear.

CAMP SHIRT

As a loose straight-cut shirt or blouse with a simple placket front opening, the camp shirt is similar to the sportshirt – but it is always short-sleeved, and with its hip-length straight hem and short side vents it is not intended to be tucked into trousers. The camp collar is in one piece, without the rise of a collar band, and is generally worn spread open, although it can be closed at the neck with a button and fabric loop. In many ways the camp shirt is the template for Hawaiian and bowling shirts.

Garibaldi Shirt

Camp Shirt

COSSACK (KOSOVOROTKA)

For centuries recruited as a border militia by the Russian Empire, Cossack soldiers across the Slavic regions had to provide their own horse and uniform, which consequently developed a number of variants around a core identity. In winter the *kosovorotka* – a thigh-length tunic – was worn with a long *cherkeska* – a belted V-neck coat. In the summer the belted Cossack tunic shirt, with a stand-up collar fastened asymmetrically, was worn with a forage cap and baggy stirrup pants tucked into soft boots.

GARIBALDI SHIRT

In the early 1860s, fervent admiration for the Italian patriot Giuseppe Garibaldi swept through the northern states of the American Union when he offered his services to Abraham Lincoln in the Civil War. As homage, the loose-fitting Garibaldi blouse came into vogue in muslin, flannel, merino, or cambric cloths – initially in red. The front was lightly pleated and the sleeves full, with a small cuff echoing the narrow collar, which was decorated with a ribbon bow.

Lumberjack Shirt

HAWAIIAN (ALOHA) SHIRT

Hawaii developed from a plantation economy to a tourist Mecca in the 1920s, initiating the evolution of casual clothing manufacture. Exotically printed English cottons and Japanese *yukata* fabrics were preferred to the indigenous *kapa* (barkcloth), and in the mid-1920s the first Hawaiian shirts were introduced. Locals preferred to use the subdued reverse side of the prints, although gaudy conversational, floral, and topographic all-over prints have come to exemplify the evolved button-through Hawaiian shirt with its soft open collar, pattern-matched patch pocket, and straight hem.

HOODIE

A relatively modern garment, although the silhouette is reminiscent of a medieval peasant's hooded tunic, the hoodie was first worn as exercise wear in the 1980s before being adopted by hip-hop culture as street style. Today, the hoodie is a ubiquitous garment worn by most societal groups and consists of a baggy jersey sweatshirt with a hood attached, typically with a drawstring around the hood and a kangaroo pocket at the front. It can be either fastened with a zipper or pulled on over the head.

LUMBERJACK SHIRT

The lumberjack or logger shirt is a workwear staple of the North American outdoors that was also adopted by the grunge movement of the 1990s. The symbolism of this classic is rooted in the pioneer spirit of the conquest of the American wilderness, defining masculinity through folk heroes such as Paul Bunyan. The shirt is defined by its practicality: dark plaid

Sportshirt

(tartan) disguises dirt; brushed cotton or wool flannel cloth is durable and warm; close-buttoned cuffs and patch pockets avoid snags.

OXFORD SHIRT

Oxford and Ivy League shirts have been synonymous with and emblematic of the privileged alumni of Ivy League schools since the 1920s. Brooks Brothers appropriated this "preppy" staple to the American wardrobe from British styles prevalent at the University of Oxford. The lustrous basket-weave cotton fabric most commonly employed for the shirt is also known as Oxford, with chambray used as a lighter alternative. The style is characterized by a button-down collar and single cuff on long sleeves. The front is buttoned through and the back is pleated to a yoke with a central hangtag.

POLO SHIRT

In 1926 tennis star René Lacoste revealed his innovative tennis shirt. Dissatisfied with the constraints of the traditional long-sleeved woven shirt, he devised an alternative in cotton jersey piqué. Short-sleeved with rib cuffs, the new shirt had a soft collar and short, buttoned placket front. The rear tail was longer to remain tucked in during play. Lacoste's shirt was marketed starting in 1933 and was soon adopted by polo players for the same reasons of utility that applied to tennis. By the 1950s it became widely known as the polo shirt.

SPORTSHIRT

The international visibility of 1930s Hollywood stars at leisure gave exposure to the open-necked sportshirt and to "slack" (free time) dressing. By 1939 the informal, loose sportshirt had even been teamed with fabric-matched trousers to create the "slack suit" for the mass market. It had one or two patch pockets and a square-cut hem for either wearing inside or outside the slacks. A sports collar could lie flat and open as it had no separate rise, while the facings that supported the buttoning at center front produced reveres.

Polo Shirt

SWEATSHIRT

Beginning in the 1920s, companies such as
L.L. Bean used patented machinery to produce
tubular single jersey fabric, which could then
be sewn into garments such as the sweatshirt
with rib trims and inserts attached by flatlock
sewing machines. Moulinée heather cotton on
the outer face of the fabric was inlaid behind
with cotton bump yarn, to be brushed into a
fleecy finish. The sweatshirt was originally a
heavy long-sleeved T-shirt worn for American
campus sports and army training, but it has
been adopted by the masses as casual wear.

T-SHIRT

The T-shirt shape developed from military
usage in World War I. The earlier tradition of
Union Combination Suits had been divided
into a short-sleeved knitted crew vest and long
johns in the latter decades of the nineteenth
century. In 1913 the U.S. Navy issued white
crewneck jersey undershirts with short set-in
sleeves, and the army soon followed. By the
1950s this piece of underwear became the
subversive outerwear of Hollywood rebels
such as Marlon Brando and James Dean. Since
then, its popularity has spread from just the
young to all ages.

TABARD (JERKIN/SURCOAT/ SUPERTUNIC)

The wearing of tabards was evident in
literature by the end of the fourteenth century.
A short, protective outer tunic, both with
and without sleeve panels, it was worn open
at the sides, held in place by ties or a belt.
When worn by liveried pursuivants (retained
heralds), the panels could be emblazoned with
heraldic devices – the original coat-of-arms.

Sweatshirt

TUXEDO (DRESS) SHIRT

In British usage the dress shirt is an element of formalwear, associated with white- and black-tie events. In America, this style is termed a "tuxedo shirt". In Britain, the formal white dress shirt can be obtained with either attached or traditional detachable stiff collars. The front of the garment has a distinctive bib panel (plastron), which is heavier than other components either from additional layers or from the introduction of pleats, piqué fabric, or starch.

VAREUSE (BLOUSE/SMOCK)

The vareuse is a tunic of hip length in coarse, wind-proofed cotton worn by mariners and is known as a fisherman's smock in the U.K. The front neck, with internal buttoning to avoid rope and net snags, has an angular double bib that supports the simple built-on stand collar. The drop shoulder sleeves are long and open, unconstrained by cuffs, and pockets are patched to the inside of the bodice. Formalized versions of the tunic are used in naval uniforms.

WESTERN SHIRT

The fitted Western shirt – and its close Tex-Mex relation, the Vaquero – is defined by the ornate counter-curves in the shoulder yoke seaming, which is further echoed in the pocket and cuff stitched detailing. At the elaborate end of the decorative scale, the embroidered country and western ranch-wear shirt is considered a kitsch version of the basic denim model. In both instances, the decoration has roots in Spanish Baroque, the influence carried into clothing by reference to saddles, tooled boots, and gun escutcheons.

Western Shirt

KNITWEAR

INTRODUCTION

Hand knitting became mechanized in 1589 with the invention of the stocking knitting frame by William Lee of Nottinghamshire. It was a process initially confined to hosiery, a definition that also included underwear such as "combinations" – known as "union suits" in the United States. Production moved from underwear to outerwear as the twentieth century progressed, and knitwear became increasingly fashion led. The relationship between fashion and knitwear fluctuates in intensity over the decades; in 1916 Coco Chanel utilized knitted jersey to create three-piece cardigan suits, setting the paradigm for chic and stylish modern dressing, and in the 1930s "designed" knitwear emerged with the introduction of the twinset, which continues to be a fashion staple. The intermeshing of loops of yarn and the resulting elasticity render knitted fabrics form-fitting and yet unconfining, providing the modern wardrobe with its ease, wearability, and practicality. In 1864 William Cotton of England developed a machine to produce garment-shaped pieces, leading to the production of fully-fashioned knitwear as opposed to the cut-and-sew method. New technologies have since introduced complex and sophisticated patterning into contemporary knitwear.

▲ These body-con knitted tube dresses in her signature pattern of bright, acidic colors juxtaposed with black stripes are from Sonia Rykiel's spring/summer 2001 collection. Rykiel is renowned for her skinny-rib knitwear and its incorporation into various garments, including knitted dresses.

▶ Knitted garments proliferated during the 1940s and 1950s with the advances in knitting technology in both the U.K. and the U.S., which replicated the fit and function of garments more usually tailored, such as this fully-fashioned two-piece suit.

CARDIGAN

A long-sleeved knitted garment that is fastened at the front, either by buttons, toggles, hooks, or a zipper, the cardigan features a variety of necklines, including crew, V-neck, and shawl. During the Crimean War, officers in the British army wore an extra knitted layer for warmth – a woolen waistcoat or vest fastened with buttons. The garment was adopted by civilians and came to be known as the Cardigan, named after the major general who had led the army.

GUERNSEY

Originally a nineteenth-century sweater worn by Channel Island fishermen, the Guernsey has become a classic design worn by both sexes. They are characteristically thick, rib-knit, close-fitting garments that are usually navy blue. When the yarn for the original Guernsey sweater was processed, it was tightly wound, and a degree of the natural lanolin oils was retained in order to make the finished garment waterproof, but this is less common today.

PULLOVER

Also known as a sweater or jumper, the pullover is a unisex knitted garment that has no fastenings and is designed to be pulled on over the head. As such, the knit must be relatively loose in order to provide the necessary stretch. The term historically refers to any garment, knitted or woven, that was put on in this way, but it now applies to any casual knitted garment.

SKINNY RIB

A fine-ribbed sweater designed to be tight fitting, giving an elongated silhouette to the wearer. Partnered with the miniskirt, the skinny rib sweater was popular during the 1960s and was usually made in one of the new synthetic yarns such as Orlon or Acrilan. Mary Quant describes herself as being the instigator of the trend for women wearing children's-sized sweaters, worn beneath her tunic-style dresses, and the look was also seen beneath French designer Pierre Cardin's space-age cut-out pinafores.

Cardigan

Sweater Dress

SLOPPY JOE

As the name suggests, this is a type of loose, baggy sweater worn by women and girls that was initially popular in 1940s and '50s America, when teenagers first started to develop a separate style from their parents. It was usually worn with a circle skirt, white socks, and brogues. The sloppy joe was designed to suggest it had been borrowed from a larger boyfriend or father. An antithesis of the contemporaneous tight-fitting sweater, the sloppy joe had a rolled collar, hem, and cuffs.

SWEATER DRESS

Popular during the 1950s, the sweater dress was an elongated version of the figure-hugging sweaters worn by Hollywood stars, and delineated every curve from neck to mid-calf. The sweater dress provided uncomplicated one-stop dressing, and could be dressed up with jewelry and the new stiletto heel, or dressed down with a patterned silk scarf tied around the neck and sensible shoes. The fashionable "sheath" dress was also interpreted in knitted fabric, particularly in textured yarns such as bouclé.

TURTLENECK (POLONECK)

A high-necked, knitted garment, often made in ribbed knit stitch. The height of the neck fold can vary, but it is constructed from a tube-shaped piece of knitted fabric that is then turned over on itself. The British version, the poloneck – named after the garment worn by polo players – is generally higher than the U.S. version, the turtleneck.

Twinset

Turtleneck

TWINSET

A two-piece matching sweater and cardigan set, with the sweater underneath usually being close-fitting and short-sleeved, the first classic twinset was attributed to Scottish knitwear company Pringle in the 1930s. With overtones of feminine respectability, and most usually partnered with a pearl necklace (particularly in the 1950s, when it was popularized by Grace Kelly) the twinset is now a contemporary fashion staple that features variations in sleeve styles and necklines while adhering to the basic premise: the two garments being constructed in the same color, yarn, and stitch.

VARSITY (AWARD LETTER) SWEATER

A key garment from the preppy Ivy League look, the Award Letter (usually the initial of the institution, e.g., Y for Yale) sweater originally denoted that the wearer had been honored as a varsity sportsman at a U.S. college. These sweaters were often borrowed by girlfriends who benefited from the association with such minor celebrities on campus. The sweaters were usually knitted, with the lettering produced in felted wool.

UNDERGARMENTS

INTRODUCTION

Essentially the history of underwear for women is a story of constriction and confinement until the twentieth century – when, in the latter half of the century, the external corset was replaced by the internal with the expectation that exercise and diet might shape the body in the way that corsets once had. Underwear is a term that encapsulates all forms of clothing that are designed to be worn next to the skin. They are largely required to be hidden, but in some cases, parts of the garment are designed to be seen – such as the embroidered sleeves of a Renaissance chemise or the lace-trimmed hem of a Victorian petticoat. Breasts have historically been either bound by strips of cloth (from antiquity onward) or held in place by the corset, stays, or pair of bodies, until the brassiere was invented in the late nineteenth century. The underwear typically worn today is a modern invention, with what we now know as knickers, with their closed gusset, only being worn beginning around the 1870s.

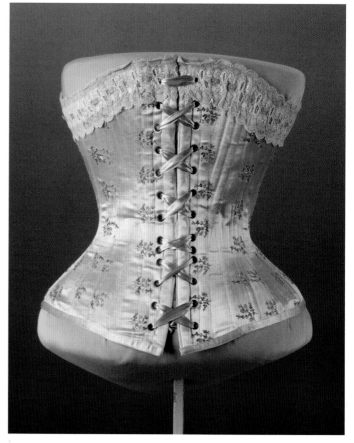

▲ A corset (*see* page 117) from a French bridal trousseau from the turn of the nineteenth century. As a trousseau corset, the fabric used would be of finer and more expensive quality than that for everyday use, and here it is a richly embroidered silk satin with lace from Le Bon Marche.

▶ One of the first proponents of "underwear as outerwear" in the 1990s – particularly with his stage costumes for Madonna's "Blonde Ambition" tour of 1992 – Jean Paul Gaultier designed this corseted silk dress with exaggeratedly pointed bra cups for his fall/winter 2013 couture collection.

BABYDOLL

A short, empire-line nightdress (or dress) usually constructed from a transparent, diaphanous fabric such as chiffon or nylon netting, and trimmed with flounces and bows at the hem and the neck. The body of the garment is typically trapeze-line. The nightdress is usually worn with a pair of shorts or underwear in a matching fabric and is named after the garment worn by the young seductress played by Carroll Baker in the 1956 film *Baby Doll* (*see* right).

BALCONETTE

Otherwise known as a demi-bra, this form of lingerie is so called because the half cups of its construction give the impression of the breasts being held on a platform or "small balcony". First invented in the 1930s, it was particularly popular in the 1950s, when it enhanced the silhouette under the fashionable tight sweaters of the day. The neckline of a balconette tends to be straight, whereas that of a similar demi-cup bra follows the curves of the breast.

BALMORAL PETTICOAT

A type of petticoat designed to be seen beneath the drawn-up hem of the practical walking skirts women wore for outdoor activities. These petticoats were popular in the 1860s and 1870s, with many different patterns being used. The Balmoral, however, was striped and was inspired, as were many fashionable objects at the time, by Queen Victoria's love of all things Scottish. The petticoat was either worn over the crinoline hoop or had hoops sewn onto it. The most common stripe pattern was a red ground with two or three black stripes.

Babydoll

BED JACKET

A garment designed for a very specific purpose – to keep the upper body and arms warm when the wearer is sitting up in bed. It was originally a purely practical garment, worn for warmth by those who were bed-bound. However, when the idea of spending time luxuriating in a boudoir was celebrated by Hollywood films, the bed jacket became a more glamorous item, being made of luxury fabrics such as satin and trimmed with feathers or lace. The jacket is usually sleeveless in order to facilitate removal without having to get out of bed, and is fastened by loosely tied ribbons at the front.

BLOOMERS

A loose, bifurcated undergarment worn on the legs and lower body. They were originally an outerwear garment, popular for a short period in the 1850s, designed to be worn under the knee-length skirts adopted by newly active women. In terms of underwear, however, "bloomer" refers to the style of voluminous knee-length knickers worn in the early twentieth century that were usually made of cotton or silk with flounced hems at the knee. The term is often confused with "pantalettes" – a type of open-gusseted, open-legged drawers worn in the nineteenth century.

Bloomers

Brassiere

BRASSIERE

The brassiere (or bra) is a garment that at its most basic level is designed to support and lift the breasts – the degree of lifting and shaping varies depending on the style of bra. Essentially it is two cups of fabric sewn together at the front, with a hook-and-eye fastening of the straps at the back. The bra can also be strapless or front-fastening. Most modern bras have wires sewn in under the cups to aid support. A form of supportive garment has been worn over the breasts since pre-historic times, but the modern engineered bra dates from the early twentieth century.

BUSTIER

An undergarment that is also sometimes adopted as outerwear. The bustier includes a short, close-fitting tunic top that is usually strapless and runs to just above the breasts, supporting them by pushing them up and against the chest. It is a shorter, more practical version of a full corset, sharing similar construction elements such as boning and lace fastening at the back.

CAMIKNICKERS

The flappers of the 1920s desired a boyish figure and replaced the hourglass corset with a flimsy combination of a camisole under-blouse and knickers – or a combination of both: the camiknicker. More recently, the camiknicker may also refer to a long pair of short-style underwear made of satin or silk, trimmed with lace. It is also known as a teddy.

CAMISOLE (VEST)

A sleeveless undergarment (although it can be worn as outerwear) designed to be worn under clothing as an insulating layer, or to be worn in bed. Either purpose has various styles – ranging from the wholly unadorned in plain cotton to those trimmed with lace and made of silk satin. The camisole can either be loose or form fitting if a stretch fabric is used. The body of the garment is held in place by thin "spaghetti straps" and typically does not offer any support to the breasts.

CORSET

The corset is a garment traditionally used to shape and hold the female form, making the body conform to the prevailing fashions, and it has been worn since antiquity in various forms, replacing the two-piece boned stays that had been worn until around the eighteenth century. The corset is typically fastened from the back by a series of lacings that are pulled tight and tied, and it runs from just below the breasts to the waist or hips, depending on the period. If a dressing maid was not available, a front-fastening corset was worn, with eyelets and hooks on a busk panel holding the two sides together while the lacing remained for tightening purposes. They are usually given their stiff shape using whalebone, wood, metal, and latterly strips of plastic, although when revived in Dior's 1947 New Look, a fabric called Powernet was used to hold the shape.

Corset

CRINOLINE

Derived from the French for *crin* (horsehair) and *lin* (linen), the materials they were originally made from, early crinolines were stiff petticoats that held out the fashionably wide skirts of the mid-nineteenth century. As these were quite unhygienic and uncomfortable, particularly in hot weather, a new version was devised in the 1850s that included a series of steel hoops, suspended by vertical cotton tapes, which formed a hollow cage beneath the skirts. By the 1870s the large crinoline had fallen out of fashion, replaced by a backward-projecting crinolette.

GARTER (SUSPENDER)

Both the garter and suspender are designed to hold a sock or stocking in place on the leg. The garter includes a narrow band of fabric, sometimes elasticated, that is placed over the stocking itself either on the thigh or on the knee (particularly when worn by men). The suspender is more complex, with a wider strip sitting on the waist with four "sling" straps hanging down that are then clipped onto the fabric of the stocking by means of a rubber button that is pushed through a metal loop.

GIRDLE (CORSELETS)

This less restrictive version of the corset was worn from the early part of the twentieth century until the 1960s. Originally meaning a belt, the girdle came to mean a tightly fitting garment that sits from between the upper thighs to just above the waist with a metal busk at the front for fastening. Far lighter and more flexible than the boned corset, the girdle held the flesh in place without the boning and lacing, instead using elasticated panels.

LIBERTY BODICE

An alternative to the more restrictive training corset that was commonly worn by children in the nineteenth and early twentieth century, the Liberty bodice was invented by an underwear manufacturer named Fred Cox in 1908 – although an adult version had been worn as part of the dress reform movement in the previous century. It included a soft knitted vest that allowed freedom of movement, was fastened with rubber buttons, and had buttons for attaching stockings and drawers.

Crinoline

Petticoat

PEIGNOIR (DRESSING GOWN)

The peignoir is an ankle-length, lightweight robe made from fabrics such as transparent chiffon or silk, designed to be worn around the home after rising from bed and before getting dressed. It is closely associated with "ladies of leisure", who had time to wear a separate ensemble while preparing for the day, specifically when combing their hair (*peignore* meaning "to comb"). It is a loose-fitting garment that is tied at the front and is decorated with lace trimming or with lace panel inserts, and is often worn with a matching negligée nightdress.

PETTICOAT

The term petticoat was first used in the fifteenth century in reference to a short undershirt or chemise, worn under clothes to protect them from sweat and body oils, but by the sixteenth century it came to generally mean a woman's underskirt. Often designed to be seen, and therefore decorated with a lace hem, the petticoat continued to be worn under women's long skirts until the 1960s, when most traditional undergarments were discarded by the young.

THONG (G-STRING)

The terms are interchangeable, but while a thong has a strip of thin fabric between the buttocks, the G-string is, as the name suggests, just a string of thread holding the fabric on the body. Originally worn to reduce VPL (visible panty line), the thong was meant to remain unseen. However, in the mid-1990s, after Alexander McQueen's "bumster" trousers set off a fashion for hipster jeans that sat very low on the hips, it became acceptable – if not desirable – to reveal the thong underwear that sat higher on the hips than the trousers.

Peignoir

HEADGEAR

INTRODUCTION

The relationship between hats and high fashion is a powerful one. The head is the site of optimum adornment, and historically, hats represented wealth and social status. Contemporary hats are an extreme commitment to style and provide an opportunity to astound, shock or beguile. Just as global fashion brands now send the latest handbag down the runway, hats are also increasingly appearing, representing a coherent fashion story. At the same time, hats have always been a significant aspect of street culture, from the flat tweed cap to the knitted beanie adopted during the grunge era of the 1990s. Hats may be pure theater, providing an audience for the wearer and evoking both admiration and awe. The designs of milliner Philip Treacy are integral to the compelling and confrontational stage performance of Grace Jones. Isabella Blow, fashion catalyst, was his muse, and Anna Piaggi of Italian *Vogue* is renowned for her espousal of Stephen Jones' eccentric and extravagant creations.

▲ These two hats designed by Philip Treacy form part of the collection of Isabella Blow – one of the great patrons of British design until her death in 2010. Blow was rarely seen in public without wearing one of Treacy's sculptural works of art.

▶ The tricorn hat is a recurring motif in John Galliano's designs for both his eponymous line and Dior – with the French Revolution and other military imagery from the eighteenth century providing constant inspiration.

Beret

BAKER BOY (NEWSBOY CAP)

Also known as a "newsboy cap", an "eight-panel", a "cabbie", or a "poor boy cap", the baker boy is similar to a flat cap, with a stiff peak but a fuller, rounder body cut from eight shaped pieces of cloth secured with a central fabric-covered button. As with a flat cap, a button may also attach the front to the brim. The style was popular in Europe and North America in the late nineteenth and early twentieth centuries among both boys and men.

BANDANA

From the Hindu word *bandhnu* – a type of tie-dying – or *bandhyna* – to tie – a bandana is a small square or length of cloth tied around the forehead or neck, initially worn as a means of holding back the hair or collecting sweat during any physical activity. The bandana is traditionally constructed from a brightly patterned check or floral pattern with a striped border in a lightweight fabric such as cotton.

BEANIE

Initially an item of workwear, the beanie is a close-fitting knitted hat that is worn pulled down to cover the ears. The name probably derives from the slang term "bean", which meant "head" in the early days of the twentieth century in the United States. U.S. designer Marc Jacobs popularized the beanie in his grunge collection of 1992, an aesthetic that mixed low- and high-end fashion, inspired by the grunge bands of Seattle.

BERET

The beret was initially a symbol of rebellion and was also known as the liberty cap or *bonnet rouge* – with its association with the scarlet conical Phrygian caps that were worn by freed Roman slaves (although this was misguided – the emancipated slaves actually wore a felt *pileus* hat). Appropriated by the *sans-culottes* of revolutionary France, the beret came to represent the archetypal disaffected Parisian existentialists, bohemians, and beatniks of the late 1940s and early 1950s. Conversely, the beret is also an item worn as part of military and school uniform.

BOATER

Made of plaited sennit or split-braid straw, and trimmed with Petersham or silk ribbon that is often striped, the boater is also known as a "sailor", "basher", or "skimmer", the latter owing to its flat crown and straight brim. Popular since the 1880s with British university students, the boater has become associated with upper-class sporting activities and is often worn as an item of uniform at independent schools in the U.K.

BOWLER (DERBY)

The bowler hat – known as the derby in the U.S. – was named after the English horse race, the Epsom Derby. First introduced by hat makers Thomas and William Bowler in 1850 for the Earl of Leicester, the bowler hat features a small curved brim with a narrow crown. Associated in Britain with bankers and civil servants since the nineteenth century, the reinforced hat was also worn by cowboys and railway workers in the American West.

Baker Boy

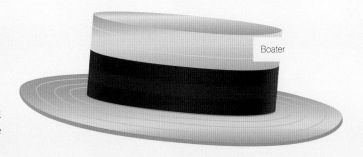

Boater

Cartwheel

Deerstalker

CARTWHEEL

Similar to the "picture" hat, although less decorated, the cartwheel hat features a low crown and a large, wide brim. Worn in summer, and most often made from straw or thin woven strips of "chip" wood, the hat might be trimmed with flowers and plumes or imitation fruit. Popular during the Edwardian era, the hat demanded support from a voluminous hairstyle and was secured with a hatpin and worn on the back of the head.

CLOCHE

From the French word for bell, the cloche was first designed by milliner Caroline Reboux in 1908. A pull-on hat usually constructed from felted wool and molded to the shape of the head, it was popular during the 1920s – when the *la garçonne* silhouette required a small head – and was worn over the newly cropped hair. It also provided a base for further decoration, very often inspired by the motifs of art deco.

DEERSTALKER

Identified with the fictional character Sherlock Holmes, the deerstalker hat was originally worn for hunting deer in the nineteenth century, providing protection from the weather. Constructed from houndstooth or herringbone tweed, the hat is close-fitting and constructed from six or eight triangular panels with rounded sides that are sewn together, with peaks at the front and back. Ear flaps are tied together over the crown with grosgrain ribbons or worn down over the ears and tied under the chin.

FASCINATOR

A hair accessory rather than a hat, the fascinator is a small, highly decorated headpiece worn perched to the front and the side of the head, attached by a comb, headband, or clip. It is the more informal millinery option for events such as weddings and commonly features faux flowers or a curled plume attached to a molded base.

Cloche

Fascinator

Juliet Cap

FEDORA

A soft felt hat with a wide brim, fedoras are typically creased lengthwise down the crown and "pinched" near the front on both sides. The name is taken from the title of a play by dramatist Victorian Sardou Fédora in 1882 in which Princess Fédora wore a center-creased, soft-brimmed hat. Fedoras have become associated with gangsters and Prohibition, which coincided with the height of the hat's popularity from the 1920s to the early 1950s.

FLAT CAP

Constructed in tweed, corduroy, or moleskin, with a rounded crown and a stiffened peak, flat caps were in common usage in both North America and Europe by men and boys of all classes during the early twentieth century, and were worn universally during the 1910s to the 1920s, particularly among the working classes. The aristocracy wore the cap primarily for leisure activities, and the style has also become fashionable with those wishing to be associated with country pursuits.

HOMBURG

A felt hat with a soft crown creased lengthwise – called a gutter crown – with a stiff, narrow, and slightly curled brim with a grosgrain-bound edge and hatband. The homburg was named after the spa town of Hamburg in Western Germany, where it was manufactured and was popularized by King Edward VII of England following his visit to Bad Homburg in Hesse, Germany, in the 1890s.

JULIET CAP

An unstructured open-work piece of lace, mesh, or crochet draped to fit the head and worn low on the forehead, the Juliet cap was a popular form of bridal headgear during the early nineteenth century. Often decorated with pearls, beads, or jewels, the cap is named after the heroine of Shakespeare's *Romeo and Juliet*. Contemporary brides are more likely to position the cap on the back of the head.

Bowler

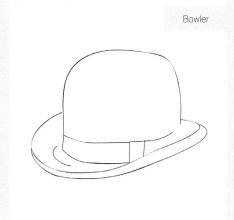

Homburg

Fedora

Trilby

Pillbox

MOB CAP

Worn by married women to cover the hair in the Georgian period – when it was called a "bonnet" – a mob cap is constructed from a circular piece of cloth, more commonly linen, gathered at the edge to form a frill. This informal style was adopted by the aristocracy in the late eighteenth century, with the fashionable yearning for pastoral ideal in dress. By the nineteenth century mob caps were solely the remit of servants and nurses.

PANAMA HAT

Originating in Ecuador and distributed through Panama, this hat is a summer version of the fedora, made in straw traditionally sourced from the plaited leaves of the *Carludovica palmata* plant. Panama hats are light-colored and lightweight, and can be rolled up for ease of storage. The hat was popularized by U.S. President Theodore Roosevelt when he was photographed visiting the construction site of the Panama Canal in 1904.

PILLBOX

Although both Dior and Balenciaga featured the pillbox hat during the 1950s, this small, circular hat was popularized by the influential First Lady Jackie Kennedy during the 1960s. It was reinterpreted by U.S. designer Halston to accommodate the style icon's signature bouffant hair style, and it was Jackie herself who repositioned it to sit on the back of the head, leaving her coiffure undisturbed.

POKE BONNET

Named for the small crown and large projecting brim that extended past the face, the poke bonnet shielded the profile of the wearer until, by 1830, a woman's face could not be seen except from directly in front. It became fashionable at the beginning of the nineteenth century and was worn by women and children of all ages. The large brim provided an ample surface area for decoration with feathers and flowers.

SNOOD

Similar in style and function to a hairnet, and particularly popular in the 1860s, a snood is a head covering of mesh or net used to gather in the hair, frequently made of very fine material to match the wearer's natural hair color. Snoods were also worn in Europe during World War II as a means of protecting the hair while working with machinery.

SOMBRERO

From the Spanish word *sombra*, meaning shade, the sombrero is associated with Mexico, Spain, and South America. Constructed from straw or felt, the sombrero has a high, conical crown and a wide brim broad enough to cast a shadow over the head, neck, and shoulders of the wearer. It is tied under the chin to hold it in place. In the American West, the sombrero featured a cylindrical crown and was decorated with embroidery.

Poke Bonnet

Top Hat

SOU-WESTER

A collapsible oilskin rain hat that is longer in the back than the front to fully protect the neck, is tied under the chin, and has a gutter front brim to keep water from the eyes. The sou-wester was typically worn by sailors and originally made of sailcloth waterproofed with a thin layer of tar. Later they were constructed from a canvas duck coated with layers of linseed oil and finished with paint. Contemporary sou-westers are generally made of a PVC-coated fabric.

TAM O'SHANTER

Named after the eponymous hero of Robert Burns's poem published in 1791, the tam o'shanter is Scottish in origin and features a tight-fitting external headband encompassing a soft full crown with the fullness worn to one side. It is usually constructed from a clan tartan cloth or velvet. A pom-pom or "toorie" decorates the center.

TOP HAT

Invented by English haberdasher John Hetherington as a modification of the riding hat, the top hat is a tall cylindrical hat with a flat top and stiff narrow brim usually constructed from a lustrous black silk or beaver cloth. It is also known as a stove pipe hat or a "topper". Associated with both the successful Victorian gentleman and the Hollywood musicals of the 1930s, the contemporary top hat is worn as part of formal dress, most notably at weddings. Milliners such as Stephen Jones have played with the scale of top hats, either supersizing them, as seen here on the left, or miniaturizing them to be worn on the top of the head as a fascinator.

TRICORN

Also known as the cocked hat, the tricorn was in general use during the eighteenth century, and was also part of military and naval uniforms. Usually made of beaver hair felt or wool felt, the hat brim had three sides that were turned up – cocked – and either pinned, laced, or buttoned in place, forming a triangle around the crown. The hat was worn over a variety of fashionable wigs.

TRILBY

A soft felt hat with the crown creased along its length that is similar in style to the fedora but featuring a narrower brim. Named after the hat worn by the title character in George du Maurier's play *Trilby* from 1894, the trilby is now worn by both men and women, and was particularly fashionable for women during the 1970s.

TURBAN

Based on winding a length of cloth around the head, and with religious connotations dating back to the fourteenth century, the turban became fashionable when couturier Paul Poiret introduced his pastiche of Ottoman court costume in 1909. The collection was influenced in part by the costumes of the Ballets Russes production in Paris of *Scheherazade* – a rewriting of *One Thousand and One Nights*. During World War II, the turban was used to constrain the hair while working with machinery.

Turban

SHOES

INTRODUCTION

Historically, the workings of the female leg
have always been mysteriously hidden, placing
emphasis on the well-shod foot. Shoes have
evolved over the centuries from a purely
practical item of dress to a decorative object
where functionality is subsumed by the
elaborate and decorative. The notion of a shoe
designer only came into being in the early
1900s – before then, shoes were the creation
of nameless cobblers and dressmakers, closely
entwined with the history of transport.
When walking or riding were the only means
of transport available, shoes were made
accordingly – it is for this reason that most
men's boots from before the nineteenth
century have heels in order to keep stirrups
in place. Traditionally, women were expected
to spend little time outdoors, and as such,
their shoes have historically been delicate,
highly decorated, and impractical, an ethos
present in contemporary shoe design with the
introduction of the 4-inch (10-cm) heel as
standard. The designer shoe – from labels such
as Manolo Blahnik and Christian Louboutin –
has achieved the same cult status as the must-
have "It" bag in the twenty-first century.

▲ Iconic shoe designer Manolo Blahnik is globally recognized for the innovative use of materials and delicate styling.

▶ Stilettos reached ever-greater heights in the 2010s, with platform soles allowing even higher heels to be worn, as seen here on a classic stiletto pump by Christian Louboutin from 2014 – a designer renowned for the trademark red sole (*see* Stiletto, page 147).

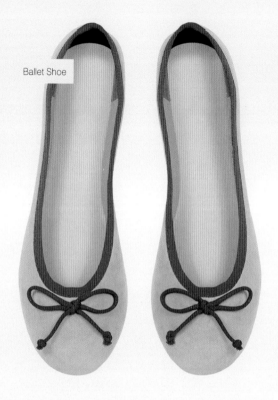

Ballet Shoe

BALLET SHOE

Based on the performance shoes worn by ballet dancers, this is a simple, soft, round-toed shoe with no heel. Decoration is limited to a single ribbon tie at the front of the vamp, although many combinations of prints and patterns are available. The ballet shoe became widely popular in the mid-twentieth century when Audrey Hepburn wore a pair with a simple black ensemble in the 1957 movie *Funny Face*, and again in the early 2000s when Kate Moss paired the shoes with skinny jeans.

BALMORAL BOOT

Queen Victoria's bootmaker, J. Sparkes Hall, first produced the Balmoral boot (named after Victoria's Scottish summer retreat) in the mid-nineteenth century. It was a narrow, low-heeled ankle boot with a toe cap made of a separate piece of leather. The boot was fastened by lacing that ran up the center front of the boot, generally with five eyelets for the laces. As the name suggests, it was a boot suitable for country pursuits – the kind of activities that Prince Albert, for whom the boot was created, would undertake while staying on the Balmoral estate.

BOAT (DECK) SHOE

A shoe constructed from quick-drying material and designed to be worn on the deck of a ship or boat, with a non-slip sole that won't damage the deck. Several styles of boat shoes have evolved in both the U.S. and the U.K. – with the latter resembling a simple cotton sneaker, or plimsoll. In the U.S., however, the boat shoe has a more elaborate design with a ridge that runs around the toe and a long stitch that runs around the uppers.

Boat Shoe

Balmoral Boot

BROGUE

The brogue is a laced shoe similar to the Oxford, but with decorative perforations and pinking applied along the seams where the vamp (the upper front piece) and quarters (the part that encloses the heel of the foot) of the shoe meet. The brogue was originally worn by Irish land laborers – with the perforations serving the practical purpose of helping the bog water that would leak in to drain away. The style spread to English estates, first adopted by gamekeepers before disseminating to the upper levels of society who wore it for country pursuits.

Gillie

CHELSEA BOOT

An ankle-length boot based on the design of a short riding boot. It is a narrow, close-fitting shape with elasticated side panels that enable the wearer to pull the boot on and off easily. The Chelsea boot was first worn in the 1960s to complement the narrow tapered trousers worn by the Mods who habituated the King's Road in Chelsea, London.

CUBAN HEEL

Usually found on a boot, particularly the cowboy and Chelsea boot, a Cuban heel is constructed from layers that are stacked up, with the size of the layers diminishing at the back as the heel reaches the ground. The Cuban heel was first seen around the beginning of the twentieth century and is now often worn by men who wish to add extra height, as it is one of the few heels that are generally considered acceptable for both men and women.

ESPADRILLE

A simple canvas shoe constructed from pieces of sturdy fabric that are stitched onto a flat or platform sole made from braided and coiled rope, hemp, or straw. They were traditionally worn in southern France and the Pyrenees, but when the jet-set started to spend summers on the French Riviera they were adopted by the fashionable as casual, disposable vacation shoes. Audrey Hepburn wore an espadrille in the 1953 film *Roman Holiday*, ensuring the popularity of the shoe, as did Grace Kelly in *To Catch A Thief* (1955), *see* opposite.

GILLIE (GHILLIE)

A traditional shoe from Scotland that is now only generally worn as a dancing shoe or as part of the highland costume, the gillie (named after a chieftain's attendant), is a flat, soft leather, tongueless shoe on which the two sides of the upper have integrated loops that are pulled together with a cord, which is then looped around the ankle and tied. Another variation is the "ghillie brogue", a traditional gamekeeper's brogue, which has an additional section above the ankles that is tied on by the same loop-and-cord method.

LOUIS HEEL

A shoe with a heel that starts out broad before tapering on all sides in a curved line to a smaller, square point. First worn by both men and women in the French court of Louis XV in the mid-eighteenth century, the Louis heel was particularly popular for shoes in the 1920s, when it was combined with a buttoned strap across the insole.

LOAFER

The loafer is based on a Norwegian style of slip-on moccasin. Bass was the first company to market these shoes to the expanding U.S. market in the 1930s, calling them Weejans. However, it was not until the peak of the preppy look in the 1950s – when loafers or boat shoes were an essential part of the style – that loafers became widespread. Teenagers took to inserting a penny into the decoration that sat on the tongue of the shoe, and as such, they came to be known as penny loafers. By the 1980s Gucci, with its horse's bit decoration, was the key loafer brand.

MOCCASIN

The moccasin shoe shares the same basic shape of all slip-on shoes, with its low-cut sides, simple aperture for the foot, and a raised vamp that is stitched in place. Originally, moccasins were worn by indigenous people of North America and were made from buckskin, which was soft but hard-wearing. The crudest form of moccasin has just one piece of skin that is gathered around the foot and sewn up, but modern versions have hardened soles, a properly stitched-in vamp, and a cuff around the edge. Decoration can take the form of tassels and beads attached to the tongue.

MONKSTRAP

With a strap-and-buckle closure instead of lacing, the monkstrap shoe is a moderately formal men's shoe that is chosen for "smart casual" occasions but not formalwear. So called because of their resemblance to monk's sandals, they are available as single or double-buckle versions.

MULE

The mule is a backless heeled shoe that is kept in place on the foot by a band of fabric or leather that reaches from the sole over the instep. Originally an indoor shoe – their construction hardly lending themselves to serious walking – they were designed to be worn in the boudoir and were originally made of luxurious fabrics such as velvet or trimmed with marabou feathers.

OXFORD

A sturdy leather shoe with its origins in the seventeenth century – when it was used to describe a half-boot – and so named because it was a common shoe for the academics of Oxford University. By the nineteenth century it had come to mean any practical, low-heeled shoe that is closed up at the front with laces or a buckle and that has a tongue beneath the fastening.

Brogue

Moccasin

Loafer

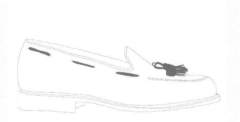

Spectator

Oxford

Monkstrap

PEEP-TOE

The screen sirens of the 1930s, such as Mae West and Jean Harlow, were the first women to wear the provocatively sexy new peep-toe shoes. The peep-toe shoe, along with the slingback, signified an eroticization of the foot, as it revealed, with the use of a cutaway at the front of the shoe, one or two toes that had been hitherto hidden away. By the 1940s the peep-toe had become a less shocking piece of design and was commonly seen on suede dancing shoes.

PLATFORMS

Shoes with platforms applied to raise the wearer off the ground by several inches have been in existence for centuries, with particularly extreme examples called *chopines* worn by Venetian women in the sixteenth century. The platform as it is known today first appeared on women's shoes in the designs of Ferragamo in the 1930s. However, it was in the 1970s when it reached its apotheosis – with the exaggerated stacked heels of the glam rock era worn by both men and women, when rock stars such as Marc Bolan wore Terry de Havilland's cartoonish designs on stage.

Peep-toe

Plimsoll

Pump

PLIMSOLL (SAND SHOE)

Several brands of rubber-soled shoes were being produced in the nineteenth century, designed for sports use and for sailing. However, they were only named "plimsolls" once the Liverpool Rubber Company started using a joining technique in which the two parts of the shoe – the sole and the canvas upper – were fixed with a strip of rubber over the seam. The resulting line resembled the "Plimsoll line" invented by Samuel Plimsoll to mark the load limit on a ship in 1876.

PUMP (COURT SHOE)

A perennial fashion classic, and the plainest of women's shoes, the pump is a low-cut, mid-heeled, slip-on shoe with little or no decoration on the upper. The toe is usually rounded but may also be pointed, according to the prevailing fashion. The term "pump" has been in use since the sixteenth century to describe such a shoe, but the meaning has taken on different forms in various countries, with pump meaning a type of sports shoe in the U.K.

SANDAL

Various types of sandals have been worn since prehistoric times. One of the most basic types of shoe, and suitable for hotter climates, the sandal is generally constructed from leather and held in place by a single strap – as with a flip-flop (also known in some countries as a thong). However it may also be a high-heeled, multi-strapped confection of many colors and decorative features, with the gladiator sandal having particular dominance in both Roman times and the early twenty-first century.

SLINGBACK

A shoe resembling a pump with the exception that the heel part is removed. The shoe is held in place by an elasticated or buckled strap running around the back of the heel. First seen in the 1930s, the slingback represented Hollywood glamour, especially when combined with a peep-toe. The slingback shoe is a summer staple and may be found in a variety of materials and heel heights.

SNEAKERS (TRAINERS)

Initially a flexible and light shoe specifically designed for use when undertaking sports activities, the sneaker has held mass appeal for decades for reasons of both comfort and style. Originally such shoes were called sneakers – because footsteps were silent when worn – in the 1860s, and the term is still used in the U.S. today. In the U.K., however, the term "trainer" (from "training shoe") is more often

used. Sneakers are similar to plimsolls, but the construction is sturdier, with greater ankle and foot support. They are either laced up or fastened with Velcro and are constructed from various synthetic performance fibers.

SPECTATOR (CO-RESPONDENT)

A type of shoe that is constructed from leathers of more than one color – usually black and white or brown and white – first popularized by Edward, Prince of Wales. However, it wasn't until the 1930s when jazz culture – with its extrovert glamour – was at the height of its popularity that the spectator shoe became widespread. The basic structure is based on the Oxford brogue, although other shoes such as Mary Janes or Chanel's classic two-tone slingback can also be called spectators if the colorway is correct.

Slingback

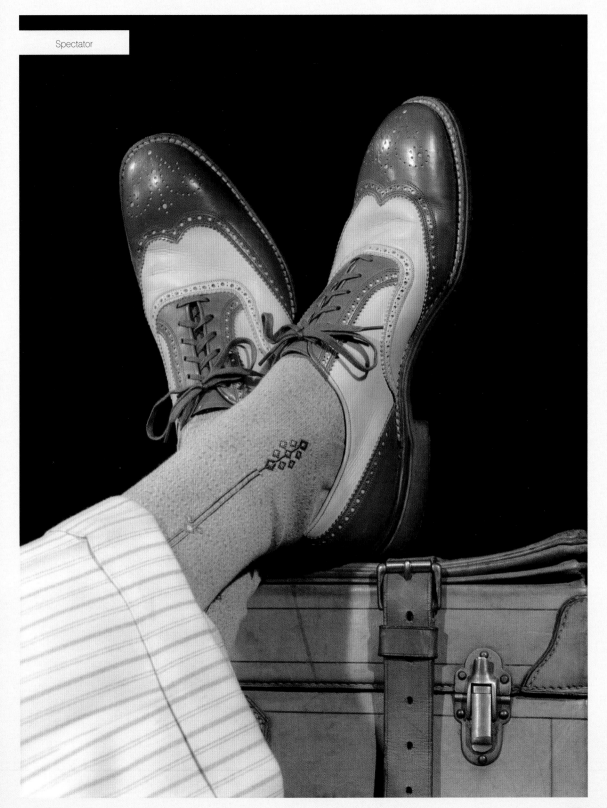

STILETTO

A form of high-heeled pump, the stiletto is a thin, sharp heel named after the stiletto blade of the Sicilian mafia – and was arguably invented by Italian shoemaker Salvatore Ferragamo in the 1950s. The stiletto has come to represent a heightened femininity – the wearer is rendered vulnerable as the heels are impossible to run in – and her foot is arched in a way that mimics sexual ecstasy. In the 1980s it was a vital tool in the working woman's wardrobe, with a sense of power being achieved by its dominatrix subtext.

T-BAR (MARY JANE)

Originally a child's shoe, but adopted by the flappers of the 1920s as a symbol of youthful exuberance and practicality. It is a mid-heeled, round-toed plain shoe with a narrow T-bar strap that runs across the front of the foot, held in place by a buckle or button. The T-bar shoe became ubiquitous during the 1930s, when most women embraced it as a practical working shoe. Manolo Blahnik created a much-coveted Campari Mary Jane stiletto in patent leather with a pointed toe in the late 1990s and once more, due to popular demand, in 2009.

WEDGE

The wedge is a heeled shoe, and the heel is constructed from one solid block that fills in the entirety of the underside of the shoe, with the sole lying flat on the ground. The wedge is commonly made of cork – particularly on lighter summer shoes – or from a lightweight wood or rubber. The upper can be made of any material but is usually leather or canvas. Wedges have been popular as both formal and

summer shoes at various points in time since the 1930s, but were diversified in the early 2010s when Isabel Marant invented the wedge sneaker with a hidden heel.

Stiletto

HANDBAGS

INTRODUCTION

An indispensable accessory, the bag has a
unique place in every woman's wardrobe.
The need for a handbag first arose during
the early nineteenth century, when the lines
of the neoclassical columnar dress were
uninterrupted by pockets, and the reticule –
a small pouch-shaped bag with a drawstring
top – was used to carry small items such as
a handkerchief. As women's lives diversified
from domestic preoccupations, a handbag
became an indispensable adjunct to a life
in the outside world. Initially crafted by
luggage makers and saddlers, it was not until
after World War I that handbags became
subject to the vagaries of fashion. In the
1920s synthetic materials such as celluloid,
casein, and cellulose acetate were used to
replicate tortoiseshell and ivory, in addition
to more traditional leather. Transparent
box-shaped bags were popular after World
War II. During the 1990s handbags became
a commodity that fueled the luxury goods
market with the phenomenon of the must-
have "It" bag, including Fendi's Baguette bag
and bespoke classics in exotic skins such as
the Kelly and the Birkin bag from French
fashion house Hermès.

▲ The Fendi Baguette bag first appeared in 1997, as part of the ailing firm's successful
rebranding. These "It" bags are marketed as individualized objects of desire, with the
basic shape being available in over 600 permutations.

▶ The Chanel brand produces a variation on its iconic 2.55 bag every season. In this
bag from the fall/winter 2005 collection, the classic rectangular quilted shape with chain
strap is given a harder edge with the use of metallic gray leather and a solid chain.

STYLES AND COMPONENTS OF DRESS

Cross-body Bag

BACKPACK (RUCKSACK)

A hands-free bag with two shoulder straps worn on the back of the body, the urban backpack or rucksack was first introduced by Jean-Charles de Castelbajac in 1984. The influential Prada backpack, the Vela, followed in 1985 – a lightweight bag in Pocona nylon with a discreet triangular logo. It was carried by both men and women and represented the fashionable version of minimalism, in opposition to the prevailing ethos of conspicuous consumption.

BUCKET BAG

So called because it is shaped like a bucket – circular, and narrower at the base than the top – the bucket bag is a hand-held accessory popularly made in natural straw, with a lidded top and a toggle-and-loop fastening. Usually carried in summer, the bag is frequently decorated with flowers or sea shells. Leather versions are stiffened to hold their shape and frequently feature double rows of stitching.

CLUTCH

Palm-sized and rectangular in shape, the clutch bag was designed to be worn tucked under the arm or clutched in the hand. It represented the modernity of the 1920s, when the pared-down silhouette of the chemise demanded a streamlined bag. Often constructed from one of the new plastics such as Bakelite, the bag featured decoration inspired by the geometric forms of art deco. The clutch bag continues to be a popular accessory for formal events.

CROSS-BODY BAG

The austere years of World War II heralded the cross-body bag, which provided hands-free storage for women conscripted into the armed services. Usually made from military canvas, the bag had long straps that were wide enough to be worn comfortably across the body. The shoulder bag increased in size and shape to accommodate the obligatory gas mask, which was compulsory luggage at all times in Britain. Bags made by the London Company H. Wald & Co. had a zippered compartment at the base of the bag to hide the gas mask.

Bucket Bag

DRAWSTRING (DOROTHY) BAG

Popular during the Edwardian era, Dorothy bags were carried only at home or for eveningwear. Often highly decorated with beadwork or embroidered and appliquéd flowers, the bags were constructed from a circle of dress fabric – often from a matching dress – gathered together by a drawstring at the top to create a frilled opening. The bags were related in type and construction to the nineteenth-century work bag, and named after Dorothy, the eponymous heroine of A.J. Munby's play of the 1880s.

DUFFLE BAG

A large cylindrical bag made of various materials soft enough to close with a drawstring at the top, with a thick strap joining the base of the bag and the top. The name comes from Duffel, a town in Belgium where the thick cloth used to make the bag originated. Originally an item of workwear, the duffle bag became a favorite of students in the 1950s and continues to be made in a variety of finishes and fabrics.

ENVELOPE

A flat, rectangular under-arm bag popular in the 1920s and '30s, similar in shape to the clutch bag but with a flap extending over the edge of the bag that is usually fastened with an invisible press stud. Contemporary envelope bags vary in size, from small evening versions to large frameless bags in pliant leather that are supported by the forearm. A detachable strap is sometimes provided.

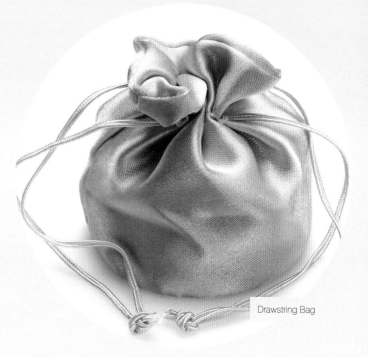

Drawstring Bag

Envelope

Minaudière

MESSENGER

Also known as a courier bag, the messenger bag is worn over one shoulder and has a strap broad enough to support its weighty contents. The bag was initially designed to transport mail and goods, constructed from sturdy canvas with interior pockets for documents. Frequently used by urban cyclists, the bag now features lightweight and impermeable high-performance fabrics and may have a padded strap for ease of wear.

MINAUDIÈRE

A small case combining both purse and powder compact, the first minaudiere was reportedly invented in 1933 by Paris jeweler Charles Arpel of Van Cleef and Arpels after noting that socialite Florence Jay Gould carried her makeup and lighter in a metal Lucky Strikes cigarette case. Usually exquisitely crafted in silver or gold and set with precious stones, the American designer Judith Leiber is associated with very luxurious minaudières, featuring whimsical subject matter, first introduced in the late 1960s.

SATCHEL

Long used by children to carry books, the satchel is usually associated with the classic image of the English schoolboy. The traditional Oxford and Cambridge-style satchel features a fold-over flap secured with two buckles, with a pocket attached to the front and an adjustable strap. The external seams feature stitching. In 2008 the satchel achieved cult status when the U.K.-based Cambridge Satchel Company began producing the bags in vibrant colors.

Messenger

TOTE

The boat tote bag was first introduced as a gardening tote by L.L. Bean in 1944. Founded in 1912 by Leon Leonwood Bean, the company built a brand on a casual style of dressing that was influenced by sportswear and the outdoors. Sometimes called a shopper, it is based on the shape of a paper shopping bag – rectangular with handles at the top. The boat tote was made in canvas and was east/west style; that is, it was broader than it was high. A taller bag is known as a north/south tote.

Tote

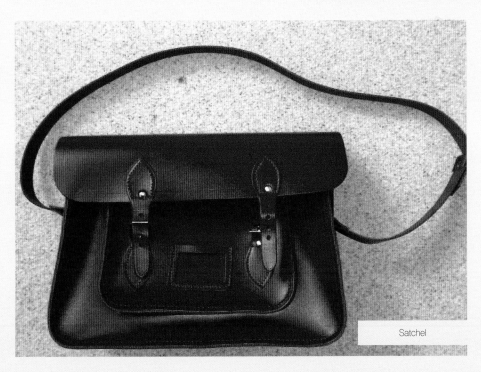

Satchel

DESIGN, TAILORING, AND STITCHING

Today, New York, Paris, London, and Milan are considered the global capitals for fashion; however, Paris has been the principal center for haute couture for over three hundred years. The roots of the modern fashion industry are grounded in seventeenth-century France when, thanks to the economic policies of Louis XIV and his finance minister Jean-Baptiste Colbert, France developed a highly successful and competitive manufacturing industry that focused on producing top-quality elite goods that were innovative in design and set the seasonal fashions.

Couture houses – founded in the mid-nineteenth century by couturiers such as Charles Frederick Worth, Jacques Doucet, and Jeanne Paquin – catered not just to French aristocracy and high society, but increasingly to a privileged international market – particularly wealthy Americans. Yet while haute couture can be seen as a continuation of the elite sartorial system of the French court of Versailles, it nevertheless emerged during a period of growing industrialization, increasing mass production in the clothing industries, and an exploding market for ready-to-wear fashion – all factors that would progressively undermine haute couture throughout the twentieth century, even with the introduction of prêt-à-porter lines. Today, haute couture clients are believed to number at just several hundred, yet the stylistic influence of the biannual Paris couture collections across the global fashion industry is beyond calculation.

Just as Paris is the center of couture dressmaking, London has long enjoyed its reputation as the capital city of tailoring. Since the eighteenth century, there has been a clear division between the dressmaking and the tailoring trades. Dressmakers were women who were highly skilled in the art of sewing, and who made unstructured clothes such as gowns and cloaks. Tailors, regulated by the Tailor's Guild, were men who made structured clothes for both sexes – clothing that often contained boning, such as corsets and coats. By the nineteenth century, tailoring had become a professional craft specializing in the use of the British woolen cloths from which suiting was made. It was the manipulation of these wool fabrics on which a tailor staked his reputation, and on which the standing of the British tailoring industry is founded.

Throughout the Victorian era, London tailors – centered at Savile Row – perfected the art of bespoke tailoring to the degree that the quality and measure of a gentleman was seen in the cut and measure of his suit. The standardization in measuring systems that occurred during the era facilitated the work of the tailor, yet it also promoted the spread of the made-to-measure system within modern tailoring.

After World War II, modern industrial cities such as Milan and New York emerged as international design centers to rival the traditional bases of Paris and London. The garment district in midtown New York had, since the late nineteenth century, manufactured affordable, ready-to-wear clothing for the masses, supported by a steady influx of immigrant labor. Thanks to its location in the heart of the city, manufacturers and wholesalers, designers and illustrators, buyers and publicists, all converged in the garment district to encourage the creation of a new style of twentieth-century fashion. Characterized as casual yet smart, American fashion promotes a style of clean lines and simple construction.

Contemporary fashion and the consumer market has been dominated by the young middle classes that demand an ever-immediate selection of affordable, yet innovative, ready-to-wear fashions. Regardless, this has not marked the end of the haute couture and bespoke traditions, which champion hand-worked techniques over machine production.

▶ A smart tailored suit – such as this 1938 offering from Balenciaga – was a wardrobe staple for any busy socialite during the interwar years.

▶▶ In 1966, Yves Saint Laurent first took the traditional male tuxedo and transformed it into "Le Smoking" – a stylish alternative to evening dress for the modern woman.

HAUTE COUTURE

INTRODUCTION

Haute couture refers to the business of Parisian custom dressmaking. Formally founded in 1868, its governing body – the *Chambre Syndicale de la Couture Parisienne* – was established to regulate the location, creation, fabrication, presentation, and dissemination of haute couture designs. Its key concern was to protect France's legacy as the catalyst for modern, original fashion design, executed at the highest level of craftsmanship. Only those designers deemed to achieve and maintain such superior standards of design and production are titled "couturier". Mainbocher was the only American designer invited to show in Paris by the *Chambre Syndicale de la Couture Parisienne* until Ralph Rucci in 2002.

The golden age of haute couture is regarded as the period following World War II through the 1950s. Supported by an enthusiastic market of wealthy American clientele, Parisian couture witnessed a period of unrivaled ingenuity in design, driven by talents such as Christian Dior, Cristóbal Balenciaga, Pierre Balmain, and Jacques Fath. Many of the houses of these designers continue to dominate fashion long after the demise of their founder, thanks to new generations of couturiers – for example, the House of Dior fostered the talent of a young Yves Saint Laurent, and was led into the twenty-first century by John Galliano. And after first working at Balmain (among others), Karl Lagerfeld has been head designer at Chanel since 1983.

▲ Inspired by classical Greek dress, Madame Grès excelled in designing minimalist, slim silhouettes. In this early gown of 1937, silk jersey is fluidly draped over the body to create a dramatic, columnar form.

▶ Employing the *moulage* technique to dramatic effect, this design, built on symmetrical lines and flowing drapery, encapsulates evening glamour. Zuhair Murad, fall/winter 2014–15.

Atelier

speaking should apply only to designers based in Paris. Specifically, an haute couturier is a designer who is a member of the *Chambre Syndicale de la Haute Couture,* which strictly regulates the location, creation, fabrication, presentation, and dissemination of haute couture designs. An Englishman is actually accredited with being the "first couturier" – Charles Frederick Worth, who dressed the Empress Eugénie and Parisian society for much of the second half of the nineteenth century.

FLOU

The *flou* atelier of a couture house is responsible for dressmaking, and is generally more concerned with the design process. The term, meaning "loose" or "fuzzy" in French, refers to the use of soft, delicate fabrics such as chiffon and silk, which must be carefully handled and draped. A *flou* seamstress requires years of precise training to acquire the necessary skills and often, in time, comes to specialize in the use of a specific fabric.

MODÈLE

This is the design template for a garment. During the conception phase of the design process, a design may be created either through sketching or draping cloth directly on a model. The design will then pass to either the *flou* or the *tailleur atelier,* depending on the hand skills that the materials and shapes required, and it is used as the basis for making the toile. It has been estimated that during the 1950s, the golden age of haute couture, approximately 6,000 *modèles* were being shown every season. *See also* Toile, page 163.

ATELIER

The atelier of a couture house is the workshop where the design and production of clothing takes place, and as such refers to both the physical space and the skilled staff working there. Notably the term atelier also refers to an artist's studio, as the atelier is an environment of creative experimentation as well as skilled craftsmanship. It is divided into two separate but equally specialized workrooms: the *flou* and the *tailleur.*

COUTURIER

Generally, the term couturier refers to a male or female fashion designer who achieves the highest level of excellence and originality in design and manufacture. Although it is generally used to refer to the leading designers working in fashion capitals across the globe, the term strictly

MOULAGE

A French term translated as "mold" or "cast",
this is the technique of direct draping on a
mannequin stand to produce a form-fitting
model that accentuates the human body.
Moulage can be a creative and experimental
process in itself, producing a design that could
be difficult to duplicate using a flat pattern.
The 1930s Grecian-style dresses of Madame
Grès are a pioneering example of moulage
design. It continues to be a popular design
technique today.

PETIT MAIN

The term *petit main*, meaning "little hand"
in French, refers to the seamstresses who
work in a haute couture atelier, under the
supervision of the *première d'atelier*, and
who are specialists in the arts of tailoring
or draping. A strict hierarchy of *petits mains*
exists within the workshop, based on training,
experience, and skill. The most skilled
seamstress bears the title *première main
hautement qualifiée*, and has the significant
responsibility of cutting the pieces for a
pattern from a textile.

PREMIÈRE D'ATELIER

The atelier of an haute couture house is
governed by one head, the *première d'atelier*,
usually a woman (*premier* referring to the male
head of a workroom, often of a *tailleur*). Their
chief responsibility is to ensure the timely and
precise execution of designs. They allocate
work to the *petits mains* in their charge,
deciding which seamstress is best suited for
the particular requirements of an individual
design. The *première d'atelier* also acts as a
vital liaison between the design studio and the
atelier, and the atelier and the salon.

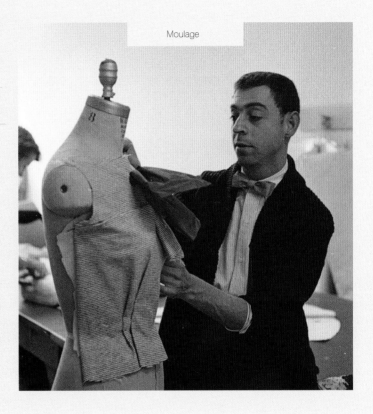

Moulage

PRÊT-À-PORTER (READY-TO-WEAR)

Clothing that is mass-produced to standardized sizes. Prêt-à-porter couture collections first widely appeared in the mid-1960s as a response to the growing economic crisis within the haute couture industry. The increasing ease with which designs could be disseminated and copied on a mass scale, and the shrinking pool of clientele with the financial means to buy haute couture, had drastic repercussions. Although Pierre Cardin was the first couturier to launch a prêt-à-porter line in 1959, it was Yves Saint Laurent who made ready-to-wear more acceptable and fashionable. Prêt-à-porter is regarded as a vital contributor to the globalization of fashion.

SALON

The term salon, meaning a reception room in French, literally refers to the building housing a couturier's workshops and showrooms, but also conveys much deeper historic connotations of culture and refinement. Since the seventeenth century, salons were gatherings of artists and intellectuals for the purpose of discussion and knowledge, held in the grand reception rooms of the palatial Parisian town houses where many modern couturiers established their businesses. The décor and ambiance of each particular salon reflects the style of each particular couturier.

SAMPLE

A sample is the first version of a garment made in actual garment fabric, and is the version of a design shown on the runway. The preferred size for samples is U.S. 4 (U.K. 8). Samples of past collections are usually stored in the

Salon

archive of a couturier, to be taken out again when desired for design inspiration or events such as photo shoots.

SILHOUETTE

The overall shape created by a garment. Silhouette is considered essential to the preliminary stages of the design process in order to determine which parts of the body will be emphasized and why. At this early stage, form and shape are given fundamental consideration, before secondary qualities such as detail and texture. *See also* pages 34–39.

TAILLEUR

Refers to the tailoring workshop of a couture house, where skilled workers are devoted to the construction of tailored jackets and coats. The tailors spend many years acquiring the complex skills relating to the measure, cut, sewing, and pressing of heavy woolen and wool-blend fabrics.

TOILE

A fitting garment, typically of muslin (cotton-calico), made from a couturier's drawn design. It is a continuation of the design process, made to confirm the designer's concept in a cheap material before the costly garment fabrics are cut. It is used as the basis for the pattern, but the term toile can also refer to the pattern itself. It is seen as an indispensable step of the classic couture practice, but it in fact is not adopted by all couturiers. Jean Paul Gaultier is notable for generally dispensing with the toile process altogether.

VENDEUSE

One of the sales staff responsible for meeting private clientele, establishing relationships with commercial buyers and selling the designs of a couture house. She does more than sell – she acts as a fashion adviser, guiding the client's taste and choice. Once a garment is ordered, the *vendeuse* acts as liaison between the design studio, the workroom, and the client, arranging for fittings and delivery.

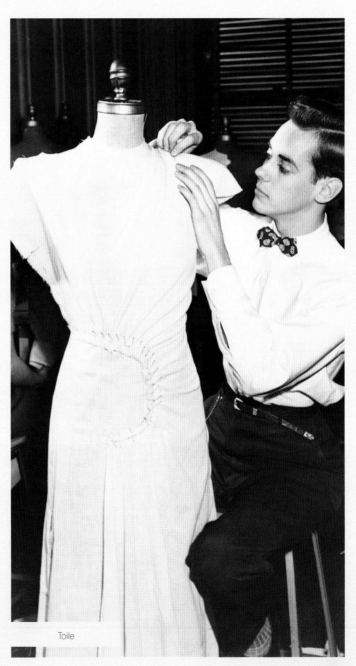

Toile

TAILORING

INTRODUCTION

Tailoring refers to the design and assembly of highly structured garments, most typically the three-piece male suit, which includes a jacket, waistcoat, and trousers. Women's jackets, as well as overcoats and riding jackets for both sexes, are also commonly tailored items of clothing. "Tailor" is a generic term in common use for what are traditionally two quite distinct roles – those of the cutter and the tailor. The cutter is responsible for measuring, cutting, and fitting the garments. The tailor makes the clothing, stitching together the separate pieces, following the pattern made by the cutter. It was conventionally believed that a competent craftsman should be proficient in both skills, and certainly in the present day, the two roles are often executed by the same person.

A well-cut tailored suit is a style icon, simultaneously displaying elegance and style, while suggesting formality and experience. Traditionally, a bespoke suit requires three fittings in order to achieve the perfect fit and balance on the body.

▲ Duchamp of London, spring/summer 2012. Since the nineteenth century, Savile Row has been the center of English tailoring.

▶ Frederico Fellini's *La Dolce Vita* (1960) catapulted sleek and sophisticated Italian tailoring to an international audience – a slim-fitting, lean silhouette cut in light, crisp fabrics, as modeled by Marcello Mastroianni.

Baste

BASTE

A baste is a tailored garment loosely
assembled using a temporary basting stitch.
Its purpose is to ascertain the fit and balance
of the tailored design on the client's body.
In bespoke tailoring, there are three types of
baste, in line with the three stages of fittings:
the skeleton baste, the shell baste, and lastly
the advanced baste.

SKELETON BASTE

The skeleton baste is, as its name suggests,
the tailored garment in its most primary and
primitive form. The essential shape and pattern of the garment is visible, and canvases
have been attached. All seams are neatly basted
together for easier adjustment. The positions
of secondary elements, such as pockets, are
marked. The fitting of the skeleton baste is a
moment for creative discussion between the
cutter and the client, allowing the opportunity
for changes to the style and fit of the garment
as necessity and preference requires.

SHELL BASTE

The shell baste traditionally corresponds to the second fitting. The shell baste of a garment is a more padded and structured form than the skeleton baste. It has been altered to reflect any necessary corrections to measurement and fit. Canvas and facings have been added to give shape where required; any areas that need shaping are eased, shrunk, or stretched to mold the fabric permanently. In a garment such as a jacket, the sleeves and collar are still only basted in. At this stage, the cut and fit have been evaluated and only require confirmation.

ADVANCED BASTE

As an advanced baste, a bespoke tailored garment is near completion. It corresponds to the third and final fitting. At this stage, all seams are now permanently sewn and pressed, with basting stitches removed. Sleeves, shoulder pads, and the collar have been set and permanently stitched. The garment has been lined and hemmed. The advanced baste is assessed on the client, and its measure is perfected. Once the advanced baste is deemed acceptable, it can be finished by completing the buttonholes and attaching the buttons.

COMMON TERMS

BALANCE

Within bespoke tailoring, balance is generally defined as the relative length of the back and front of a garment, or of two sides of a garment. Balance is considered one of the most important principles of cutting, as the balance of a design determines how it feels when worn and how it hangs on the wearer. It will vary not only with different body types, but also with different kinds of clothing, such as a waistcoat or jacket. When there is complete unison between the various parts of a garment and the body it has to cover, then balance has been achieved.

BESPOKE

The term used within tailoring to refer to a garment, usually a suit, that is hand-made from start to finish according to a client's specific measurements and requirements. Usually at least three fittings are required before completion. Bespoke tailoring is equated with premium quality in both craftsmanship and material, and is regarded as a hand-craft, rather than as a mass-produced industrial product. The term dates back to the seventeenth century, when a fabric once chosen and reserved at a retailer's establishment was "bespoke", or "spoken for", and so could not be sold to another customer.

BODY RISE

Within bespoke tailoring, the body rise is the difference between the measure of the side seam and the measure of the leg seam lengths.

Cutter

DOUBLE BREASTED

The term double breasted refers to a tailored garment such as a coat or jacket that has wide, overlapping front flaps and two parallel columns of buttons down the front. Classically, a double-breasted jacket has either four or six buttons, and is worn closed at either the second or third row. Having a heavier, broader silhouette than the single-breasted jacket, the double-breasted suit was most fashionable in the mid-twentieth century and made a revival in the 1980s. *See also* page 52.

SINGLE BREASTED

A tailored garment, such as a coat or jacket, that is closed with just a narrow overlap of fabric in the front. A classic single-breasted jacket has one to three buttons. Stylistic variations are created by the type and width of the garment lapel. It is the most common style of jacket worn in contemporary menswear. *See also* page 52.

CANVASES

The inner material used in a tailored garment to give it shape, set between the lining facing and the garment fabric. Fabrics such as linen and horsehair are commonly used as canvases within bespoke tailoring. Its use helps control the garment fabric and reduces its tendency to wrinkle and stretch.

CUTTER

The cutter is responsible for measuring, cutting, and fitting an item of bespoke tailored clothing such as a suit. A good cutter will not only take accurate measurements of a client's body, but will visually assess the client's posture and figure, make improving adjustments if necessary, and include such assessments to produce a paper pattern. This paper pattern is used by the tailor to assemble and sew the garment.

FITTING

A term used within tailoring to refer to the client's trying-on of a garment baste. During a fitting, the cutter will assess how the garment hangs on the client's body, and any minute but necessary adjustments to its balance and style will be made. Within bespoke tailoring, a suit essentially requires three fittings, in accordance with the three stages of bastes. Made-to-measure suits only command one fitting, called the single-baste.

MADE-TO-MEASURE

A machine-made tailored garment coming from a pre-existing stock pattern, but allowing the client some choice regarding style features and fit. The client can choose the type of fabric, styling options, and details such as the type of lapel. The client's measurements are taken and forwarded to a factory workshop where a semi-fitted suit is made, and then finished after a single fitting. Although a made-to-measure suit would not achieve the same high quality of fit and finish as a bespoke suit, it would be considered superior to an industrially mass-produced garment.

TAILOR

Today, the term tailor is commonly used to refer to a person working in the design and production of tailored menswear garments. However, within the bespoke tailoring trade, a tailor is strictly someone who sews – who constructs and stitches together the pieces of

cloth for a garment that has previously been measured and cut by the cutter.

TRIMMINGS

Generally speaking, trimmings are all types of decorative embellishment that may be added to garments. Ribbons, braids, lace, and embroidery all fall within this category. Within bespoke tailoring, the term also refers to all the raw materials that make up a garment – the fabric, facings, canvas – and includes fastenings such as zippers and buttons.

Bespoke

POCKETS

Originally, pockets were little bags worn by women for the carrying of small essential items, which were usually worn strung around the waist and underneath the outer clothing. Men, in contrast, wearing tailored jackets and waistcoats from the seventeenth century had their pocket bags sewn into the lining. By the 1800s, women's pockets fell out of favor as handbags grew in popularity. In modern fashion, pockets can be decorative as well as functional. Technically, pockets fall into two basic categories: patch pockets and set-in pockets.

BOUND POCKET

A type of slashed pocket that has two narrow welts visible on the outer side of the garment and a pocket bag hidden between the lining and the garment. As such, it looks like a large, bound buttonhole. The pocket itself is used to finish off the edges of the slash in the garment, so garment fabric (rather than lining) is generally used.

FLAP POCKET

The flap is a shaped garment piece attached by only one edge, in the case of pockets, to the top seam allowance.

FRONT-HIP POCKET

A variety of set-in pocket attached to the garment at the waist and side seams. It is formed of two layers – the pocket piece, which is made from the garment fabric and sewn directly into the garment waistline, and the facing, often made of lining, which finishes off the pocket opening. Front-hip pockets are a standard feature of casualwear designs such as jeans and chinos.

INSEAM POCKET

A type of set-in pocket in which the pocket bag is sewn into a seam and is usually made from a lining fabric. It is formed of two layers – an under pocket, which sits nearest the lining, and an upper pocket. An inseam pocket often hides the garment opening. Couture garments typically have zippers inside the inseam pocket.

Bound Pocket

Flap Pocket

Bound Pocket

JETTED POCKET

A variety of double-welt pocket with two narrow welts, often made of satin, above and below the pocket slit opening.

PATCH POCKET

Patch pockets appear on the outside of a garment. They usually consist of a single layer of garment fabric and can be lined or unlined. They are very versatile, often forming a design feature in their own right – as can be seen in the work of one of the most imaginative couturiers, Elsa Schiaparelli. A patch pocket that has been sewn by hand rather than machine is one of the identifying characteristics of a couture garment.

SLASH POCKET

A type of set-in pocket in which the pocket bag is sewn into a slash. As with the inseam pocket, a slash pocket is formed of two layers, an under and upper pocket. There are three types of slash pockets, which differ only in the way the pocket opening is finished: a bound pocket, a flap pocket, and a welt pocket.

WELT POCKET

A slash pocket set into the garment with a slit entrance, formed from a single welt attached at the lower edge of the opening. Welt pockets are a popular choice for tailoring.

Patch Pocket

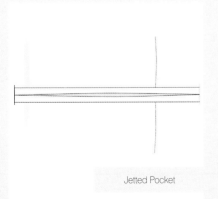
Jetted Pocket

Welt Pocket

TRADITIONAL COLLARS

"Collar" generally refers to the part of a garment that fastens around the neck. It is usually made from a separate piece of fabric, as opposed to the neckline, which is the top edge of a garment that frames the neck. Within tailoring, the collar is regarded as the centerpiece of a jacket, framing the tie, neck, and face.

ASCOT COLLAR

A very tall standing shirt collar with the points turned up over the chin. It is traditionally paired with a formal morning-dress suit, as is traditionally worn when attending the Royal Ascot races. This style of collar can also be called a "stock collar" – a stock being a form of eighteenth-century neckwear consisting of a high, stiffened band of fabric. Since the twentieth century, the term Ascot has more popularly referred to any type of silk neckcloth or cravat worn under a shirt collar and tied directly around the throat.

BERTHA COLLAR

Visually comparable to the white fitted yoke of a nun's habit, the bertha is a large, flat collar that extends from the neck outward as far as the shoulders and sweeps around in a deep curve to the opposite shoulder. Originally a plain style made in linen, sometimes with lace, and worn by the English Puritans in the seventeenth century, the bertha went through a revival in the 1940s.

BIB

Traditionally, a bib refers to a piece of fabric that covers one's chest, and as such can be applied to the top section of an apron or dungarees. Historically, the origins of the bib front can be traced back to the sixteenth century and a style of large flat collar that hung in front of a garment and covered the chest. In modern fashion, the term refers to a shirt style that features a large front section that is often decorated, embroidered, or beaded.

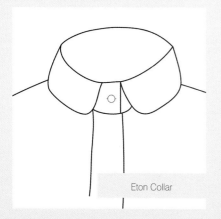
Eton Collar

Classic Collar

BUTTON-DOWN COLLAR

A variation of the classic shirt collar, the collar is buttoned down over the tie. Buttonholes are placed in the wings of the collar, through which small buttons placed high in the center front of the shirt can be affixed. It is generally regarded as a more informal shirt style.

CLASSIC COLLAR

Referring to men's shirting, the classic collar is the style most commonly seen on contemporary business shirts. The wings (the front, folded-down edges) of the collar are cut straight and point downward.

CUTAWAY COLLAR (WINDSOR)

Referring to men's shirting, the cutaway collar differs from the classic collar style in that the wings are cut away at an angle toward the shoulder, rather than straight down. It may also be referred to as a "Windsor collar".

ETON COLLAR

An Eton collar is a type of wide, stiff, turnover shirt collar with a stand. The collar has rounded edges. The design for an Eton collar is accredited to the uniform of Eton College, an English boys' school that dates back to the fifteenth century. It is a precursor to the Peter Pan collar in womenswear.

FLAT COLLAR

The general term for a collar with little or no stand around the neck, so that it falls directly on to the shoulders. A Peter Pan collar is an example of a flat collar.

MANDARIN COLLAR

A mandarin collar is a form of short, unfolded collar that sits straight up from the neckline. It is a characteristic feature of traditional Chinese clothing. The front edges of the collar are rounded and centrally meet. It started to appear on Western fashionable clothing in the twentieth century, occurring only intermittently as an Oriental motif until the 1970s, from which time it has become a popular choice for fashionable dress.

Ascot Collar

Cutaway Collar

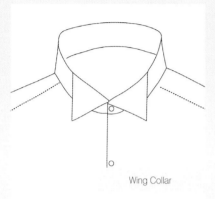

Wing Collar

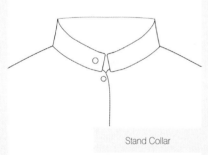

Stand Collar

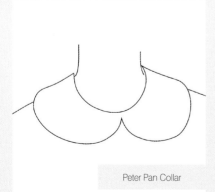

Peter Pan Collar

PETER PAN COLLAR

A type of small, soft collar with rounded corners, it sits flat on the curve of the neckline. Variations of the collar were regularly worn by children throughout the nineteenth century, but the name itself dates to the early twentieth century. The name "Peter Pan" refers to the believed use of the collar for the costume of the title character during the Broadway premiere of the play in 1905.

ROLLED COLLAR

A rolled collar is any type of collar in which the fabric "rolls" back on itself to form a stand in the back and contours the neck in front. The shawl collar is an example of a rolled collar.

RUFF

Worn as fashionable dress by both men and women during the sixteenth and seventeenth centuries, a ruff is a type of small, pleated, and starched collar that varied considerably in size and style throughout this period. The ruff originated as a frill attached to the neckband of a shirt or smock, but as they grew in size, ruffs became separate articles of dress. At their most exaggerated, immense ruffs were like "cartwheels" (as they were called in the Elizabethan court) that completely encircled the throat and framed the face. Their heyday was from the 1570s until the 1620s, but they continued to be worn in Spain into the early years of the eighteenth century. Ruffs were made of starched fine lace, pleated and supported with small tubes (called "poking sticks") of iron, bone, or wood.

STAND COLLAR

The historical term for an upright neckband or collar attached to a doublet, coat, or waistcoat.

STOCK COLLAR

Worn during the eighteenth century as part of military uniform, a stock was a shaped fabric band fastened at the back of the neck with ties, a buckle, or a hook and eye. In the nineteenth century they entered mainstream fashionable wear. Very extravagant styles reached high past the chin to graze the cheeks. *See also* Ascot Collar, page 172.

WING COLLAR

A stiff shirt collar with the tips standing up and pointed horizontally in front, as seen on a man's tuxedo dress shirt. It is worn today only with formal dress.

Flat Collar

NECKLINES & NECKWEAR

Until the sixteenth century, there was little to fundamentally differentiate between the collars and necklines of men's and women's fashions. During the Middle Ages, both sexes wore low necklines over linen chemises, and during the Renaissance both sexes wore the fashion for ruffs of various types. However, during the seventeenth century, there emerged a growing disparity between the sexes, and it is from this period that the fashion for *décolletage* for women emerged, while men's fashions covered the chest and enclosed the neck – a trend that has continued to the present day.

BATEAU

A high neckline with a wide opening, cut straight across the shoulders and following the line of the collarbone. It was originally a practical cut for sailors, and is often used by designers today on nautical-inspired garments. The style is a quintessential design element of the classic Breton striped shirt. The *bateau* neck was particularly fashionable during the 1950s, popularized by Givenchy in a cocktail gown worn by Audrey Hepburn in the film *Sabrina* (1954).

COWL

A type of unstructured, draped collar that extends nearly to the shoulders in a circular style. The style originated in the loose-hooded

Bateau

cloaks worn by medieval monastic orders. It is largely found on womenswear. The fabric is cut on the bias to achieve this style, so it works best with garments knitted in soft yarns such as angora and cashmere – fabrics that will yield and not stand out too far from the body.

CRAVAT

Today, the term cravat is generally used with regard to any type of wide neckcloth or tie worn loosely folded under the chin, often inside the shirt collar. Historically, the term referred to men's neckwear of muslin or silk, which was worn throughout the seventeenth and eighteenth centuries.

CREW NECK

Also called a round or jewel neck, this neckline is close-fitting, collarless, and in a rounded shape. The crew sits just above the collarbone, usually finished with a rib binding. Like the *bateau*, this neckline also has its genesis as a nautical garment – the term refers to the style of sweater worn by boat crew members. The crew-neck T-shirt is a modern classic of casualwear.

DÉCOLLETAGE

The term décolletage refers to the part of a woman's chest from the neck to the bust, and by extension to a style of neckline that is cut very low to reveal a woman's cleavage. Historically, women's formalwear has been designed *en décolleté* for many centuries, tracing back to the court dresses worn at the French court of Louis XIV. This trend continues today, with women's eveningwear tending to reveal far more décolletage than is generally worn for daywear.

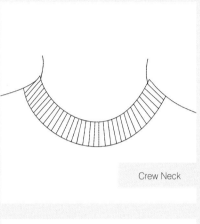

Crew Neck

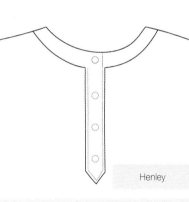

Henley

Jabot

Funnelneck

FICHU

A type of neckwear worn by French women from the later decades of the eighteenth century, a *fichu* referred specifically to a type of small black lace scarf that women knotted around their necks so that the points fell on the chest. From the early nineteenth century onward, the term came to be popularly used to refer to any type of eighteenth-century lightweight female neckwear that covered the chest, replacing the period term of handkerchief or neckerchief.

FUNNELNECK (POLO/TURTLENECK)

A funnelneck collar is shaped like a tube that encases the neck and rises up to the chin. It is usually designed for garments made in soft, elastic fabrics such as cotton and wool. A funnelneck is popularly called a turtleneck or a poloneck, and the terms tend to be used interchangeably in the modern day, but strictly speaking, there is a difference in construction. A funnelneck is grown on – it is an extension of the garment and rises above the neckline without a seam. A turtleneck/poloneck, in contrast, consists of a separate neck piece that is attached to the garment.

HALTERNECK

A modern fashion dating from the twentieth century, the halterneck is a single supportive strap of fabric that reaches from one side of a bodice, around the back of the neck of the wearer, and down to the other side of the bodice – leaving the back of the body exposed. As such, it resembles a halter worn by livestock, hence its name. The neckline can be low or high, and is a popular design feature for formalwear and swimwear.

HENLEY

A rounded, collarless neckline with a narrow central placket in the front containing a vertical row of buttons, classically no more than five. The neckline is a quintessential feature of the Henley shirt, which has its origins in the collarless undershirts worn by the rowers of the British town of Henley-on-Thames in the nineteenth century. The style was popularized for modern casualwear by designers such as Ralph Lauren.

JABOT

In modern design, the term refers to a cascade of fabric that begins at the throat and falls down the front of the shirt. The fabric can form one large ruffle, or several layers of ruffles, and today is an attached and incorporated feature of a shirt or blouse. Historically, the use of the term jabot dates back to the seventeenth century, when it referred to the lace-trimmed neck opening of a man's shirt.

KEYHOLE

A high neckline sitting on the collarbone, underneath which is a cut-out shape held closed with a hook or button, or fully attached to the neckline of the garment. It is a very versatile neckline popular with modern designers. Although a tear-shaped cut-out is the classic feature of the keyhole neckline, any shape in any size can and does appear on a wide range of clothing, from dresses to swimwear.

Halterneck

Steinkirk

PUSSYCAT BOW

A form of stand collar with very long, extended ends that can be tied into a large, loose bow. Typically associated with womenswear, in twentieth-century fashion it was most popular during the 1930s and was revived in the 1970s when it was adopted by women to make the tailored office suit more feminine.

STEINKIRK

A type of lace cravat popularly worn during the seventeenth and early eighteenth centuries; the fashion originated in France. Rather than elaborately tied under the chin, it was worn loosely twisted in front and with the ends negligently threaded through a coat buttonhole. The name refers to the Battle of Steinkirk of 1692, which took place between the French and the allied English-Dutch armies. The French were taken by surprise; the officers hardly having time to dress themselves, they had to fight with disarrayed cravats, but nevertheless achieved victory.

SWEETHEART

A heart-shaped neckline in womenswear, it is tight over the bust and dips in the middle of the cleavage. It can be worn with or without straps. It is a quintessential feature of 1950s fashion, and the name is believed to have emerged from Hollywood, where films promoted the style long after it had passed from couture runways. Its popularity endures today in contemporary formalwear.

TIE

A form of ornamental neckwear. A tie is a long piece of fabric worn around the neck, under the collar of a shirt. The width of the tie and pattern of the fabric can vary enormously, and these features are a useful stylistic indicator of historic fashion. The garment has a long history, with its original form appearing in the seventeenth century as the cravat. Traditionally confined to menswear tailoring and holding connotations of formality and white-collar employment, the tie is nevertheless popular today with both sexes.

U-SHAPED (SCOOP)

As the name suggests, a U-shaped neckline is cut deep in the front in a semi-circular U shape. The collarless neckline can be cut to various depths, some low enough to reveal the décolletage. It has recurred frequently throughout fashion history, and is a favorite feature in contemporary design as it is judged to be flattering to all body shapes. May also be called a "horseshoe" neckline.

V-NECK

A collarless neckline that is cut deep in the front of a garment and dips toward the center of the body to create a V-neck. It is a very versatile style that can vary in length as style and fit desires.

YOKE

The yoke is a design element consisting of an attached piece of fabric located at the top of a garment. One of the most popular uses in contemporary fashion is around a shirt neckline on the front and back, but it can also be applied to other clothing types such as skirts or trousers. It usually appears as an inserted, contrasting fabric panel and may be ornamented with appliqué or embroidery.

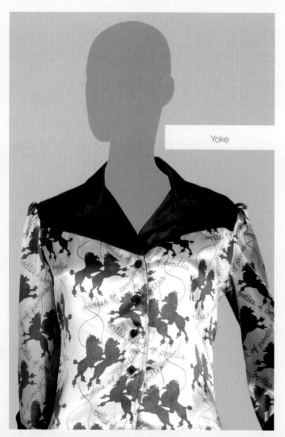

Yoke

Yoke

LAPELS

The turned-back upper part of the front of
a tailored garment such as a coat or jacket.
Within menswear, there are many different
styles and sizes of lapel, historically worn
with different styles of suit. Traditionally,
ornamentation was added to the lapel in the
form of a boutonnière – a single flower bud –
a practice fallen out of favor today when it is
reserved for only the most formal of occasions,
such as weddings.

GORGE

The gorge is the point on a jacket where the
collar is attached to the lapel, forming the
notch. The shape of the gorge will change in
relation to the shape and proportions of the
lapel itself.

NOTCHED LAPEL

A notched lapel has a wide, V-shaped opening
where the lapel and collar join – on a jacket or
coat this is approximately a third of the way
down the front. The notch allows for greater
movement and versatility in the lapel and is
notched downward, so as not to interrupt the
straight line of the lapel. Typical for single-
breasted suits and blazers, it is the lapel type most
commonly used in contemporary men's suiting.

Notched Lapel

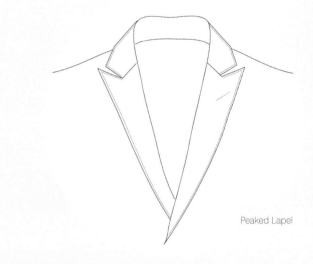

Peaked Lapel

PEAKED LAPEL

A peaked lapel is similar to a notched lapel,
but the V-shaped opening juts upward from
the lapel in a sharp point, forming a barb
or peak. Style variations are achieved by
manipulating the placement of the collar
break, the width and shape of the lapel, and
the placement of the peak.

SHAWL LAPEL

In a shawl lapel, the jacket lapel and collar
are indistinguishable, curving in one fluid,
tapering line from around the neck all the way
down to where the lapels end. It is commonly
used in womenswear design, but within
menswear tailoring, its use is reserved for
tuxedos and dinner jackets.

SLEEVES

The term sleeve refers to the part of a garment that covers the arm, or through which the arm passes. The history of Western fashion has witnessed an immense variety in styles, from the sleeves of the late medieval *houppelande* gown, which were so long and wide they almost reached the ground, to the sleeves of eighteenth-century court suits, which were cut so tight the wearer could not raise his arms above his head. Early modern clothing was cut to very basic shapes such as the tunic – the body and the sleeve were cut in one, or the sleeve was simply attached with a shoulder seam. As garment construction and sewing skills grew more advanced, so did the shape and silhouette of clothing. Sleeves were often detachable to allow for the increasing complexities of fashion. The Renaissance doublet, for example, was often worn with detachable sleeves joined at the armhole by metal-tagged laces called "points". By the 1920s, sleeves had disappeared altogether from clothing with the trend for sleeveless day dresses. Consequently, sleeves are an invaluable tool for the precise dating of historical fashion.

BALLOON SLEEVE

A development from the puff and gigot sleeves of the early nineteenth century, the balloon sleeve was originally a short-lived fashion, dating from *c.*1835–1840. It began further down the arm, having slipped off the shoulder completely by the end of the 1830s. The sleeve's rounded "balloon" shape was created by a narrow cap sleeve that billowed out and was then caught up again either at the elbow or at the wrist. The volume was created by the stiff shape of the fabric rather than from layers of voluminous fabrics. The style was revived for a brief period in the 1890s, and appears intermittently in contemporary fashion.

Balloon Sleeve

BISHOP SLEEVE

A variety of set-in sleeve cut with minimal fullness where it is set into the armseye, which then widens gradually to the wrist, where it is gathered into a tightly fitting cuff. Some versions have the fullness at the cuff designed in such a way that much of it hangs down under the wrist. It is typically executed using light fabrics such as muslin or silk, which can contain much fullness at the cuff. It is visually reminiscent of traditional ecclesiastical garb, hence the name.

CAP SLEEVE

A very short, almost non-existent sleeve that hangs over the edge of the shoulder without extending along the underside of the arm. It is usually only seen on womenswear. It is often stiffened in order to stand out from the arm slightly to create a dramatic silhouette. It is a fairly modern style, being thought to have only first appeared in the late 1920s, and may have been a stylistic development from the era's sleeveless flapper-style dresses.

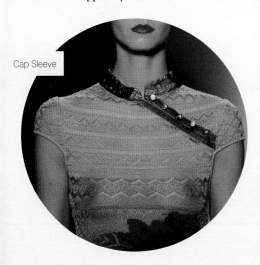

Cap Sleeve

Bishop Sleeve

Dolman Sleeve

Gigot Sleeve

DOLMAN SLEEVE (BATWING)

A type of loose cut-on sleeve that is very full under the arm, then narrows sharply to fit closely at the wrist. From the back, the sleeve resembles a cape. Although its use has a long history, tracing back to the Middle Ages, the dolman sleeve was a key characteristic of 1980s fashion. A more popular modern name for the sleeve is a batwing sleeve, due to its resemblance to the wing of a bat.

GIGOT SLEEVE (LEG-OF-MUTTON)

A variety of set-in sleeve that is cut with a very full and exaggerated rounded top that is gathered or pleated into the armhole, then tapers gradually to fit closely at the wrist. Its shape is similar to a lamb leg, and in fact it is also sometimes called by the English translation of the French name – "leg of lamb". It was one of the most defining features of fashionable dress during the 1830s, and was successfully revived in the 1890s. It is generally only seen in contemporary fashion today on wedding dresses.

KIMONO SLEEVE

A kimono sleeve is cut as an extension of the main bodice piece and is usually rectangular or square in shape. It can be either loose or close-fitting, depending on the curvature of the garment's sleeve and underarm. The term is adopted from the traditional Japanese garment of the same name. Kimono sleeves first became popular in Western dress in the early twentieth century, most notably in the designs of couturier Paul Poiret.

Pagoda Sleeve

PAGODA SLEEVE (FUNNEL)

A full type of set-in sleeve that is shaped much like the flared roof of an Asian pagoda. The sleeve is narrow at the top, where it fits the upper arm closely, then gradually flares out to become wide at the bottom. It is also known as a funnel sleeve because of its funnel shape. It is a defining feature of the early Victorian fashions of the 1850s, its full funnel shape balancing the rotund hooped skirts below.

Sabot Sleeve

Slashed Sleeve

PUFF SLEEVE

The puff sleeve was designed to help exaggerate the extremely tightly laced waist that suddenly emerged in women's fashions during the 1820s, after decades of Empire line dominance. By making both the sleeves and the skirt as voluminous as possible, the waist was made to seem tiny in comparison. At first, the puff was relatively small, but a fashion developed for a transparent oversleeve of greater volume. By the end of the 1820s, this transparent layer had become opaque, transforming the sleeve into the gigot style.

RAGLAN SLEEVE

A popular cut-on sleeve style that covers the entire shoulder. It is attached to the garment by a seam that runs diagonally down from the front neckline to the underarm, and up to the back neckline. The style is attributed to Lord Raglan, a general in the British Army during the nineteenth century who lost an arm in the Crimean War and found that this design accommodated his disability. Today, it is typically used on casualwear and sportswear.

SABOT SLEEVE

A close-fitting sleeve that curved tightly over the elbow before flaring out. The style was originally characteristic of the gown *à la polonaise* from the 1770s onward. It is named after the eighteenth-century sabot, a clog carved from one piece of wood.

SLASHED SLEEVE

A Renaissance fashion for slashing the upper material in regular slits to reveal the paler white silk or cotton underneath (and then pulling the under material through the holes). Chroniclers of the period ascribe this trend to the defeat of Charles the Bold of Burgundy in 1476 by the Swiss. The victorious Swiss plundered the rich Burgundian court for silk and other treasures, patching their damaged clothes with rich fabrics. This was known as *landsknect* fashion and it spread to all the courts of Europe. Slashing was adopted by the Punk movement of the 1970s as a sartorial expression of anarchy. Vivienne Westwood's Cut, Slash, and Pull collection was inspired by this Renaissance style.

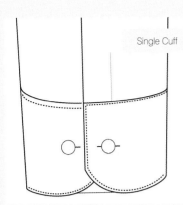

Single Cuff

CUFFS

A turned-up hem. Cuff usually refers to the finishing at the end of a shirt sleeve, though it can also refer to the bottom of a trouser leg. A traditional tailored shirt cuff is stiffened with canvas interfacing to ensure a crisp, neat appearance. In addition to the cuff, a placket is usually made in the lower sleeve to allow the garment to be put on and taken off more easily. The exception to this practice is when cuff bands are used, usually with a stretch fabric that can slide easily over the hand.

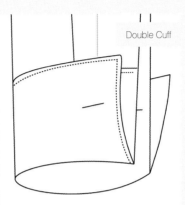

Double Cuff

Engageantes

DOUBLE CUFF (FRENCH)

The French cuff is a type of shirt cuff that folds back on itself and is secured with cuff links through two buttonholes rather than a button. It is a characteristic of a more formal shirt style.

ENGAGEANTES

Sleeve cuffs made up of scalloped ruffles of fine lace or cambric, worn singly, in double or triple layers during the seventeenth and eighteenth centuries, particularly with formal-style gowns. They were detachable cuffs, cut to hang quite short over the inner crook of the arm but long over the back of the elbow. The fashion originated in France.

SINGLE CUFF (BARREL)

A single cuff is the style commonly employed on business shirts. It can also be called a "barrel cuff", as its shape looks like a barrel. Buttons and bound buttonholes are used to fasten barrel cuffs.

CONSTRUCTION AND SHAPING

INTRODUCTION

Seams, darts, and pressing techniques are key components of garment construction in order to achieve the desired silhouette. Seams and darts shape a garment visibly, and can often be incorporated as design features in their own right. The use of darts as a technique for creating silhouette and fit is taken for granted today; however, it did not become a standard feature of dressmaking until the nineteenth century. Pressing, combined with the use of support fabrics that can add strength and weight to certain areas, shape a garment invisibly. Within couture, pressing occurs at innumerable stages throughout a design's construction and involves the skilled and careful balance of heat, moisture, and pressure on a fabric. Together, all these techniques bring life to a two-dimensional fabric pattern, shaping it to fit the planes and curves of the human body.

The term closure refers not just to the opening in a garment created for ease of wear and removal, but also to the type of fastener used to join the opening. There are many types available to the designer, and many factors to be taken into consideration when making a choice. Closures can be inconspicuous or a decorative part of the design. The selection of closure depends on the garment's design and function, its fabric, the intended effect, and the closure location. Some couturiers have even used certain closure preferences to create their signature style, such as Chanel's gilded buttons.

▲ Armani Privé, fall/winter haute couture 2014. Tiers of net and tulle are used to construct a romantic ballgown with an hourglass silhouette.

▶ The creative possibilities of construction techniques are demonstrated by John Galliano for spring/summer 2014 haute couture. Galliano's imaginative brilliance in cutting techniques allows him to rethink the form and shape of a basic silk jacket.

Dart

ARMSEYE
The sewing term for an armhole.

BACKING/UNDERLINING
A layer of lightweight, natural-fiber fabric applied to the wrong side of a garment section before the seam is sewn; its purpose is principally to provide additional support by adding weight and firmness. Backing can also be sewn into a garment to reinforce seams and to provide a layer for inner stitching, such as on a jacket collar. The term backing is used within tailoring and couture; within home dressmaking, the term underlining is more commonly used, but refers to the same element.

BIAS CUTTING
Generally, bias refers to any line that is off-grain – that is, diagonal to the crosswise and lengthwise grain of a fabric. Bias cutting refers to such diagonal cutting of fabric. In particular, the term true bias is a cut made specifically on an angle forty-five degrees to the lengthwise grain. This direction allows for the most stretch in the fabric, but the material and silhouette can be easily distorted in unskilled hands. Bias-cut dresses are a quintessential feature of 1930s fashion, epitomized in the designs of Madeleine Vionnet.

DART
Darts are used to shape a garment by taking fullness away from a seam line. They are folded wedges of fabric stitched to a point and are most often used where curves are desired over the contours of the body – at the waistline, shoulder blade, bust, and elbow. They should be precisely placed so that they point toward the fullest part of the body contour.

DRAPE

The fluid way a fabric hangs. Drapery can form a stylistic feature in its own right, typically seen on bias-cut dresses. The production process for a couture garment usually starts with "draping the pattern" – a process that involves draping several rectangles of muslin on a dress form that is padded to duplicate the client's figure. The muslin is then pinned and shaped to create the toile.

EASE

The smooth joining of two garment sections that are unequal in length without forming gathers or pleats. The term ease also refers to the amount of space in a garment that allows comfortable movement. To achieve this, a small section of fabric is purposely made fuller in one section, making it longer than the section it joins. As such, easing is a practice used to provide shaping to garment areas such as the back shoulder and the bust.

Drape

Godet

GATHERING

To gather is to pull fabric along a line of stitching so that it puckers. Gathering is when one or several loosely stitched rows are puckered to create fullness and soft, even folds. The process accordingly draws a larger piece of fabric into a smaller area – fabric is usually gathered to one-half or one-third of the original width. Gathering is most often used at waistlines, sleeve cuffs or yokes.

GODET

An extra panel of fabric inserted into a seam or cut line to achieve volume in a garment. They are typically triangular-shaped, but in practice they can be used in a variety of shapes, including a half or full circle. Utilized within womenswear, a godet creates a flare within a skirt or dress, and so can potentially act as a design feature. As such, they were an important element in dress design of the 1920s and 1930s, as typified in the *oeuvre* of Jeanne Lanvin. In contemporary fashion, they are used to create the dramatic fishtail dress style, the godet forming a fan-shaped addition to the dress train (*see also* Fishtail Skirt, page 81).

GORE

A gore is a vertical panel section used to achieve volume, generally used on skirt designs. A gore skirt is made up of a series of gores vertically sewn together – typically six to create a fitted skirt, but as many as twenty-four gores may be used to achieve a full and flowing effect. Such use of gores negates the complex exercise of cutting and sewing on the bias, but gores of contrasting pattern or color can also be used as a design theme in their own right.

GUSSET

A small piece of fabric inserted into a slit to allow greater comfort and flexibility, most typically in the underarm section of a sleeve. For maximum ease of movement, a gusset should be cut on the bias. A gusset is most commonly diamond-shaped, but it can also appear in a triangular or square form.

INTERFACING

A layer of fabric between the garment and the facing that forms the understructure and is used to stabilize and stiffen the garment fabric. It can also add body, reinforce the seams, and keep the garment from stretching out of shape. Interfacing is usually a non-woven material, available in varying weights, and can be either sewn in or fused with an iron. As a rule, it is usually only applied to certain garment areas, such as the collar, front or back openings, and hemline.

INTERLINING

A specific underlying fabric that is principally used for insulation. A fabric such as flannel or brushed collar will provide additional warmth in coats, jackets, and outerwear. The interlining should be lightweight but not thick; it should not add excessive bulk or distort the shape of the garment. It is attached by one of two ways – either by joining the interlining to the lining or by attaching it to the garment itself, which is then lined.

PADDING

Shape and volume can be added to a garment through padding. It will give definition and form to a garment, particularly when soft fabrics are being used. Padding can also be used to emphasize and flatter certain parts of the body. Certain couturiers have used padding very creatively, such as Schiaparelli in her Skeleton dress of 1938 or Christian Dior's Bar Suit of 1947, which ushered in the New Look. Contemporary designers such as Rei Kawakubo have used padding to explore post-modern silhouettes (*see* below).

Padding

Shoulder Pad

PUCKERING

A pucker is a tightly gathered wrinkle or small fold, and puckering refers to the unintentional pulling of a thread in the fabric, creating a wrinkle. Seams can be especially prone to puckering during the sewing process as a result of an incorrect sewing tension or poor-quality tools.

SHOULDER PAD

One of the most frequently used types of padding, a shoulder pad defines the shoulder area and helps maintain an even appearance over the shoulder and collarbone. They come in different shapes and sizes, as required by the sleeve design, and are typically placed between the garment fabric and the lining. A tailored pad used in jackets is made from layers of wadding enclosed in felt, and is triangular in shape. The shoulder pads employed in dressmaking are generally softer and thinner than those for tailoring.

SLEEVE BOOSTER

A sleeve usually requires some form of support to maintain its shape. A sleeve booster supports a full or exaggerated sleeve cap. It can be quite wide and full, and will extend deep into the sleeve cap.

SLEEVE HEAD

Another form of sleeve support, a sleeve head (or header) is used to bear a classic, eased sleeve cap. It forms a strip made from a variety of fabrics, from silks to hair canvas, depending on how light or crisp a support is required.

STYLE LINE

A style line refers to the structural lines in a garment. Skillfully used, they can add greatly to a design and help to establish balance or proportion. Style lines can be horizontal, vertical, diagonal, or curved.

SUPPRESSION

The term used to describe the distribution of the width of fabric at the waist of a jacket. Correct waist suppression is regarded to be crucial to the overall balance of a tailored suit and how the jacket hangs over the back and hips of a body. If suppression is too tight, the jacket may bunch and tug over the shoulder blades.

VENT

The finished opening at one end of a seam, most typically used at the wrist edge of a sleeve where buttons are placed and at the back hemline of jackets and straight skirts.

WAISTLINE

The line between the upper and lower portions of a garment is known as the waistline. It does not necessarily lie on top of a body's natural waist, but may be higher or lower as fashions dictate. Likewise, waistline seams may be straight, curved, or steeply angled toward the bust or hips. There are various ways of sewing waistlines: by a seam, by means of an attached casing, or by an insert of fabric or ribbing.

WAISTLINE CASING

A waistline casing is an enclosed tunnel-like form made to enfold elastic or a drawstring. A fold-down casing is formed by turning an extension of the garment edge inward and sewing it into place. An applied casing consists of a separate strip of fabric that is attached to the garment. They are extremely practical, as they can be adjusted to suit any required size, and can be employed in different parts of a garment – for example, the bottom of a jacket, at the waistline of a dress, or at the top of a skirt or trousers.

Vent

SEAMS

Seams are the fundamental structural element of any garment and the simplest way of joining two or more pieces of fabric together. A straight seam is most commonly used; in a well-made straight seam, the stitching is exactly the same distance from the cutting line down the entire length of the seam. "Seam allowance" refers to the distance between the cutting line and the seam line. This allowance is usually hidden inside the garment once it is sewn. Seams are also used to create shape and can be curved or cornered. "Seam finish" alludes to any technique that finishes the raw edges of a seam. There are many different types of seams, the most significant of which are listed below.

Flat Fell Seam

FLAT FELL SEAM
A strong, self-enclosed, and hardwearing seam, it is popularly used with denim garments and outdoor wear. It is a visible seam – seen, for example, on the outside of the legs of jeans – and as such is often incorporated into the design, for instance by using a thread in a contrasting color. It shows two rows of stitching on the right side and one row on the wrong side of the garment and is made by overlapping one seam allowance with the other and top-stitching them together onto the garment with two parallel rows of stitches, encasing all the raw edges.

FRENCH SEAM
With French seams, the seam and seam finish are completed in one, looking like a tuck on the wrong side of the garment. It is time-consuming to execute, but French seams provide a clean, neat finish to very fine or transparent fabrics, and are accordingly extensively used in couture ateliers. They are made by placing two pieces of material together on the wrong side and sewing a seam with a narrow seam allowance. The seam is then turned inside out, bringing the right sides of the material together. A second seam is stitched, encasing the first seam within. The seam is then pressed to one side.

PRINCESS SEAM
Princess seams are shaped seams designed to fit a body's contours. They run vertically from the shoulder seam, over the center of the bust, and down either to the waistline or the hemline. Princess seams eliminate the need for darts, as they curve outward with the bust, inward to the waist, and back outward over the hips. They accordingly demand precise measurement and execution. The silhouette that is achieved evokes the fitted Princess

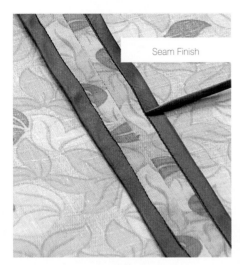
Seam Finish

Line style first designed in 1875 by Charles
Frederick Worth.

RUNNING SEAM

The most basic and common kind of seam, a
running seam is created by placing two pieces
of fabric together, right sides facing, and holding the seam allowance together with a basting
stitch. The seam is then sewn using a permanent running stitch. The seam allowance can
be overlocked to stop the edges from fraying.
To finish, the seam can be pressed open, or
both edges can be pressed to one side.

SEAM FINISH

In order to prevent the edges of seams,
facings and hems from fraying, the edges are
finished. Seams can be finished a variety of
ways, such as by overcasting or with a binding.
Overcasting by hand is time-consuming, but it
is the preferred finish within couture because
it creates a flat, soft finish that is not likely to
show on the right side of the garment.

Princess Seam

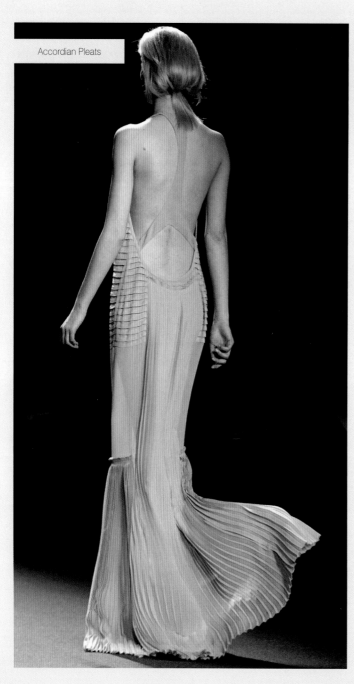

Accordian Pleats

PLEATS

A pleat is a fold of fabric made by doubling the material upon itself and then held down securely by pressing or stitching it along joining seam lines. The pleat is folded on the fold line and aligned with the placement line. Pleats are used to add volume to a garment, the amount of volume depending on the number of pleats and the pleat depth – they may appear individually, several grouped together, or around an entire garment section. They are also important stylistic features, with different styles of pleats giving a different silhouette to a garment.

ACCORDION

In an accordion pleat, the fabric is ordered in narrow folds of uniform width all facing in the same direction. These resemble the bellows of an accordion, hence the name. They are similar to the knife pleat but are much narrower. Executing the accordion pleat in synthetic fabrics tends to have more permanent results than with fabrics from natural fibers, in which the pleats quickly lose definition.

BOX

Box pleats have two fold lines and two placement lines, and accordingly, the two folds of each pleat are turned away from each other. Usually reserved for skirts, they form a strong, geometric silhouette.

CRYSTAL

A line of narrow, ridged pleats heat-set by industrial machinery into lightweight fabrics. Crystal pleats are accordingly embedded in a textile and not created by the dressmaker. They are often found on lingerie. Mariano Fortuny was an innovator in the creation and use of crystal pleating, seen on the iconic Delphos dress (from 1907), which was inspired by the pleating of a classical Greek chiton (*see also* page 71).

INVERTED

Inverted pleats are akin to a backward box pleat. They have two fold lines and share a common placement line. The two folds of each pleat are turned toward each other and meet. In contrast, the back folds face away from each other.

KNIFE

Knife pleats are all folded and sharply pressed in the same direction; every pleat is accordingly three layers deep. They are considered the simplest form of pleating, and have a long history in clothing. Nowadays, they are most frequently used in day skirts and uniforms, but they have been innovatively used for eveningwear by couturiers such as Jean Patou. Knife pleats are also called side pleats.

SUNBURST

Sunburst pleats are similar to knife pleats, but they are cut on a bias – this will give a flared effect to the garment. Typically used in skirts of lightweight fabric, sunburst pleats create a graceful, romantic effect.

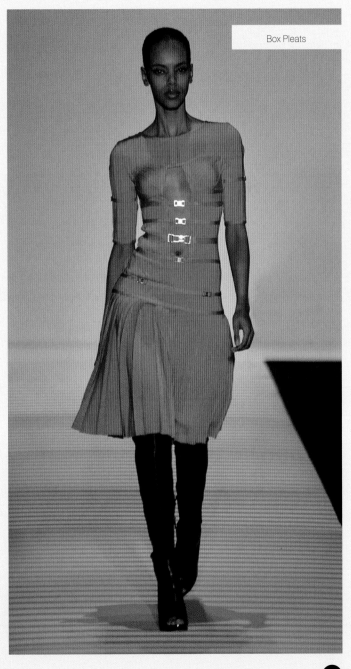

Box Pleats

Tucks

DECORATIVE STITCHING

RUFFLE (RUCHE/RUCHING)

A strip of fabric that is cut, gathered, or pleated in such a way as to produce fullness. Ruffles are chiefly decorative, although they may serve a practical purpose such as lengthening a skirt. There are two types of ruffles, differing in how they are cut. A straight ruffle is cut as a strip of fabric and produces an effect similar to gathering or pleating, while the circular ruffle is cut from a circle, and the fullness is produced on the outer edge. A ruffle is also called a ruche.

SHIRRING

Shirring is a decorative way of controlling fullness in a garment and is formed with multiple rows of gathering, which must be straight, parallel, and equidistant in order to attain the right effect. Shirring is achieved by stitching a line of loose, long gathering stitches, leaving a long tail of thread on either end. These tails are then pulled to gather up the fabric. Elastic and cord can also be used for shirring to create a flexible and comfortable fit.

SMOCKING

A sewing technique in which rows of fabric are gathered up in even pleats and decoratively stitched together at regular intervals to create a patterned effect. A section of garment is usually smocked before it is constructed. Yokes, bodices, sleeves, and waistlines are among the most popular sections to be smocked. Different ornamental effects are also achieved by using a contrasting, decorative thread and/or embroidery smocking stitches.

Ruffle

Smocking

TUCK AND PINTUCK

A stitched fold of fabric. Tucks are most often decorative, but they can also be used to shape a garment. A tuck is made when two stitching lines are brought together and stitched, creating a fold. There are several different kinds of tucks – tucks that meet, side-by-side, are called blind tucks. Spaced tucks preserve a space between each tuck. A pin tuck is a type of very narrow tuck, forming a pattern of ridges in fabric formed by a series of narrow, stitched folds placed at regular intervals. They bestow fine detail and texture to a garment.

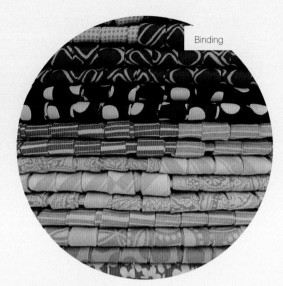

Binding

EDGE FINISHES

When a garment has cut edges, these need to be finished in some way to prevent the fabric from fraying. Three finishes are used extensively in couture and bespoke tailoring: hems, facings, and bindings. Each edge finish has a slightly different function; hems are used on the lower edges of a garment, while facings, in contrast, are most often applied to the upper and vertical edges. Bindings can be used on any garment section but are usually utilized as replacements for facings. The choice of edge finishes will depend on a variety of design specifications – from the garment silhouette and the shape of the edge being finished to its position on the garment and the type of fabric being used.

BINDING

A long strip of fabric that is principally used to cover a seam edge or to encase raw edges, such as at a hem or neckline of a reversible garment. The strip used for binding is often cut on the bias, with folded edges for binding on curved or straight edges. The use of binding ensures a neat and decorative finish. A jacket that has no lining but all of the internal seams bound is often referred to as a Hong Kong finish.

FACE

The face layer is a term used in sewing to refer to the top right side of a fabric or the outside of a garment.

FACING

Used to finish a garment's raw edge. Facing is mostly used on garment openings and when the edge is curved or shaped, such as on a

neckline or armhole edge. Skillfully placed facings contribute appreciably to the overall impression of a well-executed garment. Essentially, facing is carried out by stitching two pieces of fabric together and then turning them so that the seam allowance is enclosed. There are three types of facings: extended, separate, and bias. An extended facing, such as a plain turned-up hem, is cut as an extension of the garment section. A separate facing uses a fabric piece cut independently of the garment but cut to duplicate the required shape of the garment edge (such as a neckline). A bias facing is shaped, rather than cut, to duplicate the edge it faces.

LINING

Lining refers to fabric sewn into the inside of a garment. While the purpose of interlining is to provide insulation and support, the purpose of lining is to cover and hide the construction details of a garment's interior. For high-quality clothing, a smart lining fabric such as silk will be used. Lining accordingly brings several benefits to the garment – it increases its

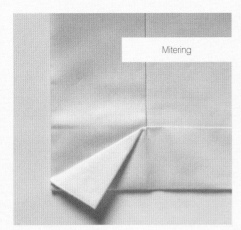

Mitering

Lining

attractiveness; it makes it more comfortable to wear; and its increases the garment's life, as it helps to retain the shape.

MITERING

A technique used for finishing corners that occur at garment edges, such as a skirt hem. Mitering refers to the diagonal joining of two edges at the corner. These slanted seams are carefully pressed to ensure a sharp corner, with the mitered piece always at a right angle to the corner's sides and then stitched in place.

WAISTBAND

The waistband anchors the garment at the waist and is a method of finishing a waistline edge. The most common form of waistband is straight and horizontal, but waistbands can also be shaped. Both types are inflexible. In contrast, stretch waistbands, which contain elastic, are flexible and allow for movement.

WELT

A strip of material that is stitched to an edge, border, or seam. Commonly used in pocket making, the welt is usually a rectangular piece of fabric – either cut separately or as a part of the pocket, which fits over the pocket opening and is sewn into the lower edge of the slash.

HEMS

Like facing, a hem is used to finish garment edges to prevent fraying or tearing, but hemming refers to the bottom edge of a garment. Hem allowance indicates the distance between the cutting line and the hemline. For a classic plain hem, the seam allowance is folded inside the garment before it is sewn in place using a hemming stitch. The hemline alludes to the lowest edge of the garment once the hem is sewn. Several different hemming techniques exist to suit different types of material, which are listed below. Hems hang free of the body and, consequently, can greatly affect how a garment drapes.

BABY HEM

A very small double-turned hem, usually measuring ⅛ inch (3 mm), this is useful for lightweight and delicate fabrics such as chiffon. It can be machine- or hand-stitched in place.

FACED HEM

Most of the hem allowance is removed in a faced hem due to the use of facing. The facing is usually a strip of lightweight fabric that is stitched to the hem edge, then turned inward so that it does not show, and secured with an appropriate hem stitch.

HAND-ROLLED HEM

When hemming very sheer or delicate fabrics such as chiffon, it is necessary to hand roll a hem. This involves rolling up the edge of the material by hand and stitching it into place using very small hemming stitches to create a very narrow hem.

LETTUCE-EDGE HEM

A form of decorative wavy hem created by stretching the fabric as the edge is sewn with a zigzag stitch; the size and frequency of the waves depend on the strength of the stretch. It is most suitable for fabrics with an inherent stretch, such as soft jersey knits. It is usually employed to edge flounces, frills, and sunburst-pleated skirts.

Lettuce-edge Hem

Piped Neckline

NECKLINES

BANDED NECKLINE

A neckline finished with a folded band is called a banded neckline. It is often used on T-shirts and casual tops, as it is so suitable for stretch fabrics. The edges of a separate band of fabric, cut to shape, are joined with the edges of the neckline and stitched together.

BOUND NECKLINE

The neckline is finished by binding it with a strip of fabric, either made from the garment fabric or a contrasting material. Binding is made with a bias-cut strip of fabric, which ensures it will lie smoothly around the shaped neckline. The seam allowance is cut away so that the bias binding adheres closely to the edge. This binding encases all the raw edges of the neckline, ensuring a neat finish.

FACED NECKLINE

The use of facing to finish a neckline is suitable for most neckline shapes. It involves cutting facing shapes to exactly fit the neckline edge; these are then attached to the garment, right sides together, and stitched. A lighter-weight fabric may be used for the facings in order to reduce bulk. Interfacing is also normally used to prevent the neckline from losing its shape.

PIPED NECKLINE

A neat and attractive finish to a neckline edge is to apply piping, a decorative trim made from wrapping a strip of fabric cut on the bias around a piping cord. The piping is stitched to the garment edge, and then a separate neckline facing is applied to the garment edge, which will hide the piping seam. Coco Chanel popularized the use of a piping finish on her suits.

Bound Neckline

Placket

PLACKET

A short, slitlike opening in a garment that allows it to be put on and taken off more easily. Plackets are most commonly found at the neck, the wrist, the top of a skirt, or the front of trousers. The slit can be finished in a variety of ways – hemming or facing are among the most commonly used. A neat finish will ensure the placket fits well, opens easily, and yet remains hidden. The term placket dates back to the sixteenth century, when it referred to a form of underskirt.

CONCEALED PLACKET

A concealed placket is designed to hide the fasteners that close the garment and are often used when a more noticeable closure would derange the overall garment design. A concealed placket has an independent underlay of fabric hidden beneath the finished edges of the garment opening. They are regularly found on shirt fronts, where they are referred to as fly-front shirt plackets.

MULTIPLE PLACKET

When two or more plackets are constructed at the same or nearby positions on a garment, this is referred to as a multiple placket. They are a necessity for multi-layered garments with a built-in foundation. A common example of a multiple placket would be zipper fasteners on the center back of a dress, and on an attached undergarment such as a slip.

ZIPPER FASTENERS

First invented by Chicago mechanical engineer Whitcomb Judson in 1893 as a "clasp closer", the modern teethed version of the zipper wasn't created until 1917 by Gideon Sundback, who worked for Judson's firm, the Universal Fastener Company. However, it wasn't until the 1930s that the device appeared in garments, primarily for children. A zipper is composed of a strip consisting of two rows of protruding teeth that are made to interlock when closed. The teeth are made to open or close by means of a slider that runs up and down the strip. A conventional zipper always has one closed end. Early forms of zippers were made of heavy metal and were confined to military use. Beginning in the 1930s, with the invention of lighter and more reliable metal forms, zippers came to be adopted by couturiers, most noticeably Charles James, who converted the zipper into a design feature. Modern zipper fasteners are made of cotton or nylon and metal. There are various ways of attaching a zipper to a zipper placket, detailed below.

Centered Zipper

CENTERED ZIPPER

The most common type of zipper placement preferred for the center front and back of a garment, this method places the zipper teeth in the middle of a seam. A 1 inch (2.5 cm) seam allowance is typically used, to which the zipper face is sewn.

FLY-FRONT ZIPPER

A fly is a type of closure that conceals the zipper or button opening in shorts, trousers, or skirts through the use of a fly shield – an attached flap of fabric. It is a very neat and durable form of closing that completely hides the teeth of the zipper. The fly-front zipper is the traditional application for men's trousers and is often used on modern womenswear. The placket has a long-established lap direction – in women's clothing it laps right over left; in men's clothing it laps left over right.

Invisible Zipper

INVISIBLE ZIPPER

A modern type of zipper that is specially designed to disappear into a seam and that has a small, thin, oval pull. When closed, the teeth lie hidden by the tape front. When properly inserted, neither it nor the stitching can be seen on the outside of the garment. It is commonly used for center backs of garments or side seams.

DESIGN, TAILORING, AND STITCHING

LAPPED ZIPPER

The teeth of the zipper are concealed using this method of attachment. It is applied using the same method as the conventional centered zipper, the only difference being the placement of the zipper in relation to the garment edge. The fabric seam at one side of the zipper is stitched close to the teeth, while the other side lies over the teeth to conceal them. Lapped zippers are most often used at the left side seam of trousers, skirts, and dresses. It is also known as an offset zipper.

OPEN-ENDED ZIPPER

An open-ended zipper comes apart into two pieces, and is usually found on clothing such as coats, jackets, and waistcoats. A special type of open-ended zipper can be applied using either a centered or lapped application. It is also known as a separating zipper.

BUTTONS AND OTHER FASTENERS

There are two basic kinds of button design: shank buttons and sew-through buttons. The lower side of a shank button has a sort of neck, or shank – a vertical protrusion with a hole in it, through which the button is stitched and attached to the fabric. The shank ensures that the button rests upright on the buttonhole without distorting it. In contrast, sew-through buttons have holes through which stitches can be made; they come in either a two-hole or four-hole design. If sewn flat, the button is rendered obsolete. In order to be utilized, the button must be raised from the fabric by means of a shank created from thread. The shank permits the button to open and close smoothly, even with bulky fabrics. Besides being utilitarian, buttons can have great decorative effect on a design.

CHINESE BALL BUTTONS

A type of decorative fabric button made by looping and interweaving a thin cord or braid to form a ball shape. They are usually paired with button-loop closures.

BOUND BUTTONHOLE

A bound buttonhole has two fabric welts that meet at the opening. The welts can be of the same fabric as the garment or of a contrasting fabric, braid, or piping. Being suitable for lightweight fabrics, bound buttonholes are often used for womenswear.

Bound Buttonhole

Keyhole Buttonhole

BUTTON LOOPS

An alternative to the customary buttonhole, button loops are loops that contain a closed button. They can be made from a variety of different materials, such as contrasting or matching fabric, decorative cords, braids, or even thread. They offer great versatility, as they can be set into a seam line or along a folded edge, individually or as a group. They are often used on sleeve cuffs.

DOUBLE BUTTONHOLE

Usually reserved for couture workmanship, a double buttonhole has two buttonholes back to back – one on the garment and one on the garment facing.

KEYHOLE BUTTONHOLE

Most commonly used in tailoring, a keyhole buttonhole is an oval-shaped buttonhole with an eyelet at one end. The eyelet, in appearance like an oval projection, acts as a larger "resting place" for the button shank. By providing more room for the shank, it ensures that the button-hole will not be distorted with use.

WORKED BUTTONHOLE

A worked buttonhole is a slit in the fabric finished with stitching. The stitches can either be applied by hand – in which case it is referred to as a hand-worked buttonhole, or by sewing machine, when it is called a machine-worked buttonhole. It has two sides equal in length to the buttonhole opening, and two ends finished either with straight bar tacks (forming a rectangular form) or fan-shaped stitches (giving a more oval form).

HOOKS AND EYES

A type of fastening device that utilizes a small hook on one side and a loop made of fabric or metal on the other side. They are often used as closures where two edges meet – for example, at necklines or waistbands – and come in a variety of sizes.

SNAP FASTENERS

A type of closure device – usually made of metal – that consists of two interlocking disks. One disk has a small projecting post (the ball) that clips into a hole in the partner disk (the socket), with an accompanying "click" (or "snap") noise. They come in a variety of forms, such as no-sew snap fasteners or snap-fastener tape. They have limited holding power. Snap fasteners are also known as poppers or press studs.

VELCRO

Velcro is a type of fabric hook-and-loop fastener principally made from artificial fibers such as polyester and nylon. It was invented in 1948 by the Swiss engineer Georges de Mestral, and is said to have been inspired from nature and how the minute hooks of a burr stuck to his coat. Similarly, one side of a Velcro fabric strip is made up of tiny hooks that adhere to its opposite partner-strip, which is composed of tiny loops. Extremely versatile and practical, Velcro is extensively used on modern athletic-wear design and children's clothing, and comes in a wide variety of different weights and sizes. It is also ideal for knit or stretch-woven fabrics, which can easily extend and distort with use.

Worked Buttonhole

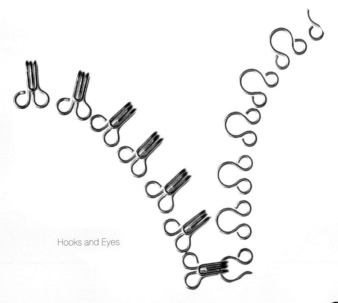

Hooks and Eyes

COUTURE STITCHES

INTRODUCTION

In an era of mass production and widespread
use of machinery within the clothing industry,
the couture and bespoke tailoring sectors stand
out for their preference for sewing by hand.
The use of hand stitching enables far greater
control and attention to detail throughout the
execution of the work, and a far higher level of
excellence is achieved as a result.

There are principally two families of hand-
sewn stitches – temporary and permanent.
Temporary stitches – generally referred to as
basting stitches, although the term tacking
stitches can also be used – are intended only
for interim use. They are used to mark the
garment, to prepare it for fittings, and to hold
the different fabric layers in position during
assembly. Thousands of temporary stitches may
be sewn into a couture or bespoke garment
throughout the course of its construction.

Permanent stitches, in contrast, are sewn
once and rarely removed unless absolutely
necessary – for example, if a mistake has been
made. Certain permanent stitches are similar,
if not identical, to those used for basting, but
they are executed with more precision.

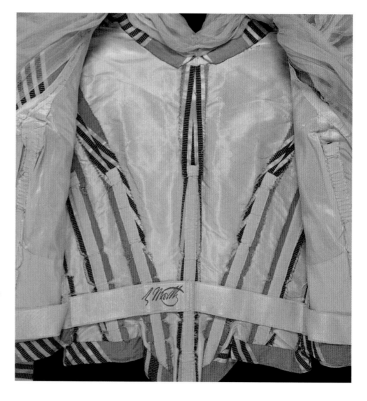

▲ Victorian clothing relied heavily on internal structural supports to create the lines of the
ideal hourglass silhouette. This late nineteenth-century silk bodice designed by Charles
Frederick Worth employs curved seams, supported with whalebone struts and waist tape.

▶ A variety of embroidery techniques, including French knots and couching, are
employed to create a pattern of geometric and floral motifs on this seventeenth-century
linen doublet with hand-worked buttonholes.

BASTING (TACKING)

A quick, temporary stitch used to hold fabric in place before the final stitching. It can also be used to mark the garment and prepare it for fittings. In couture and bespoke tailoring, most plain seams are basted together at least once before they are permanently stitched, and many are basted, ripped, and re-basted several times. There are several forms of basting stitch – even, uneven, diagonal, and slip basting. Basting is also known as tacking.

CROSS STITCHING

A variation of diagonal basting, cross stitches resemble a row of stacked diamonds. Cross stitches are created by working a pair of diagonal basting stitches in opposite directions. The pair crosses in the center to form an X. They are chiefly employed as marking stitches, but can also be used to hold folds in place. Not all couture garments carry labels, particularly skirts, so cross stitching is often used to indicate the center front of a garment to expedite dressing.

DIAGONAL BASTING

Diagonal basting consists of horizontal stitches placed parallel to each other, which produce diagonal floats on the other side of the fabric. It is used to hold or control two or more fabric layers together during construction and pressing. Diagonal stitches can be made either short or long. Short diagonal stitches, placed close together, offer the most control and are used to hold seam edges flat during stitching or pressing. Longer diagonal stitches are placed further apart and are used for tasks such as holding underlining to garment fabric to prevent shifting during construction. Diagonal stitches can also be permanent stitches.

EVEN BASTING

The most common form of basting stitch is even basting, which is similar in technique to permanent running stitches. These are short, straight stitches, evenly placed the same short distance apart. It is principally used to join two garment edges under some stress, such as on a curved seam or a set-in sleeve.

SLIP BASTING

A form of temporary, uneven slipstitch that enables patterned materials such as stripes or plaids to be precisely matched. The slip basting stitch is also useful for basting intricately curved sections, or for making fitting alterations from the right side of a garment. The garment edge to be sewn is first turned under along its seam line. This overlapped edge is matched to the seam line of the corresponding garment piece. It is attached by making a very small straight stitch in the under layer, then taking a long stitch directly through the fabric fold of the upper layer. Continue to alternate stitches in

Even Basting

this way. Slip basting alone would not keep layers of fabric from shifting during sewing, so it is also frequently reinforced with a row of even basting. *See* Slipstitch, page 222.

TAILOR'S TACKS

A common form of temporary marking stitch used to transfer marking-up details and matching points from the pattern to cut fabric sections. They are an alternative to tailor's chalk and are more time-consuming and labor-intensive, but necessary in certain situations, such as when working with sheer or delicate fabrics or using a multicolored material against which chalk cannot be seen. Tailor's tacks are created by making a small stitch with a length of double thread; this is repeated, but rather than pull the second stitch taut, a small loop is left. This basic stitch is repeated at intervals. Once completed, the thread is cut at the center point between each stitch.

TOP BASTING

Top basting is used on the right side of the fabric to hold the layers of material flat and in place for a fitting. Used instead of pressing, it allows the garment's fit and design to be easily evaluated and altered as required. Top basting usually employs the uneven basting stitch.

UNEVEN BASTING

Uneven basting stitches are used for general basting – for straight seams that don't require much control, for marking, and for basting hems. Like even basting, these are short, temporary stitches, but are placed farther apart. They are longer on one side of the fabric than the other. The uneven basting stitch is also used for top basting. *See also* Top Basting, above.

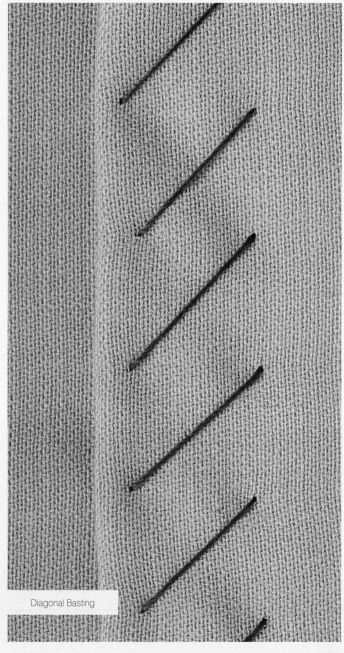
Diagonal Basting

PERMANENT STITCHES

BACKSTITCH

The backstitch is one of the strongest and most versatile of all permanent stitches. It is principally used to join seams that require both strength and elasticity, such as those used for setting sleeves. The essential backstitch technique involves inserting the sewing needle behind the point where the thread emerged from the previous stitch. There are several variations to the backstitch, including the prickstitch and the pickstitch (*see right* and page 222).

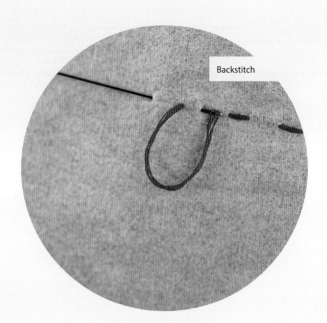

Backstitch

EVEN BACKSTITCH

The even backstitch looks much like machine stitching, in that the short stitches are even in length, with little space between them. It is the strongest form of backstitch. This stitch is used chiefly to make and repair seams.

HALF BACKSTITCH

Also referred to as the partial backstitch, it resembles even backstitch, except that the length of the stitches and the space between them are completely equal. It accordingly looks like a simple running stitch on the front side of the fabric. It is not quite as strong as an even backstitch, but is still commonly used for repairs.

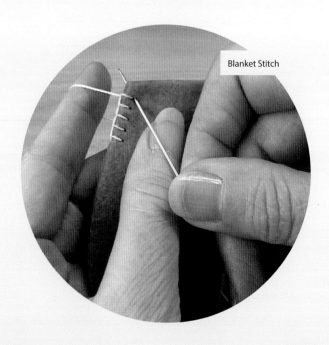

Blanket Stitch

BLANKET STITCH

The blanket stitch is versatile and has several uses – as a decorative edging, to cover hooks and eyes, and to finish thread bars. The stitch is executed by inserting the needle horizontally into the vertically positioned fabric edge. The thread is looped under the needle point and pulled taut over the fabric edge to form the stitch. For each consecutive stitch, the thread is kept under the point of the needle.

BLINDSTITCH

The most common form of hemming stitch, which can be executed easily and speedily. Blindstitches are formed by picking up with the needle just a couple of threads from the garment, then from the hem allowance, and continuing to alternate from garment to hem, maintaining an even spacing between each stitch. Tiny stitches ensure they remain inconspicuous.

BUTTONHOLE STITCH

Principally used to finish buttonholes and to make button shanks, it can also be a decorative form of edging. It is recommended to use waxed thread for buttonhole stitches, as waxing strengthens the thread and keeps it from twisting during execution. For each stitch, the needle is inserted from the back of the fabric, and the thread is looped under the needle point, before pulling taut and positioning the stitch on the fabric's edge. The stitch depth and spacing can vary as desired.

CATCHSTITCH

This stitch allows a fair measure of elasticity in a seam and is often used when hemming to hold one edge flat against another. It is formed by criss-crossing the stitches over two fabric edges. Catchstitches look like an even row of

Xs on the right side of the fabric, with two equivalent rows of dashes on the wrong side. Due to its suppleness, the catchstitch can also be used to form casings for elastic and tapes.

BLIND CATCHSTITCH

This is a stronger and more elastic version of the catchstitch, resistant to wear-and-tear. It is accordingly used for hemming heavy fabrics. It is executed using catchstitches worked between the two layers of fabric (garment and hem), as with the blindstitch.

DIAGONAL STITCH (PADSTITCHING)

Diagonal stitches are used to permanently join two or more fabric layers together. The technique is the same as the diagonal basting stitch, though the stitch length tends to be shorter. Rows of stitches are often laid out in a chevron pattern by making each row of stitches in the opposite direction to the preceding one. In tailoring, the diagonal stitch is referred to as padstitching and would be used to attach the interfacing to the outer garment fabric. Padstitching consisting of short stitches laid closely together can also help form and control the shape of collars and lapels.

DRAWSTITCH

A drawstitch is a variation of the slipstitch. It is used to join two folded edges from the right side. A short stitch is taken in one folded edge, alternating with a stitch in the other folded edge. The thread is kept taut to keep

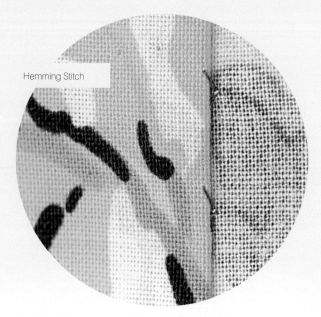
Hemming Stitch

the two edges firmly together. The drawstitch is commonly used in tailoring to attach two folded edges, such as the collar and lapel.

FELLSTITCH

A fellstitch is utilized to sew a raw or folded edge flat against the fabric below it – for example, when setting an undercollar, attaching a lining to a facing, or finishing narrow or rolled hems. The folded edge of fabric is placed and pinned in place on top of the lower layer to which it is to be joined. Short, straight stitches are made directly across the seam fold, diagonally taking the needle under the fabric and out again on the opposite side. A line of tiny stitches is visible on the right side, and a row of diagonal stitches is visible on the underside. The fellstitch is considered a precursor of the slipstitch, and was extensively used within tailoring during the nineteenth century. It is also commonly used today for appliqué.

FRENCH TACK

The French tack is similar in execution to the thread bar stitch, the main difference being that the ends of the tack are attached to two separate garment sections rather than two adjoining points in one area. The French tack employs a "thread chain" made with a hand-crochet technique. A small backstitch is made in the garment to make a loop. This loop is held open using forefinger and thumb, and thread is drawn through to create a second loop. The first loop is slipped off the fingers and tightened to make a stitch. This process is repeated until a chain of the required length is formed. The French tack is often used in tailored clothing such as coats and jackets to hold the lining and garment together at the hemline, while

retaining freedom of movement. Chanel used French tacks to keep the ends of collars and flaps from rising up.

HEMMING STITCH

A hemming stitch is used to secure a hem edge to a garment. There are two different types of hemming technique – flat or blind – that can be chosen subject to requirements. The flat hemming technique passes the stitches over the hem edge; the blind hemming technique takes the stitches inside between the hem and the garment, which ensures the stitches are invisible in the finished garment. The two most common types of hemming stitch are the blindstitch and the blind catchstitch. For hemming on ruffles or sheer fabrics, which easily distort, the slipstitch or the fellstitch are more suited.

HEMSTITCHING

Not to be confused with the hemming stitch, hemstitching is a type of decorative hem finish, traditionally used for linens and handkerchiefs. The hem edge is folded under and basted into place. Several threads are pulled from the fabric directly above the hem edge – the needle is pulled through the fabric to catch the threads – then drawn down to take a stitch through

Hemstitching

threads of fabric, then carrying the stitch back down to the lower section but slightly further up the edge. As the stitches are repeated, an evenly spaced zigzag pattern is formed, with the noticeable difference that with each stitch, the thread crosses over itself.

OVERCASTING STITCH

Small, slanted stitches sewn over a raw fabric edge in order to prevent fraying and reveling. Generally speaking, the more the fabric frays, the deeper and closer together the overcast stitches should be. Diagonal stitches are taken over the fabric edge, ensuring an even distance apart and a consistent depth.

OVERHAND STITCH

Similar to the whipstitch, overhand stitches are tiny, even stitches used to hold together two finished edges. It utilizes a diagonal stitch, placed very close together, which creates a secure and invisible seam. Overhand stitching is commonly used to attach lace edging or ribbon to a garment.

the hem edge. Repeating the stitches, evenly executed, produces a molded, ornamental border above the hemline.

HERRINGBONE STITCH

A type of hemming stitch that is strong but supple and particularly suited to working with pinked hem edges. They can also be used to join heavy interfacings to the garment fabric in coats and jackets. It is executed by anchoring the thread in the lower section of the hem, carrying it up to the upper section of the hem at a slight diagonal, picking up a couple of

Herringbone Stitch

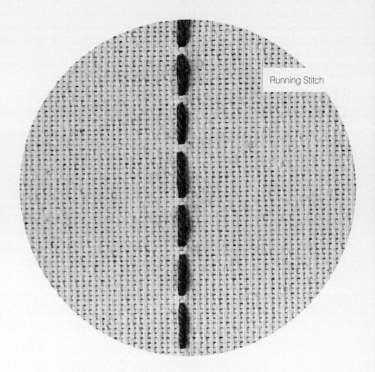

Running Stitch

PICKSTITCH

A pickstitch is executed using either the even or the half backstitch technique, with the essential difference being that the stitch is not taken through to the underlay of fabric. As such, it is intrinsically a decorative backstitch, with little strength to it.

PRICKSTITCH

A decorative variation of the backstitch. It uses the backstitch technique, but the top stitch is kept very short, like a small prick, with long spaces between them. This stitch is commonly used for setting zippers.

RUNNING STITCH

The running stitch can be considered the most fundamental stitch. It consists of short, even stitches that have a wide variety of uses. It is highly suitable for delicate sewing, such as fine seaming, tucking, and gathering. It is similar in appearance to the even backstitch, but its stitches are smaller and permanent. It is executed by drawing the needle in and out of the fabric, creating a series of evenly spaced stitches of equal length on both the right and wrong side of the fabric.

STABSTITCH

The stabstitch creates inconspicuous stitches on the right side of a garment, and is used for sewing bound buttonholes and pockets, setting shoulder pads and zippers, and joining thick layers of fabric. Stitches are created by "stabbing" the needle vertically down and up through the fabric layers and then repeating, ensuring an even distance is maintained between each stitch.

SLIPSTITCH

A stitch that is used to permanently join two layers from the right side of a garment (such as a waist seam), two folded edges on the end of a band, or one folded edge to a flat surface (such as a skirt hem). When executed correctly, the slipstitch is nearly invisible on the right side. It is formed by slipping the thread under and through a fold of fabric, picking up only a single thread on the right side of the fabric to anchor it.

THREAD BAR (THREAD LOOP)

The thread bar stitch is used to reinforce areas of stress, such as at pleat points, V-shaped openings, or at the bottom of zippers. When it is used at a garment edge, it can perform the role of a metal eye or button loop (in which case it is called a thread loop). It can be made either using the buttonhole or the blanket stitch. It is preferable to employ a waxed thread, which is stronger than normal thread. Several strands of thread are first anchored at two points in the fabric to form a loop-like thread bar. This bar is then covered with either buttonhole or blanket stitches.

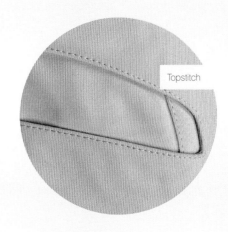
Topstitch

TOPSTITCH

Most often used very closely along garment edges, such as necklines, pockets, and seams, the topstitch is most often machine-made rather than handmade and provides a neat finish to a garment. It is usually executed as a straight stitch in the same color as the garment; however, decorative topstitching can be done in a contrasting color or in a more ornate stitch for different effects.

WHIPSTITCH

A variation of the overcasting stitch, a whipstitch is specifically used for seaming and hemming multiple layers rather than finishing raw edges. The same technique as for the overcast stitch is used, but stitches should be kept quite small and very close to the fabric edge to ensure the finished seam lies smooth and flat.

SMOCKING

Smocking is the technique of sewing embroidery stitches on a base of pleats. The result is a decorative panel with a certain amount of elasticity, making it highly suitable for garment decoration, particularly at areas of stress during wear such as at the bodice, waistline, or sleeve-wrist. Smocking should be executed before the garment is constructed. Crisp, lightweight fabrics produce the best results for smocking. There are many types of smocking stitches; among the most popular are the cable stitch, the diamond stitch, and the wave stitch. *See also* page 256.

CABLE STITCH

A pattern of interchanging straight stitches. A straight stitch is made through one fabric fold, and this is repeated with each new stitch made alternately above and below the previous one.

DIAMOND

A pattern of interlocking diamonds is made by working a large diagonal stitch, followed by a shorter straight stitch, and repeating to create a zigzag line. The fabric is then turned around, and the stitches are repeated to work a parallel row.

WAVE

A pattern of waving lines. Parallel rows of stitches are worked in blocks, creating even, straight stitches in steps up and down to create a zigzag.

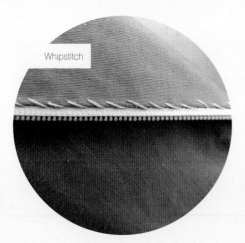
Whipstitch

EMBROIDERY STITCHES

INTRODUCTION

Embroidery is a branch of needlecraft that has a decorative, rather than functional, purpose. Embroidery as ornament for fashionable clothing reached its zenith in the eighteenth century. The skilled embroidery designers of the Lyonnais silk industry were unparalleled in their execution of beautiful and innovative designs, many of which used costly materials such as gold and silver thread, mirrored sequins and colored paste beads, and even precious jewels. "*L'Art du Brodeur*" ("Art of the Embroiderer"), a treatise written in 1770 by Charles Germain de Saint Aubin, Royal Embroiderer to Louis XV, describes the years of training and the unparalleled skill of those who worked in the industry. The treatise has retained its value as an important source on embroidery techniques. Today the most exquisite and innovative embroidery is reserved for haute couture, and is synonymous with Maison Lesage – the prestigious workshop of Parisian embroiderer François Lesage (*see also* page 252).

The extensive variety of embroidery stitches are classified into four main families of stitches – straight, looped, knotted, and isolated. Straight stitches consist of single threads lying flat on the surface of the base fabric. Looped stitches incorporate a loop – such as chained stitches or buttonhole stitches. Knotted stitches are twisted and sit on the surface of the fabric like beads. Isolated stitches may be formed by any of the previous three methods, but they are used singly.

▲ A detail of rich geometric embroidery, inspired by Tudor dress, from the bodice of a Christian Dior satin dress from his H-line collection of fall/winter 1954–55.

▶ Embroidery by the House of Lesage on a jacket by Elsa Schiaparelli from fall/winter 1937–38. Couture embroidery employs a wide range of different techniques and materials, including the use of silk and metallic threads, foil, tubes, beads and paillettes (spangles).

Blackwork

ARROWHEAD STITCH

A simple V-shaped stitch, this can be used in rows as a border or to make geometric patterns. Two diagonal running stitches are placed angled together to create a V (the arrowhead). This stitch is repeated as desired – one below the other to form a row, or making the stitches so close they are touching in order to form a shape. Although decorative, it can also be employed as a functional reinforcement stitch at points of strain on a garment – for example, at a pocket.

BLACKWORK

A distinctive form of counted thread embroidery that solely uses black thread on a white ground of linen or cotton fabric. Blackwork was extensively used to embellish clothing as well as household furnishings in the fifteenth and sixteenth centuries, especially seen on prominent garments such as ruffs and cuffs (*see* left, portrait of Elizabeth I of England, *c*.1590). During the Elizabethan period, English blackwork exalted in the depiction of botanical and animal motifs from nature. The principal stitch used for blackwork is the Holbein stitch (*see* Holbein, page 230).

CHAIN STITCH

A chain stitch is an unbroken series of looped stitches that form a chain. It is made by making an oval loop of thread that starts and ends at the same point, which is anchored by the following stitch by pulling the threaded needle through the loop. It is the principal stitch used for tambour embroidery. There are many variations of the chain stitch, including the feathered chain stitch, in which the chain stitches are slanted at alternate angles, the lazy daisy stitch, and many more.

COUNTED THREAD WORK

This term refers to any embroidery technique that requires the embroiderer to first count the fabric threads before taking a stitch in the fabric. An even-weave fabric such as linen or cotton – in which the spaces between the warp and weft threads are equal – is used. Cross stitch and blackwork are common examples of counted thread work.

COUCHING STITCH

Couching is a method used for anchoring a length of thick thread to a base fabric by taking small stitches in a finer thread over it at regular intervals. The term couching comes from the French *coucher*, meaning to lay down, just as the thick thread is laid on the fabric. The technique is used for threads and embellishments that are too thick to stitch through fabric, such as cord, wool, and metallic threads, which would be stripped if they were drawn through fabric.

COUCHING/GUIMPED WORK

A couching technique employed for metallic thread work. Guimped work refers to the application of metal thread over a raised motif. The term guimped most likely derives from the French term for the technique, *guipure*. In the past, relief shapes were cut from vellum, but today felt is generally used. Stab stitches are used to attach the edge of the motif to the fabric. The metal thread is then evenly applied row by row over the relief, with each row attached at the edge of the shape with a small stab stitch.

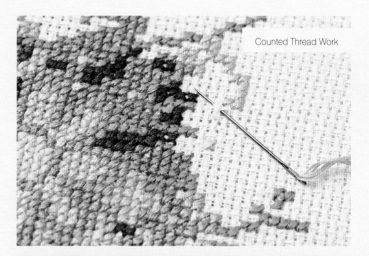

Counted Thread Work

Couching Stitch

Cross Stitch

COUCHING/OR NUÉ

A variant of couching using metallic thread, this technique is used to create complex shapes made up of colored couching stitches. The name *or nué* comes from the French term for the technique, meaning shaded gold. An outline of the design motif is first drawn on the base fabric. Metallic thread is then attached using a couching stitch. Each time the metallic thread passes over the motif outline, the couching thread is switched to an alternative color, giving shape to the motif with each stitch.

CREWEL WORK

Crewel embroidery is a decorative form of surface embroidery that uses wool – the use of loosely spun woolen thread is its defining feature. Any form of free embroidery stitch can be employed, although some of the most popular stitches include the satin stitch, the stem stitch, French knots, and couching. Crewel work can also be known as Jacobean work, as the height of its popularity occurred during the seventeenth century. During this period, crewel work was used to create elaborate and realistic scenes taken from nature, as well as for decorating home furnishings and clothing accessories such as gloves and shoes.

CROSS STITCH (SAMPLER)

Cross stitch is one of the simplest, and yet most versatile, of embroidery stitches. Often it is the first stitch an embroiderer will learn, hence it is also called a sampler stitch. It can be used for working straight lines, motifs, and intricate borders and for filling solid shapes. Cross stitch is executed by stitching two intersecting diagonal stitches to form

an X. A wide variety of different stitches and effects can be created by alternating the size of the stitch, or by only executing a part of the stitch (half cross stitch, three-quarter cross stitch, etc.). A double cross stitch creates the shape of a star. Assisi work refers to a striking technique in which cross stitch is stitched just in the background areas of a design, and the design motifs are left unstitched.

CUTWORK

A surface embroidery technique involving the cutting away of fabric areas in order to create a design. The raw edges of the cut eyelets are then sewn with a border to prevent fraying. The eyelets may also be filled with decorative stitchwork. White linen is traditionally used for the base fabric for cutwork (although cotton may also be used) and white thread for the stitches, creating an effect similar to lace. Although many different embroidery stitches may be employed, the two principal ones for cutwork are the running and the buttonhole stitch.

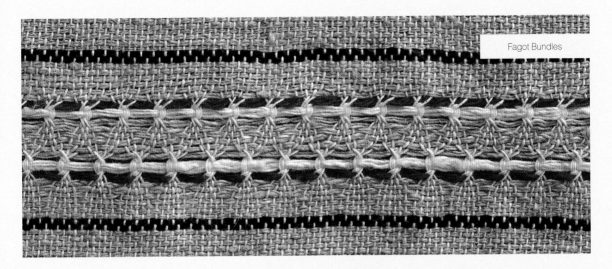

Fagot Bundles

DRAWN THREAD WORK

A variety of counted thread work in which fabric threads are drawn to one side in order to work the stitches. When warp threads are pulled, a band of weft threads are left and stitches are worked on regular groups of these, and vice versa. A variation of the hemstitch is the most common type of stitch employed.

FAGOT BUNDLES

An attractive variation of the fagoting stitch, this creates a star motif attaching two separate fabric sections. It is achieved by making two horizontal bridge stitches between the folded fabric edges. With the third stitch, the needle is brought up and passed behind the two previous stitches. The thread is pulled to tighten the loop and draw the stitches together before anchoring on the opposite folded edge.

FAGOTING STITCH

A decorative stitch used on clothing in order to join two fabric sections, leaving an open space in between. It is a decorative alternative to a seam, but is only suitable in areas of little strain, such as yoke sections or bands near the bottom of a skirt. It is similar in execution to the herringbone stitch – after anchoring the thread at the top of one folded fabric edge, it is carried diagonally over the opening and the needle is inserted through the opposite fold. It is then passed through and loops under the thread before being carried diagonally back over the opening.

FEATHERSTITCH

The featherstitch is created by a series of open half-loops of stitching taken on alternate sides of a given line, thus resembling a vine or ambling branch. The featherstitch is worked by first making a looped stitch on the surface of the fabric. The needle is brought back up just under the center of this loop, and a second loop stitch is made in the opposite direction. This step is repeated until the row of interlocking loops is the desired length. A more intricate branch is created by the double featherstitch, which creates alternate groups of loops. The chained featherstitch interlinks the loops like a chain.

FLY STITCH

A variation of the featherstitch that can be used in embroidery as an isolated stitch, a scattered filling, or a border. It is also known as a Y-stitch, thanks to its shape. A fly stitch is simply composed of two stitches – first, a horizontal long stitch that is left loose to create a loop on the surface of the fabric, and second, a short, vertical, upright stitch is made over the center of the loop and anchored slightly below.

FRENCH KNOTS

An extremely versatile variety of knotted stitch for surface embroidery. Resembling a round knot, it can be used individually, bunched in groups to fill spaces, or worked to form geometric shapes. A French knot is created by anchoring the thread at a point in the fabric, then wrapping the thread twice around the shaft of the needle. The needle is then brought gently back down through the fabric beside the original anchoring point, leaving a knot on the surface of the fabric.

HARDANGER

Hardanger embroidery is a variant of whitework embroidery executed on a cotton fabric. It combines many disciplines of needlecraft, chiefly the techniques of counted thread work, drawn thread work, and pulled thread work. Hardanger originated in Norway, and was traditionally used here to embellish linens, caps, and aprons.

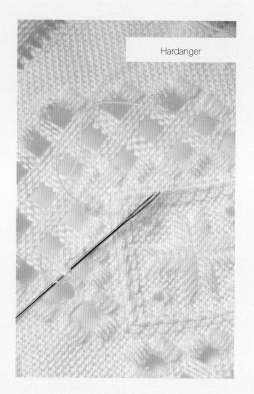

Hardanger

HOLBEIN STITCH

The fundamental stitch for blackwork, the Holbein stitch is used to develop a wide variety of blackwork patterns and looks the same on both the right and wrong side of the fabric. The stitch is based on the running stitch and is made in two stages. First, a row of running stitches of equal length and evenly spaced is made. A second row of running stitches is then made, which neatly fills the gaps in the original row to create a smooth, even line. The Holbein stitch is also known as the double running stitch.

Lazy Daisy Stitch

HUCK WEAVING

Huck weaving, also popularly called Swedish weaving, is a surface embroidery technique that consists of darning a simple geometric pattern using a variety of running and looped stitches. The stitches are not taken through the fabric but are worked on the surface. The term huck comes from Huckaback linen, the fabric on which huck weaving was originally worked.

LAZY DAISY STITCH

A form of detached chain stitch that creates a flower motif. After anchoring the thread in the base fabric, the needle is brought back down in the same hole, leaving a small loop on the surface. The needle is then brought back up through the loop and anchored with a small stitch to the side. This is repeated in a rotating circle to form a flower.

LONG AND SHORT STITCH

A variant of the satin stitch used to fill large areas of a design; it also allows a shaded effect to be given through the use of two or more shades of color. An outline of a motif is made on the base fabric. A row of alternating long and short straight stitches is made along the top of the outline, angling toward the center of the motif. In the next row underneath, the gaps made by the short stitches are filled with long, straight stitches. This is repeated until the shape is filled. The long and short stitch is traditionally used to give subtle shading to petals and leaves.

Long and Short Stitch

SATIN STITCH

The satin stitch is used as a motif filler, since it creates a smooth, shiny surface. The technique

Shisha Work

Silk Ribbon Embroidery

Whitework

involves a series of flat stitches laid side by side to cover a section of fabric. Working on the outline of a shape made on the base fabric, and starting at the widest point, straight stitches are taken diagonally from one edge to another, keeping them close together and varying the length as necessary until the space is filled. It can also be called a damask stitch.

SHISHA WORK

Shisha work refers to a form of mirror embroidery, consisting of small shapes of mirrored glass attached to a background fabric with utilitarian straight stitches, over which is a border of decorative interlacing stitches. The technique is thought to have originated in Persia around the thirteenth century, and shisha work is still extensively used to decorate traditional clothing in many regions of Asia. A combination of different stitches is used in shisha work, principally cross stitch, satin stitch, and buttonhole stitch.

SILK RIBBON EMBROIDERY

A technique that creates stitches with ribbon rather than thread. This type of embroidery was extensively used to decorate fashionable clothing during the eighteenth and nineteenth centuries, and is popular today for modern lingerie. Silk ribbon is not suitable for fine details, but a wide range of embroidery stitches can be employed – particularly the chain stitch, the fly stitch, the feather stitch, running stitches, and the French knot.

SHADOW WORK

Shadow work is a type of embroidery worked on sheer fabric, with the body of the embroidery on the back of the design so that the color of the thread shows through on the front of the fabric like a shadow between two solidly colored outlines. Contemporary shadow work principally uses the herringbone stitch, along with backstitch, which is used to outline the design motifs. Often employed to embellish contemporary clothing, shadow work is executed on a commercial scale in India.

STUMP WORK

Stump work is a form of raised embroidery. It combines a wide range of embroidery and needle-lace stitches, often wired and padded, to create three-dimensional motifs taken from nature. It has historically been used to embellish household items and certain clothing accessories such as purses and shoes. Stump work reached the zenith of creativity in the seventeenth century, during which time it was used to compose ingenious, narrative works of art.

WHITEWORK

Whitework embroidery refers to any embroidery technique in which the stitching is executed in the same color as the base fabric – which is traditionally white. It has a long history in the ornamentation of household and personal linenware. During the Edwardian era at the turn of the twentieth century, whitework was a popular embellishment for women's fashions.

Stump Work

TEXTILES AND EMBELLISHMENTS

Textiles have clothed the body since prehistoric times, when people first learned to fashion a crude needle and thread to shape skins around their body and to treat the skins so that they did not decompose. In more temperate climates, people made the first inroads into constructed textiles, with Central Asian tribes discovering a crude felting technique, or layering up strips of bark to make a woven/matted hybrid cloth for draped garments. The weaving of fibers only really became established when tribes settled in one place, as a loom was a heavy object not easily moved. Today, there is a dizzying variety of textiles and fabrics available to execute the simple function of clothing the body; from the highest-tech performance sportswear to an exquisitely handcrafted, embellished gown from a couture house, there are myriad choices of ways in which to get dressed.

The urge to embellish textiles has also been around since textiles were first worn. From decorations burned into the skins of primitive fur garments to the trims and feather excesses of the Victorian period, embellishment has been a key part of garment history, derived from the desire to individualize clothes and express creative consumption.

The textile industry today is a billion-dollar industry, with production chains stretching across the globe. Textile manufacture has always been a key part of the world's economy, with the body of the North American economy in the nineteenth century being made up of fur trappers satisfying the needs of Europe for beaver fur, and the cotton mills of northern England that fueled the expansion of the British Empire.

Textiles can be divided into two distinct groups: natural and synthetic. Essentially, natural fabrics come from four main sources – cotton, flax, wool, and silk – whereas synthetics are predominantly derived from petrochemicals. A textile's smallest component part is a fiber – a fine, hair-like filament, either natural or manufactured, that is then usually made into a yarn. A yarn is composed of twisted fibers, either singly or from various sources. The yarn or fiber is then woven, knitted, or felted into a fabric.

Besides dyeing and printing, most fabrics undergo a finishing treatment, such as brushing, to lift the nap and create a softer texture, or a chemical solution can be applied to make the fabric waterproof. The variety of finishes and treatments available today is ever increasing, with more and more niche needs being met by specialist manufacturers.

Sustainability has become a key issue in the production of textiles in the twenty-first century, as it involves the consumption of vast amounts of resources, particularly water (to irrigate the crops and process the fibers) and, when manufacturing synthetics, the use of petrochemicals. As such, there is a push for more textiles to be recycled, with brands such as Eco Age promoting sustainable style through recycling, a challenge taken up by dozens of the biggest couture houses. The provenance of textiles is also of greater concern, from factory conditions in the Far East to the harvesting of wild animals.

▶ A shiny fish-scale effect is created by the lavish use of oversized translucent paillettes – showing the transformative power of embellishment – in this fall/winter 2011–12 collection from Prada.

▶▶ A contemporary of Fortuny, and known for her Renaissance Revival designs, Mary Monaci Galenga (1880–1944) developed the technique of painting gold onto velvet and silk. By 1914, she was designing theatrical velvet cloaks, tea gowns, and textiles. This stenciled velvet detail, designed by Galenga, dates from the 1920s.

PATTERNS

▶ Showcasing the zig-zag chevron motif synonymous with the Missoni label, this pinafore-style dress with long peplum overskirt is expertly suited to display the bold, imaginative color contrasts for which the fashion house is well known.

▼ The paisley, a twisted teardrop motif that is Persian in origin but with the Western name derived from a Scottish town, is interpreted as an ornate large-scale pattern by Thakoon for spring/summer 2012.

INTRODUCTION

From the Latin *pator* (via "patron"), the term pattern originally meant "parent form": the initial design motif. The defining characteristic of pattern is repetition using either the hands or a mechanical aid such as a stencil or a block. The origin and development of all pattern are inevitably related to the culture of a particular country; the apotheosis of hand-block patterned fabrics was reached in Indian textiles in the early nineteenth century, and no other country has had such a long-standing influence on the printed cloths of other nations. In adhering to the Bauhaus principle that "form follows function", pattern may be perceived in modernist terms as anti-design, that decoration is extraneous if a garment is well designed. However, the desire for pattern is innate; indeed, one of the earliest forms of the application of pattern to the human body is tattooing. Pattern can enliven the plainest fabric, make the dullest dress desirable, and give dynamism to a safe silhouette. Whether it be woven, printed, or dyed, there are myriad patterns available in every possible colorway, and most have been utilized at some point in fashion history.

Abstract

ABSTRACT

Abstract art was a radically new art form from the early twentieth century. This aesthetic had filtered down into mainstream design by the 1920s but reached its pinnacle – when it was appreciated as being entirely "modern" – in the post-war designs of the 1950s. The word abstract means any non-objective motif that cannot be labeled anything else. Abstract prints continue to be popular today, as seen in the vibrant prints of Christopher Kane and Marni.

ANIMAL PRINT

Leopard, cheetah, zebra, python, and giraffe are all animals whose hides have proved inspiration for clothing decoration. With its wild, savage, and untamed connotations, animal print is a perennial fashion favorite, with designers such as Roberto Cavalli and Dolce & Gabbana proving its greatest champions. A more subtle effect can be achieved by the use of different colorways: for example, a black and dark brown print can harness the abstract shapes of leopard skin while rendering the pattern more sedate.

BOTANICAL

Naturalistic representations of foliage and flowers have always been a part of floral pattern design. However, it wasn't until the late nineteenth century, when Darwin's *The Origin of Species* popularized the notion of recording nature systematically and artists such as John Ruskin encouraged the idea of minutely observing nature and art, that botanical print was widely used as a dress fabric. However, with the latest innovations in digital printing, it is possible to have photorealism standards of depiction.

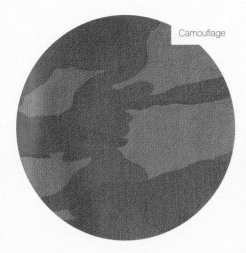
Camouflage

CAMOUFLAGE

Initially designed purely for the concealment of military personnel or equipment in a landscape, camouflage has been adopted by fashion designers since the 1980s, particularly in Stephen Sprouse's iconic day-glo treatment. Irregular patches of color are used to mimic foliage and undergrowth. The battledress of the Gulf War in 1991 introduced a new colorway, with its soft browns and yellows, compared to the dark greens and browns of the traditional pattern. Designers such as Jean Paul Gaultier have subverted the style, creating extravagant couture gowns in camouflage.

CHECKS AND PLAIDS

These are patterns made up of a series of stripes lined up at right angles, of differing or regular widths. Typical examples are gingham and windowpane check. Originally only produced on the loom, they have also been adapted into designs of greater complexity by print designers. An elaborate form is the Scottish tartan, for which there are strict rules for the formations of color and stripe. Vivienne Westwood is one designer who has used tartan to make a bold fashion statement, combining tradition with a sense of rebelliousness.

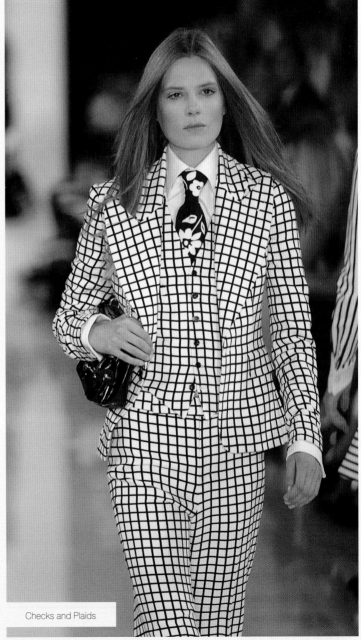
Checks and Plaids

Folkloric

CHECKERBOARD/CHESSBOARD

One of the boldest of graphic patterns, chessboard or checkerboard usually appears as a monotone print, with alternating black and white squares of regular size. The effect can be softened by breaking up the grid into smaller sections or by intersecting it with colored lines. The design was popular in the 1960s, when the bold graphic lines of the Op Art movement were appropriated for "youthquake" fashions.

CHEVRON

This pattern can be woven, stitched, or printed. When woven, it has the same construction as a herringbone twill and consists of a series of layered stripes that appear as stacked V shapes. Chevrons can also be embroidered with a zig-zag stitch, used as a decorative edging, or adapted by pushing the stripes out of alignment, creating a fractured, out-of-kilter pattern. The luxury Italian label Missoni is renowned for its raschel knitted chevron designs.

CHINOISERIE

A term to describe any design that mimics authentic Chinese designs or is a Western approximation of them. This style of decoration was influenced by the opening up of the Chinese market to Dutch traders in the eighteenth century. Recurrent motifs include pagodas, dragons, and fantastic landscapes with figures. The most recent wave of popularity came in 1997 when both Prada and John Galliano for Dior used chinoiserie elements in their spring/summer collections.

CONVERSATIONAL

A conversational print is one that is representational and has a narrative. Another term is novelty print, featuring idiosyncratic subject matter taken out of context, such as domestic artifacts, animal motifs, or cartoon characters. Generally used for childrenswear, in fashionable clothing the subject matter may have an overriding kitsch element, as seen in the aesthetic of U.S.-based designer Jeremy Scott and his appropriation of food labels as a print motif.

FOLKLORIC

A general term for all patterns with historical European or American vernacular designs as their inspiration, without referring to a specific ethnic group. Motifs include simplified, bold floral patterns in strikingly vivid colors. "Folk" dress is tied up with the notion of simpler non-Western cultures and has to do with tradition not novelty. One of the first attempts to explore the concept of folk dress in the twentieth century was instigated by the couturier Paul Poiret, who set up the Atelier Martine in 1911.

FOULARD

Foulard can either refer to the woven fabric – a lightweight silk twill – or to the pattern most commonly associated with this kind of fabric – a plain ground with a small printed pattern with a basic block repeat. This type of pattern can also be seen on plain woven fabrics and is popular for menswear, particularly for ties, dressing robes, and scarves. Foulard can also refer to a type of garment – a silk scarf – worn by women.

Chinoiserie

Liberty Print

LEAF PRINT

Leaves have been a decorative motif for as long as patterns have been worn. They can appear naturalistic but also lend themselves perfectly to abstraction with their graphic shapes and geometric lines. Some of the best abstracted leaf prints date from the modernist 1950s but, more recently, designers such as Christopher Bailey at Burberry have used the splashy informality of painted autumnal leaves to act as a decorative balance to the formal trench coat.

LIBERTY PRINT

The terms "Liberty print" and "Tana Lawn" have become virtually interchangeable, with Liberty of London's sweet sprigged floral tana cotton fabrics viewed as classic prints, never out of production since their creation in the 1930s. Named after the fine cotton produced around Lake Tana in Ethiopia, with "lawn" referring to its slight luster, Tana Lawns were originally used for childrenswear until the 1970s, when a partnership with Cacharel produced womenswear clothing with a romantic aesthetic.

PAISLEY

Paisley, with its characteristic teardrop or cone-shaped motif, is sometimes thought to be the mark made by curling the hand into a fist and printing with the little finger downwards into the cloth. The motif is also thought to represent a seed pod – a symbol of life and fertility. The pattern originated in the woven shawls of Kashmir, which were imported into Britain at the end of the seventeenth century. The Indian shawl was then copied by weavers in Paisley, Scotland.

PATIO PRINT

Large-scale floral patterns, so named because they were popular for use on patio furniture in the 1930s and 1940s. The shortage of materials during World War II meant that bark cloth was used for clothing, and the bright patio prints served as a counterpoint to this coarse fabric. Gucci revived an interest in these large splashy prints with its 1999 spring/summer collection, in which oversized exotic flowers were placed on equally oversized dresses. They were much imitated by the mass market.

PINSTRIPE AND CHALKSTRIPE

Originally pinstripe referred to a woven suit fabric that has a dark background with white parallel lines running vertically through it. However, this now refers to a pattern as well as a fabric, and pinstripes can be printed or stitched onto any material or garment. It is predominantly used for men's suiting, although many baseball teams have adopted it for their uniforms, reversing the pattern so that it appears as black stripes on a white ground. With a chalk stripe, a series of threads is used to create a thicker line that is reminiscent of tailor's chalk.

Stripes

POLKA DOT

Polka dot print is a perennial favorite – whether tiny or comically oversized, dots add a playfulness to the most serious of garments. Comme des Garcons epitomizes this dichotomy perfectly. It takes fashion entirely seriously using challenging silhouettes and fabrics, but gives them a levity with a polka dot print. The name comes from the Hungarian Polka – a dance craze in the mid-nineteenth century, when many products were also given the same name.

SPRIGGED (TOSSED FLORAL) PRINT

Small sprigs of single flowers are placed at intervals on a plain light-colored or white background, as if they had been tossed in the air and fallen at random. This pretty print was immensely popular in the Regency period, with the heroines of Jane Austen often being described as wearing "sprigged muslin" gowns as daywear. Sprigged cotton gowns have remained popular, although they are seen more on childrenswear today.

Pinstripe

STARS/CELESTIAL

Whether representative of a starry-eyed romanticism or of a space age in love with the future, celestial motifs are a recurring element in pattern design. From Chanel's 2003 star print to the rockets of the 1950s and 1960s, when space travel was a new reality, the night sky offers myriad forms of inspiration. Stars can also invoke another connotation, that of patriotism, especially when rendered in red, white, or blue, as seen in the collections of Tommy Hilfiger.

STRIPES

A basic geometric design of alternating colors, the stripe is an infinitely adaptable pattern. The history of striped clothing is mixed; in the Middle Ages, for example, stripes were seen as subversive, an indicator of something suspicious. Only those on the outside of society wore stripes, such as prostitutes and jesters; Judas was commonly depicted wearing a striped garment. Today, however, there are no such connotations, and the striped Breton top is a staple garment of most female wardrobes.

TOILE DE JOUY

This refers to any narrative scene depicted on cotton, linen, or silk. The first decorative fabrics of this kind were printed cottons from India in the late eighteenth century. These fabrics were so popular that imitation was inevitable, with the first successful imitator being Philippe Oberkampf, who set up his factory, Jouy, near the French court of Versailles. As such, the name Jouy has became synonymous with any finely printed fabrics depicting classical narrative allegorical scenes.

Sprigged Print

Toile de Jouy

TRIMMINGS

INTRODUCTION

Unlike embellishment, which is intrinsic to the garment, a trimming is an addition, providing extra detail and interest to some aspect of the overall silhouette. Many trimmings are rooted in the development of woven fabrics, particularly various braids and those fabrics woven on a narrow machine. Others are the subject of the atelier, a specialist workshop that produces labor-intensive effects such as those by the house of Lemarié, now owned by Chanel, which has supplied feathers to couture houses since it was founded in 1880. Trimmings may consist of a subtle attention to detail, such as the self-colored, hand-stitched fagoting on the bodice of a 1920s tennis dress, or represent brilliant excess, such as the plethora of swagged braids, fringes, and tassels that provided an aura of grandeur to the couture gowns of Charles Frederick Worth and the American designer Mainbocher with his Biedermeier evening dress fantasy. Modernists who agree with essayist Adolf Loos, in his defining treatise "Ornament and Crime" (1908), that "freedom from ornament is a sign of spiritual strength", eschew trimmings as interfering with the unadorned sculptural cut and line of the clothes. Other designers enthusiastically engage with their inherent variety and potential for compelling decorative effects.

▲ Christophe Decarnin designed this influential military-inspired drummer boy jacket with oversized shoulders for Balmain's fall/winter 2009 collection. The military detailing is executed with fine silver frogging on the front fastenings and the epaulettes.

▶ An outstanding example of plumasserie, this Alexander McQueen dress from his "Horn of Plenty" collection of fall/winter 2009 resembles the coat of a raven while referencing the nipped-in waist and wide hips of the 1950s New Look silhouette.

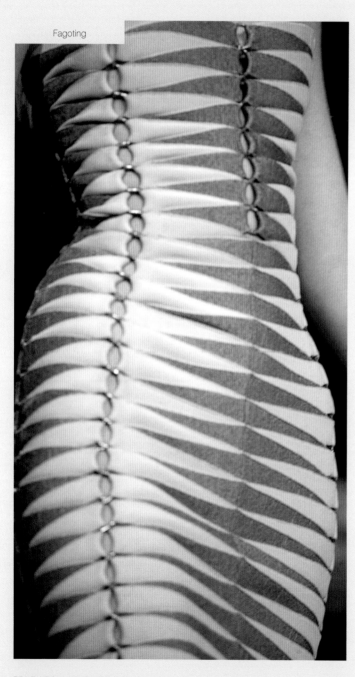

Fagoting

BRAIDING

Braiding is a simple form of narrow fabric construction created by the intertwining of yarns. This began as a handicraft until manual efforts were replaced by narrow-width looms. The flat braid structure is formed by crossing a number of yarns diagonally so that each yarn passes alternately over and under one or more of the others. Circular (tubular or round) braids are formed hollow or around a center core. Various materials are deployed, including cotton, polyester, nylon, and plastic strands.

FAGOTING

Fagoting is a technique deployed to join two pieces of material together by means of an insertion stitch, creating a see-through band between the two. Traditionally worked by hand, it was most often used in lingerie and childrenswear in delicate fabrics such as silk, satin, linen, and cotton, with the technique being popular during the 1920s and 1930s for use in lightweight summer clothing. More unusually, thicker materials may also be fagoted together, although this creates a sturdier effect.

FRINGING

Fringing consists of an ornamental border of threads left loose or formed into tassels or twists, generally used to edge clothing or material and frequently attached to a separate band. During the 1920s, with the adoption of the streamlined chemise dress, fringing was attached in layers to the whole of the garment, providing a shimmering expanse of movement when worn for the popular dances of the day. In the 1970s, fringing was associated with hippie dress, and still retains its boho aesthetic.

FROGGING

An ornamental braiding used for fastening the front edges of a garment together, frogging consists of a button-and-loop mechanism. Frogging became an important decorative feature on military uniforms from the seventeenth to the nineteenth centuries, particularly for those prestigious regiments such as the hussars. The device was much copied in women's dress of the era, particularly the pelisse. Donatella Versace included frogging in a series of bias-cut dresses for her fall/winter collection of 2014.

GALLOON

A galloon is any finished lace of various widths with a decorative scalloped edge on both sides. It is frequently constructed to allow for a silk ribbon to be threaded through the center, creating a drawstring effect typically used on lingerie and wedding gowns. When made of metallic gold or silver thread, the galloon is used for trimming military and ecclesiastical dress. The name is derived from the seventeenth-century French word *galonner*, meaning "to trim".

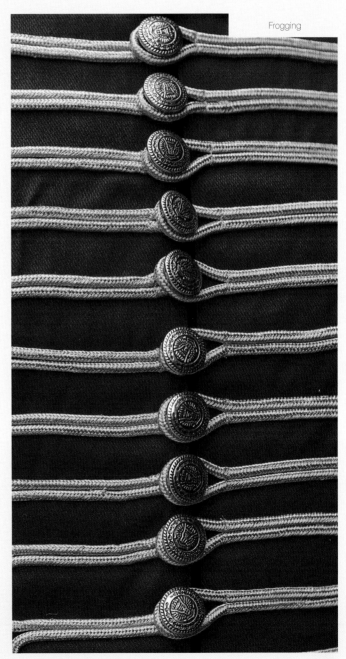

Frogging

Galloon

Passementerie

PASSEMENTERIE

During the sixteenth century in France, the first Guild of Passementiers was created and documented the art of passementerie. The tassel was its primary expression, but it also included fringes (applied, as opposed to integral), ornamental cords, galloons, pom-poms, and rosettes. Tassels, pom-poms and rosettes are point ornaments; the others are linear ornaments. Couturier Charles Frederick Worth lavishly adorned his crinolines and gored skirts of the mid-nineteenth century with passementerie.

PICOT EDGE

A popular decorative device since 1910, a picot edge consists of small points. A common sewing technique in the 1920s and 1930s, worked both by machine and by hand, it is a rolled hem with a zig-zag stitch sewn over the hem to hold it in place. It is usually worked on very fine, lightweight fabrics such as chiffon. In knitting or crochet, a picot edge is formed by a series of looped threads along the edge of the fabric, with a "picot" consisting of a single loop.

PLUMASSERIE

Feathers have traditionally been worn by both men and women, with use for male garments at its peak in the sixteenth century, when explorers returned with feathers from new and exotic species. More usually used as trimmings on a garment, the time-consuming process of creating an entire garment in feathers is one that can only be undertaken by haute couture. In 2009 Alexander McQueen constructed a knee-length dress from thousands of duck feathers dyed black for his collection "The Horn of Plenty".

Tassels

Soutache

RICKRACK BRAID

A waved or corrugated braid that was originally crocheted in the late 1800s, when variations of rickrack appeared, called waved braid. Constructed from a solid, usually contrasting, color on the ground and sewn down the center with a single row of stitching, rickrack braid was popular during the 1950s, edging the circular felt skirts of the bobby-soxer. Rickrack also has intimations of folk dress, particularly during the popularity of American West motifs in the 1970s.

SOUTACHE

A soutache is a narrow, flat, decorative braid, traditionally woven from metallic bullion thread, silk, or a blend of silk and wool. It is used in the trimming of clothing to conceal a seam, creating definition and highlighting the structure of a garment. Soutache was a particular feature used in the decoration of military uniforms. In the twentieth century, it began to be woven in rayon and other synthetic fibers.

TASSEL

Derived from the Latin word *tassau*, which refers to a clasp (as for the neck of a garment), the tassel is primarily a device to prevent the unraveling of threads. It is made by binding gathered threads together at one end with a matching cord around a suspended string, leaving the other end to fall free. Over time, tassels became increasingly ornamental. Usually placed along the hem of a garment, they are also a feature of military uniforms.

EMBELLISHMENTS

INTRODUCTION

Lavish embellishment has long been used to indicate the wealth and status of the wearer, evidenced in the sumptuous hand-embellished garments of the Renaissance court, when raised goldwork and blackwork were studded with pearls and gemstones to signify the importance of the wearer. The predilection for heavily embellished garments is also evident in twenty-first-century fashion. Couturiers such as Raf Simons at Dior, Olivier Rousteing at Balmain, and Italian label Dolce & Gabbana all exploit the specialist talents of the atelier, where the *petites mains* produce fabrics of luxurious richness and delicacy. Giving a three-dimensional quality to the surface of haute couture garments is left to the specialist Lesage embroidery atelier in Paris, which has been owned by Chanel since 2002. To the traditional techniques of embroidery, modern processes such as laser cutting have been added to the repertoire of the designer, replicating handcrafted techniques and frequently used in conjunction with other processes, resulting in a complex layer of embellishment. A contemporary resurgence of handcrafting in the twenty-first century has resulted in a concurrent renewal of interest in domestic customization, bringing a new perspective to the traditional crafts of fabric embellishment.

▲ An example of the high level of couture craftsmanship, including goldwork from the specialist embroidery atelier Lesage, now under the auspices of Chanel.

▶ The simplicity of the edge-to-edge jacket and narrow skirt showcased by U.K. designer Christopher Kane in his spring/summer 2011 collection is subverted by the use of neon brights and simulated lace – produced by laser-cutting and vinyl-coating leather.

Blackwork

APPLIQUÉ

A technique in which pieces of material are sewn or glued onto fabric to form a top layer of decoration – the word is derived from the French *appliquer*, meaning "to apply". As well as being decorative, appliqué is also used to repair damaged sections. A leather elbow patch is a classic form of practical appliquéing. In fashion, appliqué is used to suggest a certain naïve style, an aesthetic seen in designs by Marc Jacobs.

BLACKWORK

This technique was at the height of its popularity in the sixteenth century and can often be seen in portraits of the period. Undergarments such as nightdresses and coifs were routinely decorated with blackwork, particularly on the collars and cuffs to reinforce the fabric. It is created by using tightly twisted threads of silk on white or off-white fabric, and designs include repeat geometric or floral patterns or more complicated curvilinear floral designs, where shadows are formed by seed stitches.

CHAIN STITCH

With chain stitch, thread is either hand-embroidered or crocheted to form a long, continuous stitch that has the appearance of a chain. In machine sewing, the stitch that loops the threads creates a chain on the reverse of the fabric. This is a basic embroidery stitch and one of the most simple to execute. It may be used to decorate the edges of fabric if used in a contrasting color.

Couching

COUCHING

Also known as laid work, this type of
embroidery design is made by overlaying
various cords or threads over a piece of
fabric, which are then secured in place using
small stitches running over the threads and
through the fabric. The most famous of
this stitch is found on the Bayeux Tapestry,
which was created in the eleventh century.
Historically, there is a strong tradition of
couching in the Middle East, with production
centering on Bethlehem.

GOLDWORK

The technique of goldwork (otherwise known
as bullion thread) was originally used on
ecclesiastical and royal garments and, in the
more recent historic past, on military garments
and livery. Goldwork, a type of stitching done
with gold or silver thread (where a core yarn is
covered with a gold film), is used to create flat,
outlined, and raised designs. The process is
very laborious and expensive, and is used only
for high-end fashion garments.

Goldwork

Satin Stitch

LASER CUTTING

A technique used to mimic the appearance of lace or cutout work, laser cutting is created by inputting a design into a computer, which then guides an intense beam of light over the fabric, vaporizing the material, leaving a cutout design. Only haute couture labels could create the intricate and spectacular lasercut designs, initially since it was an expensive process, but with new developments, the process is now available to the mass market.

PAILLETTES AND SEQUINS

These are two types of ornament that add luster and light-reflecting shimmer to fabrics. The paillette is a long, flat or oval bead, with a hole at each end for attaching it to the garment, that is designed to dangle rather than sit flush against the fabric. The sequin, on the other hand, is usually round, with one hole at the center, and sits flat. Early paillettes and sequins were made from shell or metal. More recently, they are made from plastic.

RHINESTONES

As the name suggests, this type of rock crystal decoration was originally found in the Rhineland and was applied to garments and jewelry to lend a sparkling, light-reflecting surface texture. Imitation rock crystal is now more commonly used, and the Swarovski Company, founded in Austria in 1895, is one of the world's largest manufacturers of both cut crystal and imitation glass rhinestones. Rhinestones are a quick method of embellishing a garment, as they can be glued on rather than stitched.

SATIN STITCH

Satin stitch, otherwise known as damask stitch, is a series of close parallel lines of embroidery sewn over a printed design. It is called satin stitch because its shiny surface mimics silk satin. The thread used is generally low-twist embroidery thread, which has a soft luster. The design is often given a border of chain stitching in order to create a smooth line. This style of stitch can also be raised to create a padded surface.

SMOCKING

Sequins

A technique in which rows of stitching are used to gather up a light fabric into small folds, giving a degree of elasticity and fullness to a garment. As such, it was particularly used on cuffs, collars, and sleeves – elements of a garment that require flexibility. Smocking originated in England in the Middle Ages, with all levels of society wearing smocked garments, although the wealthy tended to only wear a smocked undershirt. *See also* pages 202 and 223.

TAMBOUR BEADING

Tambour work, a difficult and labor-intensive technique, reputedly arrived in France in the 1720s from China. The technique requires the fabric to be stretched tightly on a frame, and a tambour hook – similar to a crochet hook but with a removable needle at the end – is used to make a chain stitch, holding the bead in place. The hook is held on top of the frame, with the threaded beads or sequins underneath.

Tambour Beading

PLANT FIBERS

INTRODUCTION

A wide range of plants provide fibers suitable for processing to become textiles. The fibers can either be obtained from the stem or bark (known as bast fibers), the leaves (known as hard fibers), or, less commonly, the seeds (known as seed fibers). These plants have been harvested and cultivated for millennia in all territories of the world.

With the discovery of X-ray microscopes in the 1930s it was possible to see that most plant fibers are made up of short, tapered molecules, which explains why natural fibers generally have to be spun together into yarn before being processed into textiles.

Plant fibers are generally considered to be more desirable by the fashion industry because they are associated with several benefits, as well as a provenance that synthetics do not have, although when synthetic fibers were introduced in the twentieth century, they were heralded for their easy-care properties and novelty value. All plant fibers rely on a plentiful water supply in their processing, and, as such, can be perceived as having a high toll on the environment. Plant fibers are rarely harvested from wild sources today – most are cultivated on large plantations.

▲ Actress Gillian Anderson wearing vintage linen by Irish designer Sybil Connolly. During the late 1950s and 1960s, Connolly pioneered a technique for creating elegant garments from this traditionally practical textile whereby fine handkerchief linen was formed into micropleats.

▶ Designing for the Calvin Klein label, Francisco Costa utilizes the inflexibility of cupro to create architecturally minimalist garments for the spring/summer 2011 collection.

Bark Cloth

BAMBOO

Grown mostly in China, Indonesia, and India, bamboo is a perennial species that requires little water or pesticide and has therefore been embraced by the eco-fashion movement. Bamboo can be used in two ways to make fabric, either in its natural state or processed to become regenerated cellulose, when it is classified as a manufactured fiber. The benefits of the rarer, natural bamboo fiber are manifold, not least because it requires less processing and therefore less consumption of resources.

BARK CLOTH

A material made from the inner, more flexible bark of trees such as the mulberry. The inner bark is removed, soaked in water, and then hammered out to the desired thickness. At this stage it is ready for decoration. As a garment fabric, it is mostly used for novelty prints in the developed world, but has a wider use in tropical areas. It is widely used for garments in the Pacific Islands, where it is known as kapa cloth.

COTTON

Cotton is a seed fiber that has been cultivated for over 7,000 years, with most modern cotton coming from the short-fibered *Gossypium hirsutum* plant. Cotton is the most widely used natural fiber today, with around 125 million bales being produced annually. A large part of the world economy was based on cotton during the Industrial Revolution, and it is still an important product worldwide today. The benefits of cotton are its breathability and strength, but it has little natural luster or elasticity.

CUPRO

Cupro can be classified as both a plant fiber and a manufactured fiber known as rayon. Wood pulp is dissolved in a copper and ammonia solution, which is then made to coagulate in a chemical bath. The fibers are stretched and rinsed of copper residue with an acid solution before drying. It is a non-eco-friendly fabric since the volume of water that has to be used is untenable in most countries with high standards for clean water.

HEMP

Made from *Cannabis sativa*, a somewhat controversial plant that can also be used to make marijuana, hemp is a coarse plant fiber with a multitude of uses. To render the fibers suitable for weaving, the plant undergoes retting, a chemical process that separates the gum and woody matter from the valuable bast fibers. Historically, hemp was used in the shipping industry to make sails and ropes, since it does not rot in seawater.

JUTE

Jute is cheap, easy to grow, and easy to process, making it one of the most extensively used plant fibers. Rarely used for clothing but often for accessories, it is used widely as an agricultural textile or yarn and for carpet backing. Jute is produced and consumed mostly in India, Bangladesh, and parts of China and Thailand, as it grows so well there. When first produced, the fiber is soft and pliable, but it soon turns brittle and coarse upon exposure to moisture.

LINEN

Flax is the name of the plant, and linen is the name of the fabric from which it is produced. It is the oldest known textile, and examples of linen cloth have been found in archaeological sites dating back 30,000 years. From the Middle Ages to the eighteenth century (when cotton production became widespread), linen was the primary textile in every household. Key centers for linen production include Ireland, where production was started by French refugees in the eighteenth century.

RAFFIA

A coarse, stiff, fiber, raffia comes from the *Raphia ruffia* palm, grown in the Philippines and Madagascar. Once removed from their outer shell, the strips of straw-like fiber can be braided or woven into long strips that can then be sewn together. Commonly used in millinery, as well as more practical household objects, raffia for clothing has seen a resurgence in the twenty-first century, with bags, shoes, jewelry, and even structured dresses being designed with it.

RAMIE

From the inner bark of the Urticaceae family of plants, grown primarily in Brazil and the Philippines, the bast fiber is removed manually or by the chemical process of retting (where the fiber is left to soak in a chemical bath), and is used in various products that require a durable, strong, and resistant textile. Ramie is most useful in fashion garments when mixed with other fibers such as linen, as alone it can be somewhat stiff and uncomfortable.

SEA-ISLAND COTTON

This high-quality cotton thread has been grown in the Caribbean and the U.S. since the late eighteenth century. Due to the high nap content, it has to be combed three or four times to render it soft enough to weave, and it is characterized by its regularity, strength, and exceptionally long fibers. The main producer of commercial sea-island cotton today is the Derbyshire firm John Smedley. Originally known for its knitted underwear, the company first introduced outerwear garments in 1932.

STRAW

Primarily used in the millinery industry, with a trilby or panama being a summer staple for both men and women, straw comes from a broad spectrum of plant varieties, with rye straw being particularly useful due to its malleability. The straw fibers are braided or woven into hats, shoes, bags, and even garments. It can also be used as a decorative fiber, embroidered onto the surface of a fabric to give a lustrous embellishment that mimics gold thread.

Raffia

SYNTHETIC FIBERS

INTRODUCTION

Synthetic fibers were first commercially manufactured in the early 1900s, in the form of rayon, although Joseph Swan originally produced the first cellulose-based fiber in 1880. Further development came in 1924, when acetate began to be commercially manufactured. At this stage, all synthetics were rendered from cellulose fibers because the technology was too crude to produce anything from chemicals until later in the twentieth century. A key advance in the manufacture of synthetic fibers came with the development of X-ray technology, which enabled scientists to analyze microscopically the structure of natural fibers in order to understand how to mimic them. It was discovered that the molecules making up a fiber are long and narrow, so synthetics were produced as continuous filament fibers. This means they can be woven or knitted without first processing them into yarns.

All new fibers must be endorsed and categorized by the Textile Fiber Products Identification Act, which establishes whether or not a product is genuinely new. The producer must demonstrate how the fiber's physical composition differs from previous synthetic fibers, and its use to the textile industry must be outlined. New fibers that have similarities to established synthetics are usually trademarked in order to distinguish them from others.

▲ Renowned for his body-con dresses during the 1980s, as seen here, Tunisian designer Azzedine Alaïa utilized Lycra alongside his innovative cutting techniques to create his signature dresses.

▶ "Miracle" synthetic fibers such as crimplene – easy to launder and crease-free – were aimed at the Youthquake market in the 1960s with adverts depicting young models in quirky poses.

The world's best jersey is made of 'Crimplene'. Skirts in this marvellous fabric are fashion news of the year!

You know perfectly well that jersey is the most comfortable kind of fabric you can wear, and you also know that skirt must never bag or droop or you look like you've no clothes sense at all. Which all comes to: 'Crimplene'. This one by Laddies. Style 'Gem'. About 75/-.

'Crimplene' is the jersey that always keeps its shape. (It's pure 'Terylene'— that's why!)

ACETATE

A cellulose-based fiber, acetate was first produced by Bostonian inventor Arthur D. Little in 1894. Initially used for the visual arts – in photography and film – acetate was marketed as artificial silk. The first commercially viable production of the fiber was created by two Swiss brothers, Camille and Henri Dreyfus, in 1905. The production spread to America in the 1920s and is now manufactured under several trade names including Acele, Avisco, Celanese, Chromspun, Dicel, and Estron.

ACRYLIC

A long-chain synthetic polymer widely used in the garment industry, either as a mix yarn or by itself. The fibers are often used in knitwear, as they closely resemble the soft texture of wool and mohair. Other benefits of acrylic include its ability to hold its color through washing and exposure to sunlight and the fact that a garment made from acrylic is less likely to need ironing and can therefore be labeled as easy care.

CRIMPLENE

Crimplene is a robust and heavy material named after the valley in which it was first manufactured in the 1950s: Crimple Valley in the U.K. Crimplene is synonymous with the sculptural 1960s minidress and its ability to simply be washed and worn – perfect for a time when working women had less time for laundry. It was also popular for menswear – its ability to hold a crisp edge made it perfect for the sharp suits worn by the Mods of the 1960s.

LUREX

Lurex is the trademarked name for any yarn or fabric that has a metallic sheen, created by adding a layer of metal to parts of the fiber or the finished fabric through a laminating process in which metallic fibers are placed between two layers of a polyamide thread and then heated under pressure. Lurex fabric was particularly popular in the space-age-obsessed 1960s – with its shimmering texture lending itself particularly well to simple tunic dresses.

Acrylic

Lurex

MICROFIBER

Microfiber, invented in the 1980s in Japan, can be made from many different types of synthetic fibers, including acrylic, nylon, polyester, lyocell, and rayon. A microfiber is made by extruding the finest possible fiber from the spinnerette machine. The finished fiber is light, soft, and flexible and has myriad uses, but it is particularly suitable for silk-effect blouses or athletic wear because of its high wicking (the ability to draw moisture away from the skin) quality.

MODAL

A generic and a trademarked name for a synthetic rayon fiber made from regenerated cellulose from beech trees. Modal is rarely used on its own but is mixed with other fibers, both natural and synthetic, for different products such as nightwear and bed linen. It is a very soft yarn with many benefits, including absorbency, ease of dyeing, and shrink resistance. A leading Modal manufacturer is Lenzing, a company that proclaims its carbon-neutral production processes.

NEOPRENE

A synthetic rubber invented by DuPont in 1930, neoprene was once relegated to wetsuits and sportswear, especially by the Body Glove brand. Noted for its flexible, waterproof, and sculptural qualities, it has since been utilized by Japanese fashion designer Yohji Yamamoto, Marc Jacobs for Louis Vuitton, and spring/summer 2014 offerings from DKNY, Tommy Hilfiger and Roksanda Illinic, who formed the fabric into jackets, dresses, and footwear.

NYLON

Nylon was created for the DuPont company in 1938 in an attempt to mimic silk, although it has come to be used as a generic term for any long-chain synthetic polymer made from different solutions of carboxylic acid and amine monomers. Nylon thread is incredibly strong and, as such, has both domestic and industrial uses, including fishing wire and parachutes as well as clothing. The garment most associated with nylon, however, is the stocking, first manufactured in nylon in 1939.

POLYESTER

Invented in the 1940s, polyester is a long-chain synthetic polymer, characterized by its durability, ability to keep its shape after washing, and fast drying properties. Polyester was initially embraced as an exciting modern fabric, but over time, natural fabrics returned to favor and polyester became synonymous with cheap, ugly garments. However, its reputation has been rehabilitated more recently with the development of high-grade polyesters by designers such as Issey Miyake – who used high-twist polyester for his "Pleats Please" line.

SPANDEX/LYCRA

Lycra is the trademarked name for the flexible, manufactured polymer spandex that was invented in 1959 by the DuPont laboratories. Initially, spandex (a play on the word "expands") was used only for female foundation garments, but its fit and function made it valuable for performance sportswear, such as leotards and leggings. As sportswear became fashionable, its uses expanded, and now it is used in any form of apparel that requires stretch, flexibility, and elastic recovery.

Viscose

TENCEL/LYOCELL

While Lyocell is the current trademarked name, Tencel is the original name for a rayon fiber that was first produced by Courtaulds in the U.K. in the 1980s. The process of production, where wood cellulose fibers are dissolved in a solvent, is considered to consume far fewer resources and is therefore more environmentally friendly. The finished fabric is valued for its weight and draping qualities and for its ability to add luster to a garment.

VISCOSE/RAYON

Invented by Cross and Bevan, this synthetic fiber was first produced in England in 1892. Rayon's key ingredient is wood pulp cellulose or cotton linters. The pulp is made into sheets that are then soaked in caustic soda, shredded, mixed with carbon disulfide and sodium hydroxide, and then melted to form a viscose solution. Finally, the mixture is extruded and spun into fibers. Rayon is valued for its silk-like texture, ability to be dyed bright colors, and pleasing drape.

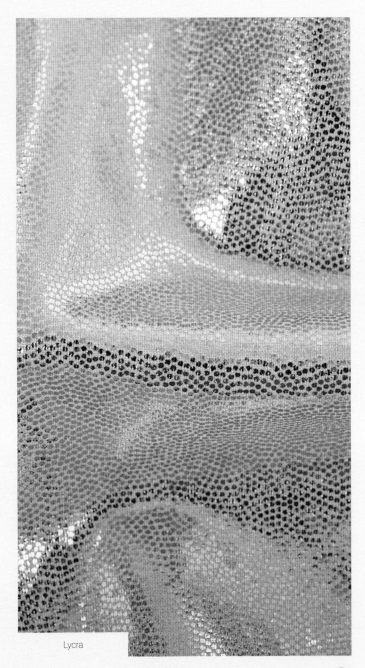

Lycra

Tencel

WOOLEN FIBERS

INTRODUCTION

Certain qualities of materials and fibers have always been reserved for the highest market levels. The most sought-after garments are generally those constructed from "noble fibers", including cashmere, vicuna, silk, and mohair. "Noble fiber" is the term used for the rarest, most expensive, and luxurious of yarns. The reason for their rarity may lie with the geographical inaccessibility of the yarn source; the relative scarcity of the breed, which might require certain climate conditions to survive; and the political complexities of the indigenous country. Noble fibers are used for both knitted and woven fabrics, from the fully fashioned twinsets by Scottish heritage brand Pringle that were popular in the 1950s to the luxurious double-breasted coat 101801, a design that remains unchanged and is offered in every winter collection since its inception in the 1980s by the Italian luxury label Max Mara. More accessible and widely used are those yarns spun from the wool of sheep. For centuries, sheep have provided mankind with both food and clothing; the fiber is durable, flexible, and ecologically sound. The type of wool that a sheep produces varies by breed, with Merino wool being the most desirable.

▲ The classic fully-fashioned cardigan is given a tailored twist with the addition of metallic buttons and a notched fully-fashioned collar in this advertisement for Scottish knitwear manufacturer Munrospun.

▶ Film star Janet Leigh epitomizes the 1940s sweater girl in a figure-hugging pastel pink sweater worn over a bullet bra.

Alpaca

ALPACA

The alpaca (*Vicugna pacos*) is a domesticated species of the South American camelid. Alpacas are kept in herds that graze on the level heights of the Andes at altitudes of between 11,483 feet (3,500 meters) and 16,404 feet (5,000 meters) above sea level throughout the year. They are bred specifically for their fiber, and have been domesticated for thousands of years. The fiber is lustrous and silky, and unlike sheep's wool, it bears no lanolin, making it hypoallergenic.

ANGORA

Angora, from the angora rabbit, is famous for its extreme softness and "fluffiness", known as the "halo". It is much warmer and lighter than wool thanks to the hollow core of the angora fiber. Typically, angora is used with other fibers such as wool to add substance and elasticity. The soft, seductive fibers in pastel colors, made up into a form-fitting garment, were a favorite of the 1940s pinup "sweater girls" such as Jane Russell and Marilyn Monroe.

CAMEL HAIR

The two-humped Bactrian camel from Outer Mongolia has a soft underlayer of hair that is warm yet light. The straighter and coarser outer coat is called guard hair. Camel hair, along with other specialty animal hair fibers, is collected during the molting season when the animals naturally shed their hairs. The hair is usually left undyed – it is a pleasing pale golden brown color. Camel hair is generally used for men and women's outerwear.

CASHMERE

The finest cashmere is from China, originating in a small district to the west of Beijing and also in Manchuria. The cashmere goat is provided with long, coarse outer hairs and a warm undercoat of fine fleece, and it is this that is plucked by hand from the underbellies of the animals. Each year, a male goat produces four ounces (113 grams), while a female produces two ounces (57 grams). A year's yield from four to six animals is needed to make a sweater.

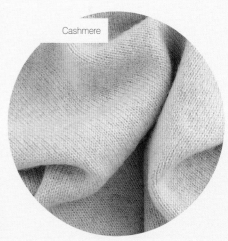
Cashmere

Camel Hair

LAMBSWOOL

Lambswool is wool sheared from a lamb between 11 and 12 months old, known as the "first-year clip". Sheep are sheared once per year, usually in the spring. The wool is trimmed in one piece, called a fleece. Sheep producers in the U.S. raise four breeds of sheep that produce fine wool, and 15 breeds that produce medium-grade and coarse wools. Though sheep producers exist in all states (except Hawaii), most sheep operations are in the West.

MERINO

One of the finest of wools, merino is noted for its whiteness and fineness and is, therefore, used for high-end knitwear. It is taken from the merino sheep, originally a Spanish breed, and is the result of the second-year clip. Australia produces around 43 percent of the world's merino wool. The fiber is ideal for performance sportswear, owing to its ability to regulate the temperature of the body, since it has excellent wicking properties.

MOHAIR

A "noble fiber" and one of the most durable, mohair is taken from the hair of the angora goat and is renowned for its high luster and surface smoothness. It also absorbs dye exceptionally well. Mohair is warm in winter, as it has great insulating properties, and remains cool in summer, owing to its moisture wicking properties. Mohair is not a soft fiber and, subsequently, it is mostly used for men's suiting and women's outerwear.

Shetland Wool

SHETLAND WOOL

Shetland wool is the clip of lambs from the Shetland Islands, situated north of the Scottish mainland, where the colder climate produces a heavier yarn. The earliest examples of Shetland yarn were left undyed in their natural colors of white, gray, and brown, and later color was introduced by dyeing the yarn with various lichens, or with madder and indigo imported to the island to produce red and blue. The patterned knitwear known as "Fair Isle" is constructed from Shetland yarn.

VICUÑA

The vicuña yields the finest, softest, and costliest natural fiber in the world. It is one of two wild South American camelids that live in the high alpine areas of the Andes. The animals are most commonly found in Bolivia, Peru, Chile, southwest Colombia, Ecuador, and Argentina. Vicuñas produce small amounts of extremely fine wool, which is shorn every three years. The fleece is sensitive to chemical treatment, so the wool is usually left its natural color.

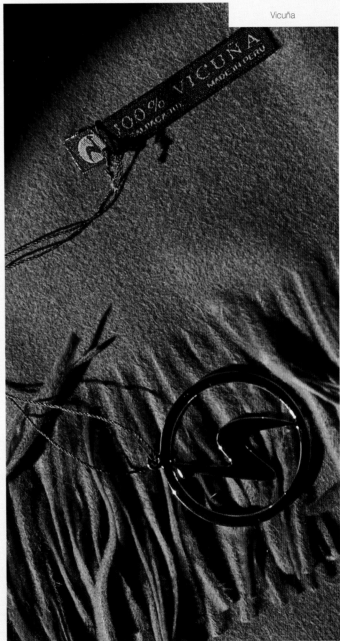

Vicuña

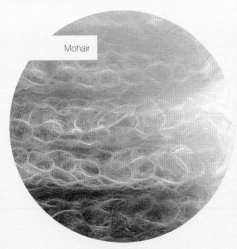

Mohair

FUR

INTRODUCTION

Fur is a controversial material in the Western fashion world, with its appeal varying over the decades. Fur tippets and stoles were an essential part of the female wardrobe in the 1930s and 1940s, and in the 1950s a mink coat was a status symbol – an item a successful husband bought for his appreciative wife. In 1965, the Italian luxury label Fendi, specializing in fur and leather goods, appointed Karl Lagerfeld as creative consultant. The designer introduced the notion of "fun fur" by shaving and dyeing the pelts, replacing the rather stuffy image of the status fur coat with fur that appealed to a younger market. However, during the 1990s fur was eschewed by designers – with infamous campaigns by PETA and Lynx spearheading the anti-fur movement.

The championing of fur by influential figures such as *Vogue*'s Anna Wintour at the beginning of the twenty-first century and the subsidization of emerging designers' runway shows by leading fur company Saga Furs have resulted in fur reemerging as a frequent element in the designer's armory. A more acceptable face of fur-wearing is vintage fur, with many women feeling less ethically compromised by wearing a long-dead mink from the 1930s, and this also jibes with the latest mania for vintage clothes. There are still some who maintain a strong moral stance against wearing fur – with Stella McCartney being the most high-profile anti-fur designer.

▲ Astrakan – the fleece of a newborn or fetal karakul lamb – is tailored into a waist-cinching coatdress by Raf Simons for Christian Dior for fall/winter 2012.

▶ The wide shoulders and masculinized silhouette of the late 1930s is fashioned from lustrous nutria fur, an alternative to the more expensive mink.

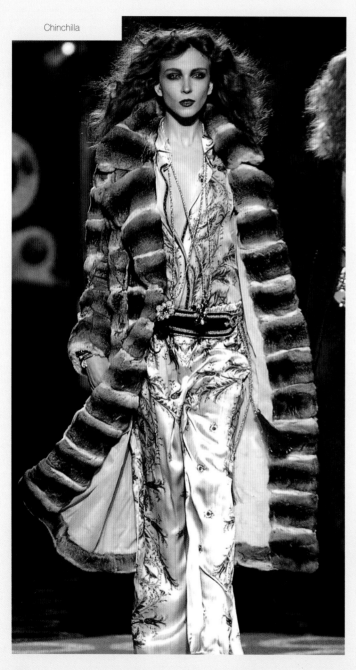

Chinchilla

BEAVER

A felted beaver fur hat of various styles was a fashionable piece of apparel for men from the sixteenth to the mid-nineteenth century. Its popularity meant that the European beaver was close to extinction by the early 1600s. Fortunately, the New World proved a valuable hunting ground, and demand was met by trappers in North America. Beaver fur, when treated, is an excellent material for hats, being glossy, waterproof, and resistant to rough, repeated wear.

CHINCHILLA

The chinchilla is a small mammal found in the Andes Mountains with a distinctive soft and fluffy fur, a quality derived from the extraordinarily high number of hairs per follicle – over 60. Wild chinchilla had been hunted to extinction by the late nineteenth century, so most chinchilla worn today is from farmed animals, including the coat worn by Madonna in 2006. Chinchilla coats are expensive, as many animals are required to make one coat.

Beaver

ERMINE

The white winter pelt of the ermine, a breed of stoat, is largely used today in ceremonial dress for both academics and peers in Britain's House of Lords. Its distinctive white fur with black tips was traditionally only permitted to be worn by royalty or the highest members of the Church, with sumptuary laws forbidding its use by anyone else in the Tudor period in Britain – a time when a new wealthy middle class was seen as becoming too grand.

FOX

Fox fur comes in many varieties and breeds, including silver. In the 1920s and 1930s screen sirens such as Carole Lombard popularized the silver-fox stole worn over the era's bias-cut silk-satin dresses. The fur tippet was also a favored accessory in outerwear, with the fox's head and tail remaining to show its origins. Fox continues to be a popular luxury textile, particularly as a trimming, where, for example, it is used to edge the hoods of parka jackets, as seen in the range of London-based designer Christopher Kane.

LEOPARD

Leopard skin is one of the most distinctive furs available and the most enduringly appealing, offering a frisson of exotica and the wild. The trend for leopard started with Elsa Schiaparelli's surreal collection of 1939, which included a hat made from the head of a leopard. A mania for leopard skin occurred when Jackie Kennedy wore an Oleg Cassini fur coat in 1961, provoking such a demand that leopards were driven to virtual extinction within a few years.

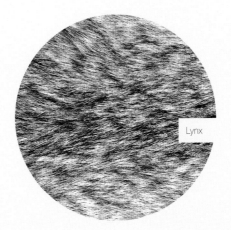

Lynx

LYNX

The appeal of lynx and bobcat fur means that the species has been hunted virtually to extinction; as such, the hunting of wild lynx is now illegal. The pelt is pale brown or gold and marked on the belly with dark brown spots – the paler the fur, the more valuable the pelt. The pelts are valued for their suppleness and soft, flexible skin, with larger furs preferred, as they give a more uniform appearance in the finished garment.

Leopard

Mink

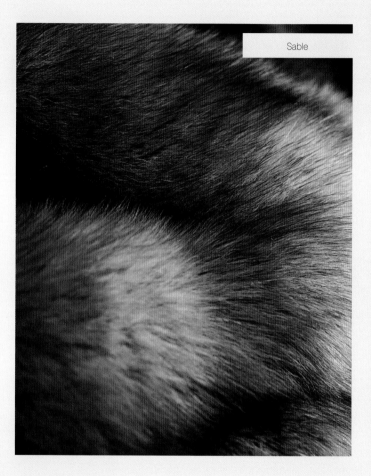

Sable

MINK

A mink coat is an enduring status symbol.
The mink is indigenous to North America
and the Far East, and there are two types of
mink commercially available: farmed and
wild, with the dark tones of the wild being
the most valued. Mink was first hunted in
the late nineteenth century but only became
fashionable in the twentieth. Dark brown is
the most recognizable shade, but breeders have
also developed lighter minks, with silver and
platinum shades.

MUSKRAT

A muskrat, or musquash, is a semi-aquatic
rodent native to North America. Its fur shares
similar qualities with beaver. It is prized for
its warmth and water resistance, as the animal
has a thick winter pelt to protect it against
the extreme conditions in its native territory.
During the early twentieth century, muskrat
was trimmed, dyed, and sold as Hudson Seal
Fur, as seal was considered more luxurious.
Today it is known as "the poor man's mink".

NUTRIA

The nutria is a rodent that was brought to
Louisiana in the nineteenth century. By the
1930s, its pelts were in high demand, worn
by stars such as Greta Garbo. In the 1980s,
when the population of nutria got out of
hand, a culling program began. Since the
nutria were being killed anyway, the pelt was
marketed as an ethical fur, and designers such
as Michael Kors and Oscar de la Renta began
experimenting with it. *See also* page 275.

PERSIAN LAMB (ASTRAKHAN)

Also called astrakhan, this is the fleece of the newborn or fetal karakul lamb, with fetal fur being the most desirable, as its texture is the most delicate. The fashion for astrakhan was first established during the nineteenth century, when the dark, shiny texture of the pelt fitted perfectly with the ornate aesthetic of the period. An inefficient way of procuring fur, since both the ewe and the lamb must be killed, it remains an expensive product.

RABBIT (CONEY)

Rabbit fur is both relatively inexpensive and easily available, used widely in high-end fashion as a trim on collars, hoods, and footwear. Rabbit is also the fur most typically used for the Russian-style cossack hat. Three types of fur are procured from a rabbit, including down hairs, which are the softest and therefore the most desirable. Rabbits are specially bred for their fur and are killed during the winter when the coat is at its thickest.

SABLE

A Slavic species of marten, the sable is one of the most valuable furs, prized for its smoothness even when stroked against the grain. It has been a luxury commodity for centuries, even passed as a gift between monarchs. Russia is its main exporter, producing both trapped and farmed sables for domestic and international markets. Rarely used for full garments now because of its value, sable is generally seen as a trim or for hats.

Astrakhan

SKIN

INTRODUCTION

Animal skins have been worn by humans since we first lost our full-body covering of hair. Prehistoric people would kill an animal and then tan the hide, fashioning crude body coverings from it to protect them from cold, heat, and sun. Examples of needles made of reindeer or mammoth bones have been found from the Paleolithic period, evidence that skin has been fashioned into garments for at least 40,000 years. Despite an alternative being found when fabrics were first crudely woven, skins have continued to be worn for various reasons, not least because the rarity of some animals makes their hide highly desirable.

Skins are generally put through a tanning process, using either vegetable or mineral methods. The raw skin is first cured in salt to halt the decomposition process before the skin is soaked in water for up to two days. Hair and fat are then removed, either manually, chemically, or both, in a bath of lime before further soaking to remove the lime solution. The hide is then tanned, either using traditional tannins (a vegetable tanning process) or by chrome tanning. The latter process is faster and produces a softer, more malleable end product.

▲ Identified by the metal pendant logo, the red Lady Dior formal frame bag is constructed from dyed and patented crocodile skin.

▶ Renowned for his enthusiastic adoption of all types of animal pelts and skins, Italian designer Robert Cavalli introduces a snakeskin trench coat partnered with a leopard-print shirt in his fall/winter collection of 2014–15.

CALFSKIN

Leather taken from a cow that was less than
three years old when slaughtered is known
as calfskin. The relative youth of the animal
means that the skin is soft and pliable,
especially when it is taken from the belly.
Its softness and fine grain make it suitable
for expensive luxury goods as well as for
bookbinding. The finest grade of calfskin is
known as *veau velours* in French, in reference
to its soft, velvetlike texture.

CHAMOIS

Chamois is a multipurpose leather that is not
just used on apparel but also extensively for
cleaning – whether jewels or dirty windows.
It is a very soft, porous leather valued for
its flexibility and warmth, especially in the
making of gloves. These properties also make
it a useful material for performance sportswear
– as it is sweat-absorbing and cushioning, it
makes the perfect fabric for cycling shorts.

CROCODILE/ALLIGATOR

There are many different species of crocodile,
including the porosus saltwater, which is used
by most couture houses. Each species provides
a different type of leather with specific
characteristics, with the most valuable part
being the belly. As the market for luxury goods
grows, fashion houses are struggling to keep
up with demand, and many companies such
as luxury brand LVMH Moët Hennessy are
acquiring their own farms in order to maintain
a quality supply directly.

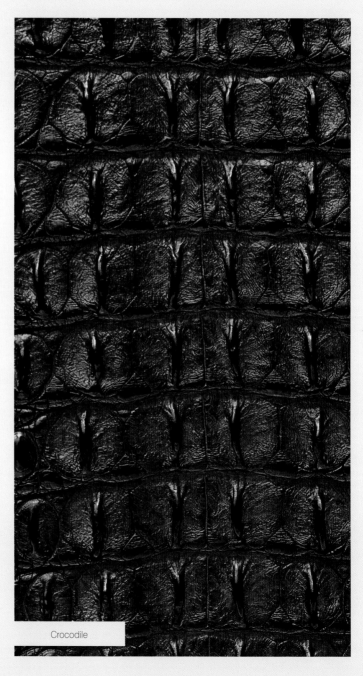

Crocodile

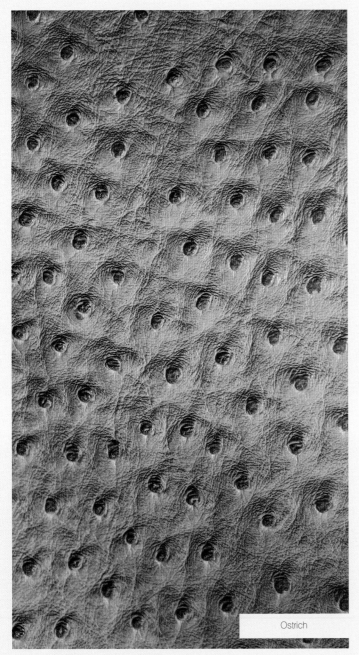

Ostrich

OSTRICH

At French luxury house Hermès, an ostrich-skin Birkin bag is the most expensive variety of an already extraordinarily expensive product – testament to the enduring desirability and exclusivity of this animal skin, the texture of which is made up of the emptied hair follicles that form bumps across its surface. The quality and price of the leather vary according to where on the body the skin has been harvested, with the skin closest to the head having the densest spot pattern.

PATENT

Patent leather was first invented in New Jersey by Seth Boyden in 1818. It is a lacquering process that gives the surface of the leather a glossy, reflective finish, which is impervious to water and easy to wipe clean. It is used primarily in footwear – especially men's formalwear – and a patent Mary Jane shoe is a perennial favorite for children's partywear. Patent leather usually comes in black, but the leather can be dyed any color.

PONYSKIN (COWHIDE)

Ponyskin, a by-product of the meat industry, can mean both the actual skin of a horse or pony or cowhide dyed to resemble it – the latter is the most common. First widely used in the 1960s, ponyskin has a shiny, flat-grain fur that combs in one direction. Classic ponyskin has large black and white spots or rough stripes but can also be found in any other color or pattern that naturally occurs on a horse.

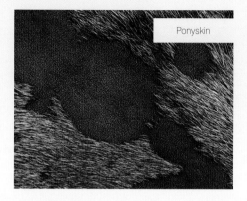

Ponyskin

SHAGREEN (CHAGRIN)

This term refers to any type of rough skin from the back of an animal (derived from the French for "rump"), but now refers to the skins of sharks or rays. Its rough and durable texture means it is the perfect leather for goods that are going to be handled repeatedly, such as bags or, historically, sword handles. It can also mean a type of silk that is woven to mimic the texture of sharkskin, known also as shagreen.

SHEARLING

A type of sheepskin that comes from a yearling lamb that has been shorn only once, which means the wool fibers are more uniform in length and shape. The pelt is worn with the skin on the outside and the shorn wool fibers on the inside of the garment, although this can be reversed. Shearling coats in a leather biker-jacket style have been popular in the 2010s, designed by influential French luxe-hippie label Isabel Marant (see opposite, far right, fall/winter 2012).

SHEEPSKIN

A type of leather in which the wool fibers are left intact, sheepskin makes a perfect insulating material, with the dual benefit of waterproof skin and the warmth of a wool fiber. In clothing, it is used for outerwear or hats, making a bulky silhouette. The sheepskin boot was a ubiquitous form of footwear in the early twentieth century and continues to be popular today. The skin can be processed, with the fibers being chemically straightened, to resemble beaver or seal fur.

Sheepskin

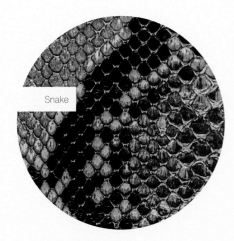

Snake

Shearling

SNAKE

The world's largest consumer of snakeskin products is Europe, with European fashion houses importing over 100 million dollars worth each year. Snakes are rarely farmed commercially, as they are too expensive to rear in captivity, so they are mostly hunted in their natural habitat – in places such as Malaysia and Indonesia. Many designers, particularly Gucci and Jimmy Choo, regularly use snakeskin in their collections. Snakeskin has a fine ombre pattern of mottled stripes in either silver or cream tones.

SUEDE

The term suede comes from the French *gants de Suède* – Swedish gloves. It is a type of leather that has been treated to give it a napped, soft texture and it is harvested from the belly of an infant animal – usually lamb or calf, although other animals can be used. The skin is turned inside-out, with the waterproof layer facing inwards. The surface facing outwards is then ground down, revealing the softer, velvetlike layer below.

SILKS

INTRODUCTION

One of the "noble" fibers, silk is valued for its
strength, lightness, luster, and ability to carry
vivid color. The domestication of the *Bombyx
mori* moth started nearly 7,000 years ago in
China, when silkworms began to be cultivated
for the gossamer strands contained within their
cocoons. As no single fiber is uniform, in cross
section the fiber is more triangular than round,
with the prism-like surface intensifying the
effect of any color. The weight of silk may range
from gossamer-thin to thick satin, its qualities
varying from the crisp malleability of tussah
silk to the figure-hugging of silk jersey.

Underpinned by the notion of exclusivity,
silk was first used in fashion for the knitted
stockings worn by European courtiers and
royalty in the sixteenth century. Costly and
elaborately patterned silks were produced in
the silk manufacturing centers of Italy and
Spain in the seventeenth century and London's
Spitalfields in the eighteenth century. With the
first successful power looms for plain weaves,
such as taffeta, operating in Switzerland by the
early 1860s, silk became more widely available.
Despite the invention of "art silk", made by
polymer chemists mainly from fossil fuels in
the 1930s, silk nevertheless remains the most
desirable of fibers.

▲ The shocking pink of this evening gown, designed in 1953 by Elsa Schiparelli,
is overlaid with a transparent white organza silk that is embellished with a scattering
of floral sprigs.

▶ The sculptural qualities of gazar are deployed by Parisian couturier Cristóbal
Balenciaga for his signature mid-century, high-waisted bubble dress and cloak
from 1961.

Crepe de Chine

CHAPA

Variously known as Chapa, Chappa, Chappe, or Schappe silk, the name is derived from a Swiss term for waste. Chapa silk is a weft-ribbed cloth composed of the coarse outer and the flimsy innermost filament, together with defective cocoons. These are converted into a form of silk staple that is spun rather than "thrown" after a malodorous degumming process of fermentation, known as schapping. The waste-product nature of this silk means that it is relatively cheap.

CHIFFON

At only 0.4–0.5 oz (12–15 grams) per yard (meter), silk chiffon is a plain weave, with a slight crepe handle that has a sheer open mesh, resulting from the use of alternate S- and Z-twisted threads of filament silk. It can also be produced in slightly heavier weights – around 0.6 oz (17 grams) – as a two-color shot cloth. Although a lightweight fabric, chiffon is capable of supporting heavy beading, making it popular with designers for luxurious eveningwear.

CREPE DE CHINE

The surface of crepe de chine gains its rough texture from the filament yarns that have been highly twisted in either an S or an Z direction. The opposition of torque between adjacent threads leads to small hollows and curls in the weft behavior, creating the crepe handle of the fabric. The fabric was notably popular in the 1920s and 1930s for eveningwear thanks to its ability to cling to the outline of the figure, particularly when cut on the bias.

DUPIONI

A crisp, relatively coarse fabric with an
irregular surface, dupioni is generally used
for semi-tailored garments such as women's
shirts, jackets, and bridalwear. It is produced
from silk formed by two worms united to spin
a single cocoon. The thread is rougher than
regular silk, and contains many irregularities
where the fibers from the two cocoons
are combined. The material has almost no
stretching ability, which means that very exact
measurements are required before cutting out
any pattern.

GAZAR

Gazar (also known as gazaar) is a heavy,
stiff silk capable of holding large folds
or shapes, with a resistant quality and a
smooth, matte texture. It is made with
high-twist double yarns woven as one. The
Parisian couturier Cristóbal Balenciaga
developed gazar in collaboration with Swiss
textile firm Alexander. Renowned for the
sculptural quality of his clothes and masterful
manipulation of fabric, Balenciaga featured
silk gazar in his collections throughout the
1960s, until he retired in 1968. *See also*
page 285.

Gazar

Chiffon

Georgette

GEORGETTE

Silk georgette has a grainy texture with a "dry" feel. It is a lightweight fabric constructed with a twisted yarn, usually with 2,000 to 3,600 tpm (twists per meter), generally made of two threads of raw silk. It is heavier than chiffon and similar to silk crepe, but it is not as soft or lustrous as crepe. Georgette is durable but snags easily. It drapes very fluidly and falls into soft ripples.

ORGANDY

A light, fine, white cotton fabric with a stiff, translucent finish, particularly suitable for garment details such as cuffs and collars. The characteristic stiffness of plain-woven, lightweight organdy was originally produced by retaining an amount of residual silk gum (sericin protein) on the filaments from the silkworm cocoon through to the finishing processes of the constructed cloth, including dyeing and printing. The transparent quality of silk organdy lends itself to use for evening and wedding gowns.

ORGANZA

Heavier and stiffer than organdy with a crisp handle, organza is a sheer, thin, open-weave transparent fabric that holds its form well when making dramatic shapes. It has a smooth, flat finish; is strong and durable; and gets its stiffness from tightly twisted yarns. It requires special sewing techniques for seams, facings, and hems, as they can be seen from the outside of the garment. It is mostly used for interfacing, bridal veils, and undergowns.

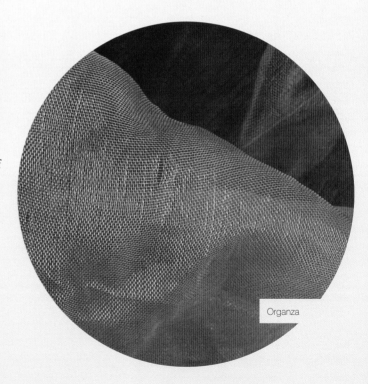

Organza

Pongee

Shantung

PONGEE

Also known as China silk or Habutai silk, this is a plain-weave silk first used as a lining for kimonos. It was originally handwoven of single warp yarns and filling yarns of hand-reeled silk, which made it slightly irregular. Habutai usually has a natural, ecru color and is known to wrinkle less than other fabrics. It sews relatively easily and doesn't show pin marks. It is best for lingerie, dresses, blouses, and light jackets.

SHANTUNG

This silk is named after a province in eastern China, where in its original form it was made from the undomesticated *Bombyx croesi* worm. Shantung silk has an uneven texture and a handwoven appearance. Later it came to be made from silk waste and was one of the simple cloths power-woven in Shanghai and Japan during the interwar period. It shares many characteristics of silk dupioni, but is finer and features less prominent slubs.

THAI SILK

American entrepreneur Jim Thompson founded the Thai Silk Company in 1948 as a cottage industry to help the post-war Thai economy. His workers produced handwoven cloth in bright colors and tones that had an immediate appeal for post-war designers including Parisian-based couturier Pierre Balmain. Costume designer Irene Sharaff used Thai silks for *The King and I* (1951), disseminating the shimmering silks to a wider audience. By the 1970s, Thompson's factory was the largest handweaving factory in the world.

TUSSAH SILK

A type of wild silk harvested from the *Antheraea* species of moth. Since the worm is not grown in a controlled environment, the moth hatches from the cocoon and interrupts the filament length, resulting in short and coarse fibers. Tussah silk was closely associated with London store Liberty & Co and thus with fashions of the aesthetic and artistic movements of the late nineteenth century. Mariano Fortuny used tussah silk for his series of flowing, figure-hugging Delphos dresses in the 1920s.

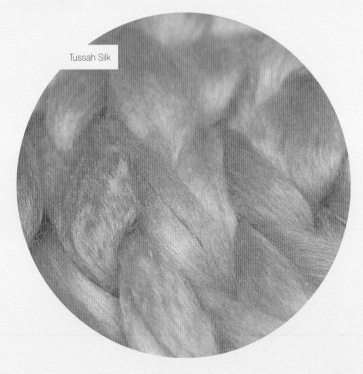

Tussah Silk

KNITTED FABRICS

INTRODUCTION

Knitting is one of the oldest techniques for making fabric, and one of the earliest to become mechanized, with the first knitting machine invented by Reverend William Lee in 1586. Knitting was a key manufacturing industry during the Industrial Revolution, and knitting technologies today continue to evolve. These are becoming increasingly specialized, and, as such, knitting manufacture is increasingly diversified.

Most manufacturers buy in the yarns, although there are some exceptions, such as American Apparel. Knitting can be executed on anything from a simple pair of knitting needles to computerized machines with 4,000 needles.

Traditional knitting meant only simple garments could be made – a sweater or a pair of socks. Modern technologies mean it is possible to have form-fitting, easy-flowing garments that offer a greater degree of movement than more restrictive weaves – clothes that reflect the greater physical freedoms experienced in the twentieth and twenty-first centuries. The weight of a knit is measured by its gauge, and its gauge depends on the number of needles per inch that the knitting machine has. The finer and closer the knit, the greater the number of needles.

▲ Subverting a simple purl-plain stitch, iconoclast designer Alexander McQueen fashions a chunky cropped top with a tubular hood for his "Overlook" collection for fall/winter 1999.

▶ Emphasizing the fully-fashioned lines of the raglan sleeves, German designer Jil Sander creates a statement sweater for fall/winter 2012.

ARAN KNIT

The Aran Islands, off the west coast of Ireland, are renowned for their distinctive cable knitwear. Designed to be worn by the fishermen that operated off the coast, these garments are hardwearing, bulky, and warm, and were, originally, waterproof, as they were knitted from untreated wool that still contained its natural lanolin oils. The predominant colorway is cream, although natural dyes are sometimes used. Aran sweaters were popular worldwide in the 1950s and 1960s, favored by fans of the Beat Poets.

ARGYLE

A distinctive diamond pattern knit with overlapping diamond lines, strongly associated with a certain type of golfing sweater. The design is derived from the tartan patterns of the Argyle clan of Scotland, but it was then appropriated by sports clothing manufacturers. Argyle knits were worn by the Duke of Windsor, a great golfing fan, and he, along with Pringle of Scotland, popularized the design in the 1920s in both the U.S. and the U.K.

BOHUS KNITTING

Bohus knitting is a style of fine-gauge hand-knitting devised in Sweden in the 1930s. The state, addressing the economic depression, set up a home industry based around hand-knitting in the town of Bohus. The first products were simple gloves or socks in plain yarn. However, the patterns became more intricate, and the yarn used, such as angora, became more expensive as their reputation grew. Production reached its peak in the 1950s, the era of the sweater girl.

Aran Knit

Bohus Knitting

CABLE STITCH

A knitting stitch that produces a series of columns in the fabric, which resemble heavy rope cord or cables, created by passing two or more groups of adjacent wales over and under each other. Cable knit is commonly used for sweaters and hosiery, with the padded texture of the fabric creating an exceptionally insulated garment. A cable-knit jumper is a key part of the preppy look devised by brands such as Ralph Lauren.

FAIR ISLE

Fair Isle knitting has come to mean any knitwear design with horizontal layers of geometric patterns, whether hand- or frame-knitted, but it also refers to a technique of knitting developed on the Fair Isles, where fine yarns are doubled up to produce a warm but lightweight fabric suitable for the harsh climate. Fair Isle is traditionally knitted from colors that could be made on the islands, such as madder, indigo, brown, and yellow.

FULLY FASHIONED

This is a machine-knitted fabric in which a garment is shaped during the knitting process. It is a useful method of production for when the close fit of a garment is required, as the piece of fabric falls from the machine in a more or less fully formed shape – valuable when making hosiery, seamless knitted garments, and tightly fitted sweaters. Fully fashioned knitwear and hosiery are made on a flatbed knitting machine and then seamed.

Cable Stitch

Intarsia

HIGH-PILE KNITS

A type of jersey knit that mimics the appearance of fur, which appears in retail stores and in collections such as Louis Vuitton's 2011 fall/winter collection. The process involves the insertion of a sliver (a loosely twisted strand of fibers) into the knit material as yarn passes through the needles, so that it is caught up within the knit structure. The fabric can then be dyed or printed with the appropriate animal skin design.

INTARSIA

This term is derived from the Italian word for inlaid design. Intarsia is knitted on a flatbed machine set up with special yarn carriers and is made up of solid blocks of color within the fabric. Most intarsia knits are jersey in structure, as intarsia is easier to make with only one needle bed in action. This style of knitting is useful for color blocking and for inserting areas of text into a knitted design.

JERSEY

Originally a simple knitted fabric with a flat, plain surface on one side and a textured reverse, produced on a single set of knitting needles. First manufactured on the island of Jersey, this fabric was originally made of wool, but today it has has a looser definition, meaning any knitted fabric without a rib knitted on a plain-knit machine. Because the knit can unravel if a single yarn breaks, jersey fabrics are susceptible to runs and holes.

LACE STITCH

Apart from its meaning as a type of lace
weaving stitch, lace stitch is the technique
whereby a plain knitted fabric is given an
open or raised texture by the transference
of a needle loop to an adjacent needle,
mimicking the effect of lace. In the nineteenth
century, instigated by Queen Victoria's
fondness for it, Shetland knitted lace became
extremely fashionable, famous for being so fine
that a shawl could be easily drawn through a
wedding ring.

POINTELLE

A delicate rib fabric with a small openwork
design, typically executed in a chevron pattern
that mimics the look of lace, created by the use
of transfer stitches as the garment is knitted.
Pointelle is generally used as an accent on a
garment, adding texture and interest, rather
than fully covering the body. It is commonly
used in undergarments, and hosiery. Its open
texture makes it a suitable knitted fabric for
warmer climates.

PURL-KNIT (GARTER STITCH)

The most basic of all knitting techniques,
purl-knit fabrics are a combination of both
knit stitches and purl stitches. They are
produced on flat or circular machines, or by
hand, with a double-headed set of needles that
move from side to side of the knitted fabric.
The resultant fabric has a regular surface, with
the purl stitches standing out from the knit,
and little elasticity. Its flat structure makes it
suitable for sweaters.

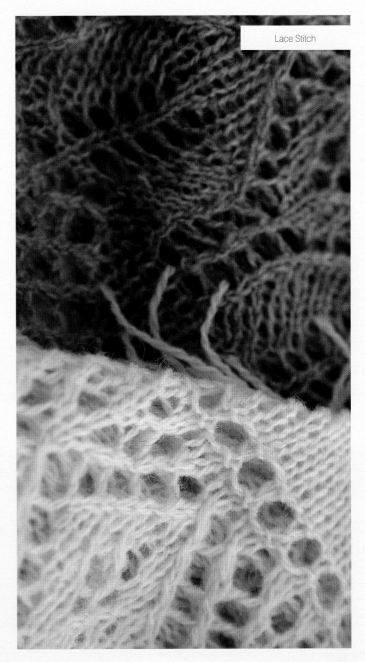

Lace Stitch

Waffle Knit

RASCHEL KNIT

This warp-knit technique is derived from the name of the raschel machine, which can produce an almost infinite number of patterns, from a fine lace-like material to heavy blankets, although the fabric created is often coarser than those knitted by other means. The machine has one or two needle bars where the fabric is pulled down from the knitting area. Raschel knits are often used for performance sportswear and foundation garments, when the yarn mix includes spandex.

RIB KNIT

Ribbed knitting has an elasticity that is useful for parts of a garment that need to stretch and snap back into place, such as collars, cuffs, and hems. It consists of columns of knit stitches alternating with columns of purl stitches, knitted by hand or machine. The degree of rib can vary from barely discernible to distinctive, with most garments, such as ribbed roll-neck sweaters, having vertical ribs around ¼ inch (6 mm) wide.

WAFFLE KNIT

Also known as honeycomb fabric, waffle knit is often used for thermal underwear, as it is a good insulator. It is formed by alternating knits and purls to make raised bumps in the fabric, which join up to make squares as the fabric is formed. The waffle-knit sweater has become popular in recent years, appearing in collections by designers such as Isabel Marant, with an oversized men's waffle knit adding a textural androgyny to a look.

WARP KNIT

Unlike most weft knits, warp-knit fabrics are much more rigid, flat, and close, and are often claimed to be run-resistant. This is due to the yarns running lengthways but in a zig-zag pattern so that loops are formed by crossing over two lengths or wales instead of one. Specific examples of this type of fabric include Tricot and Milanese. Their sturdy nature makes them perfect for hosiery and other hardwearing garments.

WHOLEGARMENT KNITTING

Technology today has advanced to the degree that it is now possible to knit entire seamless garments on one machine. This process was first commercially viable when technology became more readily available in the 1990s. This method of manufacture is incredibly efficient, as there is no need for cut-and-sew assembly, reducing the wastage of yarns. While designers have embraced the possibilities of wholegarment knitting, the main bulk of seamless knitting produces sportswear, underwear, sleepwear, and swimwear.

Rib Knit

Raschel Knit

WEAVES

INTRODUCTION

Weave technology has been evolving since at least 7000 BCE. The craft of weaving has subsequently occupied the attention and industry of every major civilization since, and the vocabulary of trade in woven textiles has infused every tongue with esoteric and evocative terminology – from bombazine to tenterhooks, from dimity to dupioni.

At a basic level, weaving is a simple binary technique: each thread is placed either under or over the path of other threads that it encounters at a right angle. However, any attempt to classify the variety of woven fabrics has to first distinguish the basic structure underlying any permutations of fiber, coloration, density, or finish. It is also necessary to identify the orientation (transverse or longitudinal) of individual component threads as they are formed into cloth on the loom. Warp yarns pass along the length of a fabric; weft yarns are inserted as filling across the warp as groups of warp threads are lifted to create a shed. The conventional categories are plain, twill, satin, and jacquard, but when variations in fiber and color, in the sequences and thicknesses of threads selected, and in applications of after-treatments are factored in, innumerable fabrics of incredible diversity can be created.

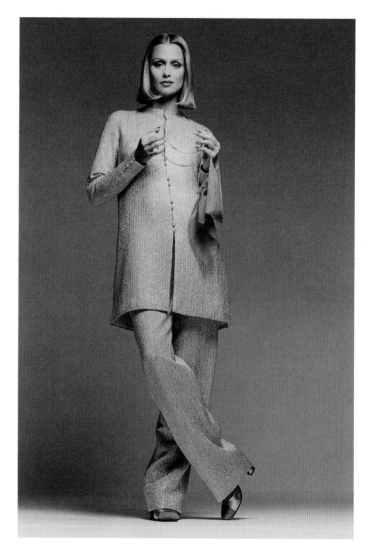

▲ American model Lauren Hutton exemplifies the pared-down minimalism of designer Halston in this lamé tunic-and-pants combination.

▶ Actress Sarah Jessica Parker wears a classic grey bouclé suit from Chanel's autumn/winter 2008 collection. The surface of the tweed has been distressed and antiqued, particularly at the elbows, giving the luxury garment a deconstructed feel.

Brocade

BARATHEA

Wool and silk barathea are two distinct materials; the pebbly, broken twill fabric of silk barathea is used for neckties, whereas the more widespread wool barathea is used for tailored formal attire – military uniforms, blazers, and black-tie suitings. Woven with a twill hopsack structure in worsted spun wool, the fine, granular texture produces a matte surface with a faint, irregular twill. Both warp and weft are comprised of two-ply (folded) yarns, adding further subtle texture.

BOUCLÉ

A bouclé fabric has a complex surface texture derived from the curling loops created in the component bouclé yarns within the cloth structure. These yarns are composed of multiple bundles of fibers, of which one bundle advances into the twist at a faster rate than the others – buckling up into prominent loops alongside the slower core in the twist. This tactile dimension has been exploited in coats and sweaters – and in the classic Chanel cardigan suit.

BROCADE

Brocades are elaborately figured, multicolored cloths woven on a jacquard loom, allowing warp threads to be lifted individually to produce patterning. The fabric is generally lustrous and highly ornamented. Raised areas can be produced, or alternatively, warp threads can render color imagery by floating above a simple base weave. Historically, brocades were symbolic of luxury and wealth, but contemporary digital production methods mean that their use is now widespread, particularly for eveningwear.

CHAMBRAY

A fine, plain weave, chambray is generally made with cotton, having a dyed color in the warp and natural or white in the weft filling. This results in a very small-scale mottled check pattern, as the two shades cross in the woven structure. There are a variety of permutations in the patterning that may be produced with the two component yarn colors. The name originates from the French commune of Cambrai, which also produced cambric fabrics.

CLOQUÉ

Fabric with a raised, puckered surface can be described as cloqué, which is created by layering two cloths that are intermittently connected. Either by exploiting differential shrinkage – for instance, using wool in opposition to cotton – or by placing additional structural elements in only one element, the cloth is forced into relief with embossed areas, patterned by jacquard selection mechanisms. Variations in cloqué fabrics are used across the spectrum of clothing, from swimwear to lamé evening gowns for the red carpet.

CRETONNE

Slightly heavier than chintz, cretonne is a cotton weave most frequently associated with bold, floral-printed upholstery fabrics. Intermittently, it is used in plain weave or twill as a sturdy printed fabric for fashion. In the early 1920s, day dresses and even men's resort shirts were made with flamboyant large prints on cretonne. The cloth originated as a white fabric, with a warp of hemp and a weft of linen, in the French town of Creton.

Chambray

DAMASK

Although there are exceptions, damask fabrics, which originated in Damascus in the Middle Ages, are usually monochrome. They rely on the variegation in the reflective quality of the surface structure of the material to reveal the figurative jacquard patterning, with identical yarn incorporated in the warp and weft axes of the cloth. The cloth is reversible – exchanging matte and shiny zones between faces. Originally in silk, damask cloth is now produced in many fibers.

Damask

DOBBY (WEAVING) FABRIC

Dobby fabric is a relatively simple woven cloth produced on a dobby loom. This type of loom can be fully automatic or operated manually by artisan workers. Warp threads are distributed, for pattern selection purposes, through arrangements of heddles grouped within up to 30 separate shafts. When one or more shafts is raised, the heddles will lift the warp threads, making a gap through which the weft (filling) yarn can be inserted to create a pattern.

Dobby

DUCHESSE SATIN

Duchesse satin is a warp-faced satin fabric that is characteristically stiff, lustrous and substantial, usually woven in silk or rayon acetate – both glossy, continual filaments. In duchesse satin, an 8-end satin float repeat is used in the warp, optimizing the ability of the filament yarn to reflect light by minimizing the interlocking of individual floats into the weft. Duchesse is favored for formal dress occasions, from wedding dresses to red carpet gowns.

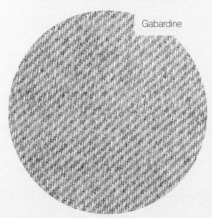

Gabardine

FIL'COUPÉ

When isolated pattern motifs are required on a sheer fabric, the conventional method is to leave the pattern yarns free to float in warp or weft direction between motifs. The distance from one motif to the next dictates the length of float, and at a certain point this becomes too weak and compromises the transparency of the ground. This problem is resolved by the simple act of cutting away the superfluous loose yarns to make fil'coupé.

FLANNEL

Flannel is a soft wool cloth that has been subjected to various finishing processes – washing, milling, calendering and pressing – to first lift a "nap" of fibers from the body of the yarn in the weave and then to compact the nap back into the surface, obscuring the woven structure. In the middle decades of the twentieth century, the cloth was a staple in the male wardrobe, becoming synonymous with pants (trousers), the semi-formal weekend attire of most males.

GABARDINE

A generic term for firmly woven warp-faced cloth in 2/1 and 2/2 twills raking steeply across the face of the cloth, made from wool or cotton as well as blends of various fibers. It also refers to a water-resistant fabric, patented by Thomas Burberry in 1888. Extant methods of chemical proofing – including rubber – had been applied to cloth, but Burberry's innovation was to proof the yarn (originally fine cotton) before weaving it into a breathable twill.

Fil'coupé

GINGHAM

Gingham is characterized by a simple small-scale check created by the intersection of identical warp and weft stripes in blocks of a single color, cut by equal blocks of white threads. The result is a balanced checkerboard of solid white squares and solid colored squares, separated by half-tone squares of the woven mixture of white and color. In cotton, gingham is used traditionally as a shirting, for summer childrenswear, or as an element of Western style.

GROSGRAIN

Inserting a coarse weft filling across a fine warp creates plain-weave fabrics with a ribbed or corded texture. Between taffeta at the lighter end of the scale, and ottoman at the heavy, grosgrain displays a distinctive furrowed appearance, whether it is in a wide acetate ribbon for millinery trims or as yardage in silk for ties and ball gowns. Additional surface texture can be created by impressing moiré patterns into the repetitive grid of the weft ribs.

HOUNDSTOOTH CHECK

Houndstooth check is Scottish in origin and produced in a wide variety of fibers. It is one of the core color-and-weave patterns in the lexicon of classic tailoring fabrics, with its small-scale tessellated pattern in two colors, created by interlocking striped bands of warp and weft, grouped respectively in blocks of four ends opposed to four picks of alternating colors. It is synonymous with haute couture garments of the 1950s and with Sonia Rykiel's collections.

Gingham

Houndstooth Check

IKAT

Ikat is an ancient Malaysian method of weaving that uses a resist-dye method on the fibers before they are woven, with areas of the warp that will make the desired pattern being sealed off – either bound tightly with yarn, or obscured by wax or clay so that they remain undyed when they are placed in the dye bath. When woven, distortion arises at the edges of the dyed pattern, making an intriguing shimmering effect.

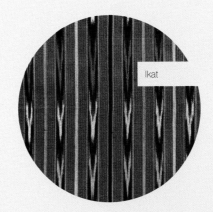

Ikat

JACQUARD

Before the invention by Joseph Marie Jacquard of his eponymous punch card selection system in the nineteenth century, any complex weaves required the laborious hand selection of groups of warp threads on a draw loom. Since then, the term jacquard has evolved to signify not only the selection mechanism but also any resulting fabrics that display a level of versatility of free design. Digital jacquard devices have now overtaken the purely mechanical processes of the original.

Jaquard

KENTE CLOTH

Kente cloth from Ghana, traditionally worn by Ashanti royalty but appropriated by hip-hop groups in the 1980s, is the product of a method of strip-weaving. The cloth is assembled from long narrow bands of geometrically patterned weave that have alternating sections of longitudinal (warp-faced) and transverse (weft-faced) stripes and color blocks. The strips, usually in cotton or silk, are aligned in such a way that creates a continual checkerboard fabric from the component strips.

Kente Cloth

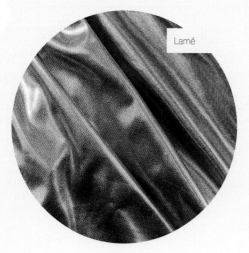

Lamé

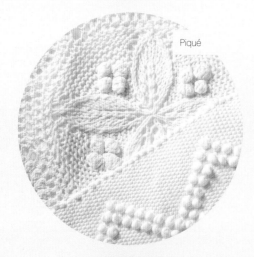

Piqué

Satin

LAMÉ

Lamé is the term generally used for any metallized cloth. The metallized yarn is maintained in flat ribbon form on the surface of the fabric in order to retain as much reflective quality as possible, evoking the theatrical exuberance necessary for the kitsch golden tuxedo suit photographed for the cover of Elvis Presley's *Greatest Hits* album of 1959. Lamé – be it silver or gold – has become synonymous with showbiz extravagance, a mainstay of glitzy Las Vegas entertainment.

LAWN

Cotton and linen garments have traditionally been produced in a sheer, plain-weave fabric known as lawn, which was also the classic material for handkerchiefs before the advent of paper tissues. The cotton yarns may be simply "carded" or given the secondary, additional treatment of "combing", which produces a stronger, finer and more lustrous yarn that generates the same characteristics in the fine cloth. The fabric is used white or dyed, and is often printed.

PIQUÉ

The term piqué means cotton piqué, traditionally used in formal shirtfronts owing to its ability to absorb starch. Piqué is a dobby weave with a similar structure to the heavier Bedford cord. Warp ribs are created as alternate groups of warp threads make plain-weave sections with the weft, before the next alternate warp section has the weft floating behind, sometimes bulked with a warp wadding yarn. Piqué variations include waffle, birdseye and Marcella, which is double faced.

SATEEN

Sateen denotes a cloth that is predominantly faced by weft floats, their intermittent binding into the warp arranged in such a way as to avoid legibility as a defined twill texture and to maximize the presence of the weft yarn on the face of the fabric. The resulting surface, particularly if produced in crisp cotton, has a certain degree of sheen, as the dominant, compacted surface of floats generates little shadow from texture.

SATIN

To create a glossy surface, satin fabrics are constructed with warp-faced floats that lie as an almost continual surface of reflecting yarn filaments. Satin, as a term, is used loosely to characterize any cloth with a smooth finish that catches the light in any fiber. Thus, silk satin, rayon satin and polyester satin are all possible. Technically, satin is a weave structure that has a dominance of warp floats anchored into the cloth in a scattered configuration.

SEERSUCKER

The term seersucker derives from the Persian words *šir o šakar*, meaning, literally "milk and sugar", which suggests the contrast between the smooth and textured areas in this classic summery cotton cloth. The puckered areas can be either simple stripes or checks, with colors in a corresponding distribution. If two separate warps are woven together under different tensions, the sections that are less taut will become corrugated. Alternately, sections can contain yarns of differentiated shrinkage in order to create puckered checks.

Seersucker

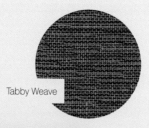

Tabby Weave

Taffeta

SERGE

Serge is a piece-dyed 2/2-twill cloth that has the same weight and number of woolen threads showing on the surface in both warp and weft directions. Loose surface fibers are then removed by singeing or shearing to expose the texture of the twill running from bottom left to top right. Serge occasionally occurs in fibers other than wool – its name derives from the Latin *serica*, meaning "silk" – but the dominant usage is in wool for military uniforms.

SHARKSKIN

The terms sharkskin and pick-and-pick fabric are interchangeable, with the latter more commonly used by British tailors. The cloth is produced with worsted yarns, including wool and mohair. The structure is normally 2/2 twill, with both warp and weft threads alternating in color in each axis, either from white to black or, perhaps, from navy to charcoal, which produces the appearance of a hybrid tonality with one or more colors intensifying as the cloth falls into shadowed drape.

TABBY WEAVE

Tabby (plain) weave is the most basic of woven cloths. Alternate (even) warp threads are raised to create a shed, permitting the insertion of the lateral weft thread across the cloth. This weft pick is beaten up (compacted) with the comb-like reed, then trapped by lowering the shed and first warp selection. The next pick is inserted when the alternate (odd) warp threads are raised. This simple binary sequence is repeated throughout the cloth production.

Tapestry

Tartan

TAFFETA

Taffeta is a plain weave that uses yarn of equal thickness, but with the warp more densely packed than the weft. This results in a fabric with an indistinct horizontal ribbing that is used for linings or, if woven more closely, for dresses, often with a subtle shot-effect generated by the interplay of warp and weft colors. The crisp, rustling character of the fabric is best achieved with filament yarns such as spun silk or acetate rayon.

TAPESTRY

Tapestry is a labor-intensive process, in which colored threads – anchored into a hidden infrastructure either with shuttles, needles or fingers – are used to create decorative and narrative configurations. Throughout the evolution of industrialized textile methods, the pursuit of labor- and cost-saving processes has focused on mechanizing tapestry production, with jacquard mechanisms and digital control finally allowing this, with some looms having as many as 10,000 individually activated warp "hooks" for weft patterning.

TARTAN

While there are many checkered cloths, those called Scottish tartans have specific characteristics. True tartan is woven from wool, with the same stripes in both warp and weft axes, constructed in 2/2 twill weave. The distribution of colored threads in the warp of an individual tartan has a regular repeat, within which there are points where the color sequence is mirrored. When this same sequence is inserted across the twilled warp, the pattern is symmetrical.

Tweed

TWEED

Tweed is a type of rough twill, originally woven in Scotland and Ireland and traditionally associated with aristocratic outdoor pursuits thanks to its durability and water resistance. Harris and Donegal tweeds are both heritage fabrics valued for their naturally dyed tones and complex patterns derived from fiber blends. Tweed, particularly the Norfolk jacket, was adopted by aspirational middle classes in the twentieth century, and in the early twenty-first century a tweed sports jacket is a key part of the hipster "young fogey" look.

TWILL

There are a variety of widely used fabrics – from silk foulard to denim – that fall within the general description of "twill". This term essentially means any woven fabric with a diagonal texture created by the dominance of surface floats progressively moving either to the left or right along the cloth. This construction means that more yarn floats across the surface than is interlocked into the weave, making it denser and more resilient than plain weave.

VELOUR

Although *velours* is simply the French word for velvet, velour has gradually come to mean something separate. Until the 1970s, velour was a heavy, cotton velvet used for plush drapery. This usage was subverted in the hippie era, when men and women alike adopted the cloth for dandyish apparel. Since that period, several fabric types have come to be known as velour, the name suggesting the handle and behavior of the cloth rather than simply the technical structure.

Twill

VELVET

Velvet is identified by the short, dense pile of its surface that is created in a variety of fibers and by various means. Historically, plain silk velvet was produced on looms with two separate warp beams under different tensions. The ground cloth was interlaced from one beam, while the yarn from the second beam was elevated by grooved metal blades standing vertically in the shed. The bridging loops were then cut with a blade across the grooved metal to make the pile.

WORSTED

In use for over a thousand years, worsted – originally a geographical reference to Worstead in Norfolk – has become a portmanteau term for both yarn spun by particular methods from long-staple, parallel-combed wool, and for cloths made from such yarns. Worsted spinning is seen as a premium technology, producing – with its additional processes of ginning and combing – fine, strong yarns to the extent that worsteds, worsted suitings and fine worsteds are considered luxury fabrics.

Worsted

Velvet

NON-WOVEN FABRICS

INTRODUCTION

The common denominator of all textiles that are termed "non-woven" is the simple absence of any need to organize fibers into yarns before they are converted into fabric. This direct non-woven approach of assembling fibers straight into textiles occurred pre-industrially, as well as in the era of cutting-edge polymer engineering, and is generally dependent on a type of friction or application of heat or water that amalgamates the fibers into a mass.

There are ancient examples of non-woven fabrics that are virtually natural textiles, such as matted hair and bark cloth. Both types represented prehistoric opportunities to create forms of cloth with minimal technological intervention. In the search for something new, modern designers have turned to this ancient method of producing fabric, at the same time as pursuing technological advances in other non-woven techniques. Felted fabrics are increasingly used by mainstream fashion designers, who value it for its strength, the fact that it can take on strong dyes, and its ability to be manipulated into strong sculptural shapes.

Non-woven industries have developed alternative fabrication systems, adopted for many useful purposes. With the diversification of synthetic polymers for fiber production, and hybrid composites made to meet a specific technical need, such as performance sportswear, there are now many non-woven garment fabrics with characteristics not present in yarn-based, structured textiles.

▲ Providing warmth and protection while remaining light in weight, ultrafine fiber wadding is used for contemporary outerwear as seen in this padded parka by British company Hunter for fall/winter 2014–15.

▶ Popular during the 1960s, the "disposable" paper dress was a short-lived trend, and provided an ideal canvas for Pop Art words and images. The Souper dress was inspired by Andy Warhol's screen prints of Campbell's Soup cans.

Nylon Reinforced Paper

ARTIFICIAL SUEDE

Invisible to the naked eye, polyester "ultra-microfibers" were first developed in the 1970s. These filaments are assembled into loose parallel bundles and set in a polyurethane binder. Filaments held together in this way can undergo further processes: heating, curling, chopping and needle punching, creating a soft material with the character of natural suede. The polyurethane is dissolved and the false suede is reimpregnated with adhesive binder. The polyester material can be laser-cut and etched, or patterned by heat impression.

NYLON REINFORCED PAPER

During World War II, American forces used paper maps reinforced with melamine. In the 1950s this innovation led to disposable protective garments of layered paper reinforced by nylon threads. Patents and trademarks proliferated: Kaycel, Dura-Weve and Tyvek all vied for domination in the "Paper Caper" craze for disposable minidresses of the mid-1960s. Scott Paper Co. delivered half a million sleeveless paper shift dresses at $1, while in 1964 the Mars Manufacturing Co. engaged Andy Warhol to design his Brillo and Fragile paper minidresses.

SPUNLACED NON-WOVEN FABRICS

These are also known as water-entangled fabrics, used principally for disposable goods, although natural fiber "eco" interfacings are also produced this way. Sheets of loosely assembled cut fibers, or batt, are bonded together by the mechanical force of high-pressure water jets. In some products the technique is used to merge layers of different fibers, such as wood pulp and polyester staple. Patterned lace effects are created by moving the batt over perforated conveyors.

WADDING (BATTING)

Wadding (otherwise known as batting) describes a loosely assembled, bulky mass of fibers that have usually been carded to form a dense cushion of fibers. This can then be used to add structure to garment form, such as shoulder pads. Polyester and nylon fiber "batt" of various weights and thicknesses is frequently used as insulation in general clothing and performance sportswear. Blends of ultrafine fiber wadding, such as Primaloft, offer calibrated insulation characteristics to correspond with climatic requirements.

WET PROCESS FELTS

When subject to moisture, heat and friction, any volume of loose animal hair will begin to tangle and come together as a result of the interlocking of the microscopic surface scales on individual fibers. In due course, the mass will become permanently matted into an irreversible felt structure. This natural phenomenon has been exploited for millennia – from the creation of nomadic clothing and housing in Mongolia to the complex manufacturing of Stetson hats in Texas from rabbit and beaver fur.

Wadding

Spunlaced Non-Woven Fabrics

LACE

INTRODUCTION

Highly prized, owing to its intricate structure, delicate appearance and the labor-intensive process of its manufacture – whether by hand or machine – lace comes in many forms, with the most basic techniques dating back to early Abyssinian times. However, lace making as we know it today began in earnest in the fifteenth century, and reached a high point of artisan craftsmanship in the eighteenth century, before becoming largely mechanized in the nineteenth.

Associated with important rites of passage, such as the christening of a newborn infant or the traditional white wedding dress, lace has only an intermittent appeal in fashion. For the fashionable woman of the *belle epoque* era at the turn of the twentieth century, the ultra-femininity of the lace blouse was an essential item of her wardrobe. The fabric was little used in the modernist 1920s and 1930s, but found favor again in the 1950s, particularly for the newly popular cocktail dress. With the twenty-first century preoccupation with heritage and provenance in fashion, lace is once again appearing on the runway. London-based luxury label Burberry has featured leavers lace from the only remaining U.K. lace manufacturer, Cluny Lace, as have Italian label Dolce & Gabbana and U.S. label Ralph Lauren.

▲ The traditional scrolls and floral motifs of Cluny lace are particularly appropriate for bridalwear; Sarah Burton for Alexander McQueen incorporated hand-made Cluny lace, as well as Chantilly lace, in the wedding dress for the Duchess of Cambridge's marriage to Prince William.

▶ Marc Jacobs plays with the innate femininity and delicacy, and the traditional scale, of broderie anglaise, combining it with pastel organza and matt crocodile skin for Louis Vuitton spring/summer 2012.

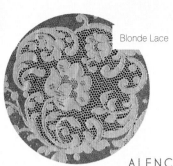
Blonde Lace

ALENÇON LACE

A royal lace workshop was established in Alençon, Normandy, in the seventeenth century in order to increase domestic production and reduce foreign imports. The main characteristic of the lace is a fine net ground and intricate floral patterns. The process of construction involves drawing the design on paper, creating the stitches on the net, then finally cutting away the paper before polishing the stitches with a lobster claw. This process takes around seven hours per centimeter, so most Alençon lace is machine-made today.

ANTWERP LACE

In the seventeenth century, the women of Antwerp, Belgium, produced this continuous bobbin lace to trim and decorate their caps. Its distinctive pattern, also known as Flanders lace, or Pottenkant, consists of bold sprigs of flowers, often in stylized pots, made in one piece or connected by bards, with an outline worked in a flat, heavy thread known as cordonnnet, and a complex tessellated ground that was stitched at the same time as the pattern.

ARGENTAN LACE

Argentan, also made in Normandy, is very similar to Alençon, but has a flatter, bolder pattern. It is also characterized by the "bride picotee", a thin buttonhole bar border decorated with a row of small pearls, a technique that was learned from the Venetians, who had been brought over to teach the Argentan workforce. As for Alençon, the French Revolution led to the collapse of the industry, and there are few workshops producing the lace today.

BATTENBERG LACE

This heavy style of lace originated during the Renaissance, when it was used as a trim for garments and for table decorations. It is made up of openly worked linen tapes, which are then coiled and looped in very open patterns. The tapes are then held in place with linen thread bars. From around the 1860s, this type of lace was renamed Battenberg lace, and the machine-made version was used in drapery.

BINCHE LACE

Another Belgian lace, binche was considered very fine and beautiful, and much desired in the eighteenth century. It is a type of bobbin lace made in one continuous narrow strip. Binche can also refer to a type of lace in which a machine-made net has flat sprigs of bobbin lace appliquéd onto it. It was developed in the seventeenth century to mimic the higher quality valenciennes lace with its spider and rosette backgrounds. As such, it was also known as fausse valenciennes.

BLONDE LACE

So called because it was unbleached and had a cream rather than white appearance, this type of lace was first made in the mid-eighteenth century. The background is usually a hexagonal silk mesh with coarse threads making up the body of the floral design. It is also known as Nankin lace, as the floral patterns mimicked the Nanjing Chinese silks that were being imported at the time. Black-dyed pieces were at the height of popularity during the French Revolution.

Broderie Anglaise

Chantilly Lace

BOBBIN LACE (PILLOW LACE)

One of the two main types of lace, bobbin lace is made on a pillow or cushion. The design is outlined by pins on the cushion, and the pattern is constructed around them by the interlacing and drawing of threads. This was the most common, domestically practiced form of lace making, as it required very little in the way of specialist equipment. It evolved from the sixteenth-century Italian practice of passementerie, or braid making.

BRODERIE ANGLAISE

Meaning "English embroidery", broderie anglaise is also less commonly known as Madeira work. This decorative technique was created by embroidering white designs on linen, cambric or cotton with punched eyelets, to give the cloth texture, or cutout holes that are then bound with buttonhole stitches. Today, the fabric is mostly associated with the ingenue aesthetic and children's clothes – adding a sense of playfulness to plainer garments and a lightness to simple cotton dresses.

BRUSSELS LACE (POINT D'ANGLETERRE)

One of the most famous varieties of lace, Brussels lace can be produced by either the needlepoint or bobbin technique. When the two techniques are combined, it is known as point d'Angleterre. Both variations are made on hexagonal grounds, with the bobbin lace having elaborate brides and toiles, and raised, braided cordonnets. It is created by outlining the design with thread on the pillow first, with the background worked into and around it.

CARRICKMACROSS

There are two versions of this Irish lace. One is called carrickmacross appliqué, in which muslin or cambric cloth is cut into a pattern that is then sewn onto a net ground and outlined with a cordonnet. The other is carrickmacross guipure, an embroidered technique whereby the design is cut away and the separate parts of the design are joined by bars. Both types of lace have been in production in County Monaghan in Northern Ireland since around 1820.

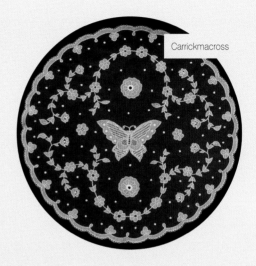

Carrickmacross

CHANTILLY LACE

Chantilly is famous for its fine bobbin lace. The manufacture of Chantilly lace was at its peak in the seventeenth century, when grenadine silk, which has a dull surface with no luster, was woven into delicate scrolls, foliage and flowers with a fine flat cordonnet outlining details. Chantilly was often made of black thread, which made it a popular mourning fabric. Besides the traditional linen and silk threads, Chantilly lace is now made with synthetic yarns.

CLUNY LACE

Cluny lace is light and delicate in structure and tends to follow traditional designs of geometric scrolls and flowers, with picots also appearing frequently. Originally a needlepoint lace made in Le Puy in France, it now refers to a bobbin lace that can be either handmade or machine-made – in linen-cotton thread or plain cotton. The name refers to the fact that most historic examples of it reside in the Cluny Museum in Paris.

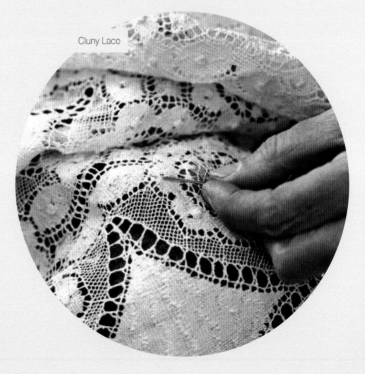

Cluny Lace

Cutwork

Guipure

CROCHET

For this simple method of mimicking lace, a hooked needle is used to work yarn into a continuous series of loops, which can then be joined together to make a fabric of any size, whether trimming for a garment or the entire garment itself. Crocheting has been practiced in Europe from the sixteenth century, but reached its peak of popularity as a domestic hobby and decorative fashion in late eighteenth-century America, introduced by Irish immigrants in the 1840s.

CUTWORK

Cutwork can be divided into two types, although in essence it means a fabric in which the design has been created by cutting out sections of woven fabric. Antique or Italian cutwork refers to fabric in which squares are cut out then stitched to keep the fabric from fraying. The other, more complex type of cutwork is where embroidery is combined with open areas of fabric that are filled with either embroidered net, drawn thread work or plain buttonhole stitches.

DRAWN THREAD WORK

Usually executed on linen fabric, this is a decorative technique in which threads are drawn out to the side and fastened to the remaining fabric, to create patterns with either plain or elaborate stitches, with further stitching executed around the area as a framing device. In some cases, the space that the drawn yarn leaves is filled with thread of a different color. There are many varieties of design, from basic hemstitching to elaborate patterns that cover the fabric.

324

Leavers Lace

DUCHESS LACE

Also known by its original name, Bruges lace, this white pillow lace is immensely popular for bridalwear because of its elegant, attractive patterns that have little visible ground. It is one of the more difficult laces to make, with each separate element of the design, whether foliage or scrollwork, made separately and then joined together, allowing for greater detail in the design. It is quite similar to Honiton lace, but finer and with occasional raised threads.

GUIPURE

There are several definitions of this coarse patterned lace, both of which are derived from the old French word for "cover with silk". The most common type does not have a mesh or net background, or bars, but rather has the tapes of the design held together by connecting threads. Less frequently, guipure can also refer to needlepoint or bobbin lace tape in bold, large designs over a coarse net ground.

HONITON LACE

This bobbin lace derives from a small Devon town that was settled by Flemish refugees in the sixteenth century. Characterized by delicate floral and foliate designs on a net ground (later machine-made), with the sprigged sections joined by plain stitches or bars, it was particularly popular as a fabric for babies' bonnets in the nineteenth century. There was a huge surge in popularity when Queen Victoria commissioned her wedding dress to be made from Honiton lace in 1840.

LEAVERS LACE/ NOTTINGHAM LACE

A machine-made lace from Nottingham, which, during the Victorian period, was the center of world lace production. Nottingham was the home of the stocking frame, but when men's hose fell out of fashion, the frames were altered to make lace instead. Originally, it was a domestic enterprise, before the lace was sent to the factory for finishing. Later in the nineteenth century, with the use of a leavers machine, the lace was both manufactured and finished within the factories.

Honiton Lace

MACRAMÉ

An ancient craft, macramé became immensely popular in the 1970s, with bags and other accessories made from this knotted fabric being an essential element of the hippie look. The term is derived from the Arabic *migramah*, meaning "embroidered veil", which explains its original usage. The fabric is made by simply knotting the yarn – either cotton string or wool – and arranging the knots in different variations to create a pattern with small or large holes.

MECHLIN LACE

Also known as Maline lace, named after its town of origin, this fine, open mesh bobbin lace of hexagonal shape is usually made from silk, cotton or synthetic yarns. Similar to tulle, but with a much larger hexagonal weave, this lace can be embellished by emphasizing the joins to create a polka-dot effect. It is similar in appearance to Brussels lace, although its ground and characteristic floral patterns are made simultaneously, in one piece.

NEEDLEPOINT

One of the two main types of lace, needlepoint is, as the name suggests, created by the use of needles and thread alone. A pattern is drawn on paper before linen or cotton thread is then sewn onto it, following the drawn design. The various elements of the design, including loops and picots and bars, are then assembled and connected with threads until, finally, the stitches attaching the lace to the paper are cut.

Macramé

Reticella Lace

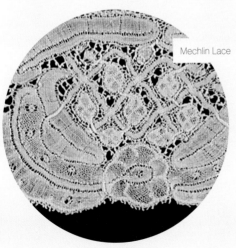

Mechlin Lace

RETICELLA LACE

A development from cutwork lace, early reticella – the first recorded use of which dates from a will of 1493 – has large, open squares of pattern cut from the background cloth. The holes, rather than the ground, are then decorated by embroidery stitches and threads pulled together. Later examples are made on a grid made of thread instead of a solid fabric ground. This type of lace is characterized by geometric patterns of squares or circles, finished with scalloped borders.

SCHIFFLI (SWISS EMBROIDERY)

Schiffli, otherwise known as chemical lace, is a type of machine-made lace or embroidery, although the term also refers to the loom on which it is made. To mimic lace, a net ground is embroidered with lines of yarn, otherwise known as shuttle embroidery. Once the design is completed, the ground is removed or burned out, leaving the raised design behind. The machine is operated by the designer, with the pantograph being manipulated by hand.

TULLE

Tulle is exceptionally fine, lightweight net fabric primarily used for ballet tutus, in millinery, and for volume under wedding or evening dresses. Tulle can be made from silk, cotton or synthetic fabrics and is formed of hexagonal mesh – a lace ground without a pattern. Tulle was first produced in Nottingham in the 1780s. However, to Nottingham's detriment, the first bobbinet machine factory opened in Tulle in 1817, and the fabric came to be known by that name instead.

TREATMENTS

INTRODUCTION

Unlike embellishment, treatments change the nature of the base cloth to create visual impact while retaining the wearability of the material. This approach differs from the various alternative means of constructing fabrics to produce patterned surfaces such as embroidery, print and weave – and is achieved through erosion, as with the technique of devoré and acid washing, or with disturbing the surface of the cloth to create pleats or a pile. Methods of application of treatments of cloth have emerged, subsided and reemerged throughout the history of craft and manufacture. Many of the techniques and processes have their provenance in ancient crafts, referenced by the contemporary designer but with the addition of a modern aesthetic, as with the space-dyeing of yarn to create the polychromatic warp-knitted stripes of Italian luxury label Missoni. Sometimes the cloth will go through several processes in different countries: woven in India, embroidered in China and, finally, shibori-dyed – the ancient "shaped resist" method of stitched and bound cloth that is then dip-dyed before finally being made up into a garment – in Japan. Contemporary technology offers a greater diversity of treatments; these are often modern solutions to previously esoteric processes, such as the then-secret method of printing used by Italian-based designer Mariano Fortuny for his Delphos gowns.

▲ Leading exponent of the devoré printing technique, British designer Jasper Conran showcases the labor-intensive process in this simple columnar evening dress from the 1990s.

▶ The light-reflecting, swirling surface texture of moiré is captured by Swiss-born designer Victor Stiebel in this couture wedding dress and train from 1963.

Chintz

ANTIQUING

A process by which a piece of cloth or a garment is made to look worn or worn-in, to give the appearance of vintage provenance. The process can vary between chemical and physical, such as stonewashing or acid washing – a popular treatment for denim jeans in the 1980s – or grating with a metal file. It is also possible to render a fabric antiqued by soaking it in anything that contains tannins, including tea or coffee.

CHINTZ

Chintz fabrics were originally printed cotton fabrics, plainly woven, and only occasionally glazed. These vivid, block-printed or hand-painted fabrics, originally made in India, depicted realistic flora and fauna and were highly prized in the seventeenth century. The term "chintz" now applies to any woven cotton that has a glazed surface. The glaze effect can be done either by application of wax or starch or by a stronger chemical process in which a resin is pressed onto the surface.

CRAQUELURE

In textiles, the technique of craquelure is commonly used to create an artificially aged or distressed surface and a mottled, jagged surface pattern. This requires an inflexible laminated or glossy pigment to be applied to the base cloth, which then dries and cracks under heat or as the result of a chemical reaction. The resulting garment has a stiff handle that is best used on formal haute couture gowns or as a small decorative area on a T-shirt.

DEVORÉ

Devoré is usually applied to velvet fabric, although the technique can be used on lace and cotton. A pattern is achieved by applying a chemical solution to the velvet pile in certain areas that then dissolves the fibers, leaving just the woven ground visible. Devoré reached its peak of popularity in the 1920s, particularly for shawls and evening gowns, and Jasper Conran's designs in the 1990s led to a revival in interest in this fabric.

EMBOSSING

To emboss a pattern onto fabric, a process called calendaring is used, in which the fabric is passed through a pair of heated rollers bearing the design. The heat and the pressure from the rollers press the pattern into the fabric, which is then fixed permanently with resin finishes. Some fabrics are embossed to mimic more expensive jacquard or dobby weaves, or they can be treated with resins in order to make the embossing design permanent.

MERCERIZATION

A chemical process used on cotton fabric in order to impart luster, improve its ability to hold dye and improve its strength and durability. The effect is produced by holding the material under tension, while a cold sodium hydroxide (lye) solution is applied. This makes the cell walls of the cotton fibers expand and increase their surface area, thereby improving their ability to reflect light. Mercerized cotton is the khaki fabric commonly used for chino trousers.

MOIRÉ

Moiré refers to a process that creates a watery, light-reflecting pattern on the surface of a fabric, produced by pressing engraved rollers onto the cloth, which then crushes parts of the fabric. Most commonly used on silks, this process can also be used on cottons, rayon and other synthetic fabrics or can be mimicked by either printing or weaving. Watered silks, as they were known, were at the height of fashion in the eighteenth century.

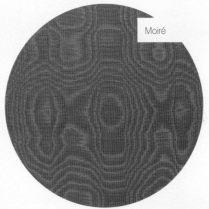

Moiré

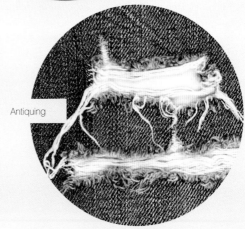

Antiquing

NAPPING AND SUEDEING

A mechanical process in which a fabric, either woven or knitted, is brushed with rotating wire bristles to form a soft, raised surface. It is often used in sleepwear because the raised fibers trap more air and are therefore more insulating. Suedeing is a similar process, although sandpaper-like rollers are used to make a surface that mimics suede. The napped flannel shirt, with a plaid design, was a key look in the grunge movement of the 1990s.

OMBRÉ

The technique of dyeing cloth or a finished garment, so that the color gradually fades from light to dark or from one color to another across the fabric. When printing, this is done by a dip-dyeing process or by painting on a dye when the cloth is wet, so as to soften the transition between shades. The same effect can be achieved through weaving, with different tones being arranged in the warp of the loom.

PANNÉ VELVET

Italy and France have been the centers of panné velvet production since the Middle Ages. France enshrined the laws of which materials should be used in the fabric in 1667, issuing a decree that it must be made of organzine and boiled silk. A lightweight variety of velvet, it has a pile that is flattened by a roller at the last stage of production, leaving an extremely lustrous finish.

PLEATING

Fabric is folded back on itself and pressed into layers, with two folds making up one entire pleat. It is a method that introduces both movement and volume to garments. There are various types of pleat, including box pleats, which usually emerge from the waistline, and knife or accordion pleats, which are flat but add movement rather than volume. Mariano Fortuny was famous for his secret method of creating fine, shimmering pleated fabrics.

PLISSÉ

A method of producing a puckered effect on a fabric, obtained by shrinking sections of the cloth through the application of a sodium hydroxide solution. The sections of the cloth that are not painted will then crinkle. Alternatively, the fabric can be treated with a resist chemical that will then protect the area from shrinkage when the whole fabric is dipped in a solution. This is a useful way of creating texture and volume without additional fabric being required.

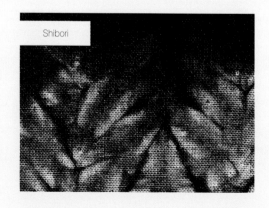
Shibori

Quilting

QUILTING

Quilting has been a traditional domestic occupation for centuries, but it has more recently been utilized in fashion garments – in particular, the padded riding jackets at Barbour. The method is to take two or more layers of cloth, usually with some sort of padding between the layers, such as down, cotton blankets or synthetic fibers, and to stitch through all the layers to create a design in relief, as the top layer gets pulled toward the bottom.

SHIBORI

This decorative tie-dye technique was invented in Japan in the eighth century. Elaborate printed patterns are created by gathering up folds of fabric, holding them in place with stitches, and then dyeing the piece as a whole. Further decoration is added by the use of resist dyeing and repeated over-dyes. The art of shibori is one revered in Japan, even in the present day, with master dyers producing kimonos, dresses and scarves.

SPACE DYEING

Also known as dip-dyeing, individual strands of yarn are dyed with one color or more at irregular, planned intervals and then fixed with a mordant, which has to be calibrated for the various dyes used. The finished effect is that of a design that is wholly organic and unplanned. The random nature of the design is best suited to crocheted or knitted garments, and the size of the stripes depends on the thickness of the yarn used.

YUZEN

Yuzen is a decorative dyeing process, using paste-resist methods, named after its seventeenth-century Japanese inventor. While the process remains a closely guarded secret, the effect is well known, with its bold lines, rich, true colors, and clear patterns being held in high esteem. This process, known as yuzen birodo, is carried out on velvet fabric, where the tufted fabric is dyed and then the pile is cut away to create shadows and texture.

Yuzen

Space Dyeing

PRINTING

INTRODUCTION

Printing is the process by which a pattern is transferred onto a piece of cloth or a finished garment other than by straightforward dyeing. Examples of printed fabric appear in prehistoric times – there has always been a compulsion to add decoration to otherwise plain fabrics and a desire to render garments individual with a striking pattern. Techniques can range from simply placing fingerprints of pigment onto a plain background to the most complex abstract and photorealist prints. With the industrialization of the fashion process in the early twentieth century, fashion fabrics required a speedy turnover. This was facilitated by the invention of the screen-printing process by Samuel Simon, who took out the first patent in 1907. This relatively cheap and less laborious method of printing cloth revolutionized the textile printing industry and liberated designers from the limitations of expensive block-printing methods or engraved roller machines, which required long runs to be commercially viable. Further inventions and patents followed, and by the 1930s, screen printing works were set up throughout Europe and America. Print design was further democratized by the introduction of digital printing, which allowed the designer to transfer a design from computer to cloth in a single step.

▲ Leading print designer Mary Katrantzou deploys digital printing techniques in this multi-directional, polychromatic, hyper-real floral design on a mini bubble skirt for spring/summer 2012.

▶ Created in a *coup de théâtre* runway show for spring/summer 1999, Alexander McQueen carefully positioned the model between two choreographed jet sprays of color to produce an instant decorative effect.

Block Printing

AIRBRUSH (SPRAY PRINTING)

A technique of applying color to a fabric that involves the blowing of dyes through jets over the cloth. This can be done by hand, at an artisan level, creating fine pictorial images. It can also be used on a larger scale, creating shaded effects on larger pieces of cloth. An iconic example was Alexander McQueen's Dress No. 13 from 1999 – a plain muslin dress that was spray painted by two robots during the fashion show.

BATIK

This resist-dye technique is a method of fixing a handmade pattern onto fabric by painting it with melted wax and then dyeing it. The wax is either applied to the fabric from a metal bowl with a narrow spout or is brushed on. Once the piece of fabric or garment has been dyed and fixed, the wax is removed physically or chemically. Batik originated in Indonesia but is now used in fashion to suggest a "naïve" or "ethnic" aesthetic.

BLOCK PRINTING

A block of wood, linoleum or metal is carved or engraved with a pattern in reverse, then thinly covered with a color dye paste before applying by hand onto the fabric. The size of the block can be either one repeat in size or can contain many repeats and be as wide as the cloth itself. The block must be made to line up with the previous print perfectly to make a seamless repeat.

DIGITAL PRINTING

Much like a domestic computer printer, digital fabric printing allows the fabric surface to be decorated with micro drops of dye that are released in jets from the print head. The use of nanotechnology means that incredibly finely detailed pattern or images can be printed and photo-quality results created. Designers such as Mary Katrantzou and Basso and Brooke are two of the foremost practitioners of digitally engineered printing with their striking, vibrant and eye-catching designs.

DISCHARGE PRINTING

To create a pattern on a colored ground, the already dyed fabric has a bleach solution painted on to strip away the color, leaving the treated areas white. It is also possible to replace the background color with a new color, as long as the dye applied to the fabric has bleach-resistant pigments. It is different from resist printing in that color is removed from the dyed fabric, whereas resist printing stops the fabric being printed in the first place.

Batik

HAND PAINTING

A highly skilled artisan method of decoration, or domestic customization, where dyes can be hand painted directly onto a fabric. This method of decoration allows for a great deal of individualization and can be as loose or as formal as desired. The finished garment must be cared for with caution, as the dyes are not easily fixable. Hand-painted garments are usually only seen in couture collections because they are so expensive to produce.

Mélange

HEAT TRANSFER PRINTING

A mass-production printing method best suited to synthetic fibers such as nylon, polyester and acrylic. Rolls of paper are printed with the design using disperse dyes. These dyes are then transferred, or sublimed, onto the fabric when it comes into contact with the paper at a temperature of around 392 degrees Fahrenheit (200 degrees Celsius) in a heat transfer printing machine. This method can also be used for customized printing, with individualized designs printed onto sheets of paper.

KALAMKARI (REPEATED DYEING)

Also known as qalamkari, kalamkari is a type of hand-woven cotton fabric from India that is either block printed or decorated by hand. The Srikalahasti variety of fabric is entirely hand drawn, with the design first painted on with a pen and then filled in with natural dyes, which are fixed by being presoaked in myrobalan and cow's milk before the decoration. After each color is applied, it is dried then washed, and this is repeated several times.

MÉLANGE/VIGOUREUX PRINTING

Mélange printing (*mélange* means "mixture" in French) is a method of printing fibers or yarn to give a shaded or blended effect in the finished woven or knitted fabric. Slivers of yarn are threaded through a machine with raised bars so that only certain parts catch the (usually black) dye. The alternative name, vigoureux, comes from the name of the man who invented the machine in the French weaving town of Reims in the 1860s.

OMBRÉ

Ombré, or gradient technique dyeing, is the technique of producing a gradual shaded effect on a fabric or garment by varying the intensity of the dye or the length of time a fabric is immersed in a dye vat. The same effect can be achieved by spraying with a dye solution. Although ombré is seen as a domestic method of dyeing, haute couture has occasionally embraced the aesthetic, with many designers, such as Christopher Kane, using it in 2012.

Kalamkari

Resist Printing

RESIST PRINTING

This is a general term that refers to any type of printing in which a design is created by preventing a dye from reaching certain parts of the fabric. This can be achieved by covering the patterned area with either a chemical or physical substance, such as resin or wax. The finished piece of fabric is left with a dyed background and a white patterned area. An alternative method of getting the same result is to piece-dye the fabric.

ROLLER PRINTING

A high-speed method of mass-production printing, with machines capable of producing more than 6,000 yards (5,490 meters) of fabric per hour. The cloth is passed through engraved, hollow cylinders that can discharge multiple colors onto the fabric simultaneously. The cylinders have very high tolerance, which means very delicate patterns can be made without the dyes running into each other. This can be done on either a single side or on both sides, using duplex printing machines.

Roller Printing

Screen Printing

SCREEN PRINTING

Flatbed printing consists of laying a flat screen of mesh prepared with blocking solution onto fabric. The color paste is squeezed through the mesh, leaving a gap where the blocking solution appears. The screen can either be applied to one garment or used to make a repeat pattern. Roller printing makes for a much faster production method, as the fabric moves through the rollers containing both the treated mesh screens and the color paste continuously.

VAT PRINTING

A commercial method of dyeing large quantities of fabric. All dyeing can be done in a vat but, technically, vat dyeing refers to a class of chemical dyes that are applied to natural fibers in an oxygen-free bath at temperatures of 122–140 degrees Fahrenheit (50–60 degrees Celsius). Vat printing can only be applied to plant fibers, as animal fibers cannot withstand the alkaline bath in which the fabric must be placed in order to fix the dye.

GLOSSARY OF SEWING TOOLS

INTRODUCTION

The earliest sewing tools were needles made of bone, using thread made from animal sinew (a strong and extremely waterproof substance). These were employed when animal skins and fur were the principal materials worn. As woven cloth from a loom replaced skin and fur, different tools were developed, often specially adapted to suit the textile and the environment.

Shears were later invented to cut cloth and were more effective than a knife. Needles of metal were substituted for those of bone, which were not fine enough for closely woven cloths. Fine needles were expensive – even up to the medieval period, they were precious objects that were coveted and cared for. However, a regular sizing system for needles was not developed until the nineteenth century. Historically, linen thread was a popular choice for sewing, until cotton thread became widely available from around 1815.

Small pins, used for holding two pieces of cloth together before and during sewing, were extensively used. Before the era of mass-produced clothing, pins were also essential items in a fashionable woman's wardrobe, necessary to construct and support an item of clothing while being worn – from which came the term "pin money", which dates back to the seventeenth century and which is still in use today.

AWL / STILETTO

A small, sharp instrument used to make points – very small round holes – in a pattern by punching through the fabric. Commonly used for indicating the position of eyelets or keyhole buttonholes. Can also be called a "stiletto".

BODKIN

An instrument shaped like a long, blunt needle and used for threading elastic or piping cord through a loop or casing.

CURVE

Called a hip curve, or curve square in the U.K., this is a measuring tool that measures curves, seam allowances, and buttonholes.

FRENCH CURVE

A pattern-drafting tool used for drawing or altering curved areas on patterns, such as collars and pockets. It can be made of wood, plastic, or metal.

HABERDASHERY

A term used to describe the miscellany of items used to complete a garment. They can have functional purposes, such as bias binding to finish edges or buttons, snaps, and zippers for closures. Needles, threads, and shoulder pads equally fall within the scope of haberdashery. The term also refers to decorative trimmings, such as ribbon, lace, and beads.

NEEDLE BOARD (VELVET BOARD)

A type of pressing tool consisting of a board containing a bed of closely bunched steel wires mounted on a backing of heavy canvas. It is used to press napped fabrics such as velvet, corduroy, and brushed cotton, while protecting the nap. When napped fabric is placed face down on the board, the wires fit between the nap and keep it from matting.

NEEDLES

A long, slender, metal tool with a pointed tip at one end and an eye hole at the other. There are an immense variety of sewing needles available to suit the different requirements of fabric and thread being used. Generally speaking, the finer the fabric, the finer the point of the needle. Needles are graded by size; the larger a number, the shorter and finer the needle.

PATTERN

A flat paper or card template representing a two-dimensional plan of a garment. Using a pattern, garment parts can be accurately transferred to fabric, before being cut out and assembled. Common practice is to develop a pattern from a design sketch using a block. A pattern cutter adapts the block to create a template that includes construction details such as seam allowance, style lines, pleats, pockets, etc.

PATTERN DRILL

A pattern-cutting tool. It is used to punch holes in the pattern in order to mark the position of darts, pockets, etc. After laying the paper pattern on top of fabric, the position of the punch holes can then be marked with chalk or thread onto the material.

PIN

Small, thin, straight pieces of metal with sharp ends, pins are used to temporarily fix pieces of paper or fabric together. They come in a variety of lengths to suit different types of cloth – generally, fine and loosely structured fabrics such as net or tulle require a longer pin to ensure they do not fall out.

PINKING SHEARS

A specially designed set of shears with notched teeth that cut a fray-resistant zigzag edge. They can be used to neaten the raw edges of seams or to provide a decorative touch.

PRESS MITT

A type of pressing tool, formed like a padded cushion in the shape of a glove and made of a scorch-proof, heat-resistant material. It contains a pocket for the hand. The tool is employed when pressing small curved garment surfaces, such as rounded sleeveheads.

ROTARY CUTTER

A cutting tool that is particularly useful for cutting through several layers of fabric at once or for cutting out long lengths of material. Often used in quilting, it consists of a handle with a very sharp circular blade that rotates.

SEAM RIPPER

A tool used to cut and open up a sewn seam without damaging the fabric. It is designed with a point balanced with a small, curved, extremely sharp blade. The curved blade can fit under a stitch and quickly break the thread, while the point is utilized for picking out threads. It can also be used to open buttonholes.

SEAM ROLL

A seam roll is a pressing tool, comprising a cylindrical-shaped molded cushion used to press open long seams and seams in very narrow areas. It can also be slid inside a sleeve to iron out wrinkles. It is usually made from cotton and wool.

SERGER (OVERLOCKER)

A type of sewing machine with the specific purpose of trimming and finishing seams in one action. Unlike a conventional sewing machine that forms a stitch with a bobbin and single thread, the serger works with a cutting blade (for trimming), loopers (which create thread loops), and multiple needle threads to form an overlocking stitch. The standard model employs two needles and carries four thread spindles. Some models can simultaneously stitch a seam while trimming and finishing it.

SET SQUARE

A pattern-drafting tool shaped like a right-angled triangular plate that ensures true right angles. As well as drawing lines at right angles, it can assist in finding the bias grain of a fabric.

SEWING MACHINE

A machine used to stitch fabric together with thread at speed, thereby replacing hand-stitching. Although the first prototype was invented in the late eighteenth century, Issac Singer is credited with developing a practical mass-produced model in the 1850s that revolutionized both the industrial clothing industry and home dressmaking. The mechanism is based on the shuttle-hook and bobbin assembly, which essentially loops two threads together to form a stitch. Computer technology allows modern machines to offer a wide range of functional, decorative, and embroidery stitches. The couture and bespoke tailoring industries make it a point of honor to use a sewing machine in their work as little as possible.

SHEARS

Shears are fabric-cutting scissors that have long, straight, sharp blades to cleanly and quickly cut through the material without snagging. They are designed with molded handles that sit at an angle to the blades, to ensure the blades sit parallel to the cutting surface and keep the fabric flat and even.

SLEEVE BOARD

A type of pressing tool, this narrow, padded board clips onto a conventional ironing board. It is primarily used for pressing the long, straight seams of sleeves that have been sewn closed, but it is also handy for narrow areas such as necklines and sleeveheads.

SLOPER (BLOCK)

A two-dimensional template of a garment design in its most basic form – it has no style lines or seam allowance. Usually called a block in the U.K., it is constructed using measurements taken from a size chart or from a measured model. Made on either paper or fabric, it can be later modified into a more detailed design. In the U.S., it is most often made from heavy paper called oak tag, whereas in Europe it is created from muslin (cotton-calico). The sloper is used as a guide for adjusting the fit of other garments and for developing designs. A designer will develop a set that reflect his or her particular aesthetics and which can be used each time a new collection is formulated. A couture house or tailoring firm may cut a bespoke set for an individual client.

STAY TAPE

A type of sheer, narrow fabric tape. It is sewn onto garment edges such as necklines, armholes, and seams in order to stabilize them and prevent them from stretching.

TAILOR'S CHALK

Chalk has been used by tailors for centuries as a way of transferring a pattern onto cloth or for conveying pattern markings or alteration lines. It can be easily and lightly brushed away from the fabric without leaving a mark. Modern chalk wedges are available in various colors; it is important to choose one that will stand out against the fabric.

TAILOR'S HAM

A type of pressing tool, so called because of its evocation of a round ham joint. A firmly stuffed cushion, usually made of cotton and wool, it will help press round shaped parts or seams on a garment. It is particularly useful for areas such as bust darts or for molding collars.

TAILOR'S POUNDING BLOCK

A type of pressing tool considered vital within tailoring. It consists of a rounded wooden block used to obtain sharp creases in heavy fabrics. After the heavy, bulky edge of a garment has been pressed with a steam iron, it is pounded with the block. The pounding helps to set the crease as the steam evaporates, so that the fabric will maintain the crease once dry. Pounding blocks come in a number of shapes and sizes.

TAILOR'S SQUARE/L-SQUARE

A measuring device in the form of an L-shaped ruler, it is used for finding the bias or straight grain of fabric, for altering patterns, or for squaring off straight edges.

TAPE MEASURE

Essential for taking body measurements, modern tape measures are made of flexible, synthetic materials or glass fiber. Their flexibility allows curved lines to be measured. The tape measure was invented in the early nineteenth century and started to be adopted by tailors after 1820. It was an important step toward a universal standardized measuring system.

THIMBLE

A tool used in hand stitching, a metal thimble protects the middle finger from needle pricks.

THREAD

Available in an immense variety of materials, colors, and thicknesses. Natural materials include cotton and silk; synthetics include polyester and nylon. It is vital to choose the right sort of thread for the job. Clothing is usually sewn with threads of lesser strength than the fabric so that if the seam is put under pressure, it will break before the garment. Generally, cotton thread is used for cotton, linen, or wool fabric; silk thread is used for silk or wool. Polyester is an all-purpose thread suitable for most natural and synthetic fabrics.

THREAD CLIPPER

A type of cutting tool, this small spring-loaded device is specifically used to cut threads. It can be held in the palm of the hand while sewing. It is less commonly called a weaver's scissors.

The publishers would like to thank the following sources for their kind permission to reproduce the pictures in this book.

Key: t=Top, b=Bottom, c=Center, l=Left and r=Right.

All images are Shutterstock except the following:

Page 3 Print Collector/Getty Images; 4l Heritage Image Partnership Ltd/Alamy; 4r ABACA/Press Association Images; 5l Ray Tang/Rex Features; 5r Stephane Cardinale/People Avenue/Corbis; 7 Victor Virgile/Getty Images; 9l Wikimedia Commons; 9r Antonio de Moraes Barros/Getty Images; 10 Heritage Image Partnership Ltd/Alamy; 11 Keystone/Getty Images; 12 Imagno/Getty Images; 13 Time Life Pictures/Getty Images; 14 © Carlton Books; 16 Photoshot/Getty Images; 17 © Carlton Books; 18 © Carlton Books; 19r Popperfoto/Getty Images; 20 Tristan Fewings/Getty Images; 21 Fairchild Photo Service/Condé Nast/Corbis; 22 Michel Dufour/Getty Images; 24 Vittorio Zunino Celotto/Getty Images; 25 Florilegius/Mary Evans Picture Library; 26 Jean-Pierre Muller/Getty Images; 28 Nick Giordano/Getty Images; 30 Rose Hartman/Getty Images; 31 Chicago History Museum/Getty Images; 32 Victor Virgile/Getty Images; 33 Bill Ray/Getty Images; 34 © Carlton Books; 35 Bettmann/Corbis; 37 John Chillingworth/Getty Images; 38 Mary Evans Picture Library; 39t Keystone/Getty Images; 39b Historical Picture Archive/Corbis; 41 London Stereoscopic Company/Getty Images; 42 © Carlton Books; 43 DEA Picture Library/Getty Images; 44 Steve Eason/Getty Images; 45t Interfoto/Alamy; 45b Pascal Le Segretain/Getty Images; 46 Edward Miller/Getty Images; 47t Silver Screen Collection/Getty Images; 47b Kristy Sparow/Getty Images; 48 AFP/Getty Images; 49t AFP/Getty Images; 49b Wikimedia Commons; 50 Reg Lancaster/Getty Images; 51 Sasha/Getty Images; 52 Doug Kanter/Getty Images; 53r SanneBerg/Thinkstock; 54l Mary Evans Picture Library; 54r Luis Dafos/Alamy; 55 © Carlton Books; 56 Andrew Cowie/Getty Images; 57 Marie Hansen/Getty Images; 58 The Advertising Archives; 59 Frazer Harrison/Getty Images; 60 EyeOn/Getty Images; 61t Slaven Vlasic/Getty Images; 62 Everett Collection Historical/Alamy; 63r Condé Nast Archive/Corbis; 64l Heritage Images/Getty Images; 64r Andreas Rentz/Getty Images; 65t Wikimedia Commons; 65b Time Life Pictures/Getty Images; 66 Wikimedia Commons; 67 Nicola Swann/Mary Evans Picture Library; 68 Print Collector/Getty Images; 69 Metropolitan Museum of Art, New York, USA/De Agostini Picture Librar/Bridgeman Images; 70 Antonio de Moraes Barros/Getty Images; 71l Mary Evans Picture Library; 71r © Carlton Books; 72 Genevieve Naylor/Corbis; 74 © Carlton Books; 75t Chirag Wakaskar/Getty Images; 76 Stefania D'Alessandro; 77l Chaloner Woods/Getty Images; 77r Mary Evans Picture Library; 78 Bertrand Guay/Getty Images; 79 © Carlton Books; 80 Kristy Sparow/Getty Images; 81l Gisela Schober/Getty Images; 81r Slaven Vlasic/Getty Images; 82 © Carlton Books; 83l Antonio de Moraes Barros/Getty Images; 83r Hulton Archive/Getty Images; 86 Nicolas Khayat/Enigma/Rex Features; 87 The Advertising Archive; 88 Condé Nast Archive/Corbis; 89r Francois Gragnon/Getty Images; 90 Jemal Countess/Getty Images; 91 © Carlton Books; 92 Popperfoto/Getty Images; 93l Mary Evans Picture Library; 93r Mary Evans Picture Library; 94l Mary Evans Picture Library; 94r Mary Evans Picture Library; 96 Pascal Le Segretain/Getty Images; 97 Wikimedia Commons; 99 Nat Farbman/Getty Images; 100 Jemal Countess/Getty Images; 101r Slaven Vlasic/Getty Images; 104 Jens Noergaard Larsen/Getty Images; 105 Victor Virgile/Getty Images; 106 Reuters/Corbis; 107 © Carlton Books; 109 Popperfoto/Getty Images; 110 © Carlton Books; 111l Edward G. Malindine/Getty Images; 111r Pascal Le Segretain/Getty Images; 112 Chicago History Museum/Getty Images; 113 Ernesto Ruscio/Getty Images; 114 Chaloner Woods/Getty Images; 115t AFP/Getty Images; 115b Glasshouse Images/Alamy; 116 Nina Leen/Getty Images; 117 Wikimedia Commons; 118 Imagno/Getty Images; 119 London Stereoscopic Company/Getty Images; 120 Chaloner Woods/Getty Images; 121 Gjon Mili/Getty Images; 122 Carl Court/Getty Images; 123 Benoit Tessier/Reuters/Corbis; 125t Larry Busacca/Getty Images; 126l Archive Photos/Getty Images; 126r Nina Leen/Getty Images; 127t James Devaney/Getty Images; 128 Wikimedia Commons; 131 Mary Evans Picture Library; 132 ABACA/Press Association Images; 133 Heckmannoleg/Thinkstock; 134 Dusko Despotovic/Corbis; 135 Ed Reeve/VIEW/Corbis; 137 Wikimedia Commons; 138 Jmkphotography/Thinkstock; 139 Paramount Pictures/Sunset Boulevard/Corbis; 143l © Carlton Books; 143r Vadim Balantsev/Thinkstock; 144 Kirstin Sinclair/Getty Images; 145 ClassicStock/Alamy; 148 Peter Horree/Alamy; 149 Stephane

Cardinale/People Avenue/Corbis; 151t Chelsea Lauren/Getty Images; 154t Lester Chen/Getty Images; 155b Cambridge Satchel Company; 156l Albin Guillot/Getty Images; 156r Michel Dufour/Getty Images; 158 The Metropolitan Museum of Art/Art Resource/Scala, Florence; 159 Antonio de Moraes Barros/Getty Images; 160 Sharok Hatami/Rex Features; 161 Allan Grant/Getty Images; 162 Popperfoto/Getty Images; 164 Ray Tang/Rex Features; 165 Archive Photos/Getty Images; 166-69 www.roryduffybespoke.com; 171 Volkan Sengor/Getty Images; 175 Fairchild Photo Service/Condé Nast/Corbis; 176 Archive Photos/Getty Images; 178 Corbis; 179 Michael Ochs Archives/Getty Images; 180 Wikimedia Commons; 181 Leon Neal/Getty Images; 184 © Carlton Books; 184 Wikimedia Commons; 185r Arun Nevader/Getty Images; 186t Keystone/Getty Images; 187-89 Wikimedia Commons; 190 Victor Virgile/Getty Images; 191 Charles Platiau/Reuters/Corbis; 192 Randy Brooke/Getty Images; 193 Jon Levy/Getty Images; 194 Venturelli/Getty Images; 195 Camera Press; 196 Pascal Le Segretain/Getty Images; 199l Threads; 199r Mary Evans Picture Library; 202 Wikimedia Commons; 203r Carlos Alvarez/Getty Images; 204 Wikimedia Commons; 205l Peter Anderson/Getty Images; 205r Dominique Charriau/Getty Images; 209t Danny E. Martindale/Getty Images; 211 © Carlton Books; 212 © Carlton Books; 213t © Carlton Books; 213b Markus Brunner/Getty Images; 214 © Victoria and Albert Museum, London; 215 © Victoria and Albert Museum, London; 217 Peter Anderson/Getty Images; 218t Image Republic Inc./Alamy; 218b Lisa Pay; 220 Make it Coats; 221b © Carlton Books; 223t © Carlton Books; 223b Wikimedia Commons; 224 © Victoria and Albert Museum, London; 225 © Victoria and Albert Museum, London; 226 Wikimedia Commons; 227b Lela Wilson/Thinkstock; 231 Wikimedia Commons; 232b Wikimedia Commons; 233 Randy Brooke/Getty Images; 234 © Carlton Books; 236 Randy Brooke/Getty Images; 237 Rex Features; 238 Stefania D'Alessandro/Getty Images; 243 © Carlton Books; 245t © Victoria and Albert Museum, London; 245b Spiderplay/Getty Images; 246 Rex Features; 247 Fairchild Photo Service/Condé Nast/Corbis; 249r Juan Ignacio Laboa/Thinkstock; 250 © Victoria and Albert Museum, London; 251r Francois Guillot/Getty Images; 252 Thierry Orban/Corbis; 253 Fairchild Photo Service/Condé Nast/Corbis; 254 © Victoria and Albert Museum, London; 255t Alamy; 256b © Carlton Books; 257 Victor Virgile/Getty Images; 258 Dave M. Benett/Getty Images; 260 Craig Ellenwood/Alamy; 261 Andreas Rentz/Getty Images; 262 Sipa Press/Rex Features; 263 Antiques & Collectables/Alamy; 265 Victor Virgile/Getty Images; 266 imageBROKER/Alamy; 267l Science & Society Picture Library/Getty Images; 267r Eugene Tochilin/Thinkstock; 268 Illustrated London News Ltd/Mary Evans Picture Library; 269 Silver Screen Collection/Getty Images; 270 Cris Bouroncle/Getty Images; 271l Genevieve Naylor/Corbis; 273r Roux Olivier/Sagaphoto.com/Alamy; 274 Hendrik Ballhausen/dpa/Corbis; 275 Condé Nast Archive/Corbis; 276l Corri Corrado/Rex Features; 279 Hulton Archive/Keystone/Getty Images; 280 Pascal Le Segretain/Getty Images; 281 Antonio de Moraes Barros/Getty Images; 284b Scott Liddell/Thinkstock; 285l Julien Hekimian/Getty Images; 286 © Victoria and Albert Museum, London; 287 Chicago History Museum/Getty Images; 288 Condé Nast Archive/Corbis; 290t Dinodia Photos/Alamy; 292 Ken Towner/Evening Standard/Rex Features; 293 Victor Virgile/Getty Images; 294b Hugh Threlfall/Alamy; 296 © Carlton Books; 298t James Ferrie/Thinkstock; 298b Popperfoto/Getty Images; 299 WireImage/Getty Images; 300 Condé Nast Archive/Corbis; 301 James Devaney/Getty Images; 305 Joshua Lott/Getty Images; 309 Scott Wintrow/Getty Images; 310l Prisma Bildagentur AG/Alamy; 313bl © Carlton Books; 313r Keystone/Getty Images; 314 Danny Martindale/Getty Images; 315 Louisa Gouliamaki/Getty Images; 316 Rolls Press/Popperfoto/Getty Images; 317 Robertus Pudyanto/Getty Images; 319 Stephane Cardinale/People Avenue/Corbis; 320-22 Wikimedia Commons; 323t Holmes Garden Photos/Alamy; 323b Clunylace.com; 324t DEA Picture Library/Getty Images; 324b Wikimedia Commons; 325t Universal History Archive/Getty Images; 325b Wikimedia Commons; 327t Wikimedia Commons; 327b MCLA Collection/Alamy; 328 © Victoria and Albert Museum, London; 329 © Victoria and Albert Museum, London; 333c Bob Krist/Corbis; 334 Antonio de Moraes Barros/Getty Images; 335 Steve Wood/Rex Features; 336 Frazer Harrison/Getty Images; 339 Dinodia Photos/Alamy; 340 Travelib prime/Alamy; 341l RGB Ventures/SuperStock/Alamy.

Every effort has been made to acknowledge correctly and contact the source and/or copyright holder of each picture. Carlton Books Limited apologizes for any unintentional errors or omissions, which will be corrected in future editions of this book.